Other Books and Series by Jeff Bowen

Applications for Enrollment of Chickasaw Newborn Act of 1905
Volumes I thru VII

Cherokee Intermarried White 1906 Volume I thru X

Applications for Enrollment of Creek Newborn Act of 1905
Volumes I thru XIV

Applications for Enrollment of Choctaw Newborn Act of 1905
Volume I, II & III

Visit our website at **www.nativestudy.com** to learn more about these and other books and series by Jeff Bowen

I0221967

APPLICATIONS FOR ENROLLMENT OF CHOCTAW NEWBORN ACT OF 1905

VOLUME IV

TRANSCRIBED BY
JEFF BOWEN

NATIVE STUDY
Gallipolis, Ohio
USA

Other Books and Series by Jeff Bowen

1901-1907 Native American Census Seneca, Eastern Shawnee, Miami, Modoc, Ottawa, Peoria, Quapaw, and Wyandotte Indians (Under Seneca School, Indian Territory)

1932 Census of The Standing Rock Sioux Reservation with Births And Deaths 1924-1932

Census of The Blackfeet, Montana, 1897- 1901 Expanded Edition

Eastern Cherokee by Blood, 1906-1910, Volumes I thru XIII

Choctaw of Mississippi Indian Census 1929-1932 with Births and Deaths 1924-1931   Volume I
Choctaw of Mississippi Indian Census 1933, 1934 & 1937, Supplemental Rolls to 1934 & 1935 with Births and Deaths 1932-1938, and Marriages 1936-1938 Volume II

Eastern Cherokee Census Cherokee, North Carolina 1930-1939 Census 1930-1931 with Births And Deaths 1924-1931 Taken By Agent L. W. Page Volume I
Eastern Cherokee Census Cherokee, North Carolina 1930-1939 Census 1932-1933 with Births And Deaths 1930-1932 Taken By Agent R. L. Spalsbury   Volume II
Eastern Cherokee Census Cherokee, North Carolina 1930-1939 Census 1934-1937 with Births and Deaths 1925-1938 and Marriages 1936 & 1938 Taken by Agents R. L. Spalsbury And Harold W. Foght Volume III

Seminole of Florida Indian Census, 1930-1940 with Birth and Death Records, 1930-1938

Texas Cherokees 1820-1839 A Document For Litigation 1921

Choctaw By Blood Enrollment Cards 1898-1914 Volumes I thru XVII

Starr Roll 1894 (Cherokee Payment Rolls) Districts: Canadian, Cooweescoowee, and Delaware Volume One
Starr Roll 1894 (Cherokee Payment Rolls) Districts: Flint, Going Snake, and Illinois   Volume Two
Starr Roll 1894 (Cherokee Payment Rolls) Districts: Saline, Sequoyah, and Tahlequah; Including Orphan Roll   Volume Three

Cherokee Intruder Cases   Dockets of Hearings 1901-1909 Volumes I & II

Indian Wills, 1911-1921 Records of the Bureau of Indian Affairs Books One thru Seven;
Native American Wills & Probate Records 1911-1921

Other Books and Series by Jeff Bowen

Turtle Mountain Reservation Chippewa Indians 1932 Census with Births & Deaths, 1924-1932

Chickasaw By Blood Enrollment Cards 1898-1914 Volume I thru V

Cherokee Descendants East An Index to the Guion Miller Applications Volume I
Cherokee Descendants West An Index to the Guion Miller Applications Volume II (A-M)
Cherokee Descendants West An Index to the Guion Miller Applications Volume III (N-Z)

Applications for Enrollment of Seminole Newborn Freedmen, Act of 1905

Eastern Cherokee Census, Cherokee, North Carolina, 1915-1922, Taken by Agent James E. Henderson   Volume I (1915-1916)
Volume II (1917-1918)
Volume III (1919-1920)
Volume IV (1921-1922)

Complete Delaware Roll of 1898

Eastern Cherokee Census, Cherokee, North Carolina, 1923-1929, Taken by Agent James E. Henderson   Volume I (1923-1924)
Volume II (1925-1926)
Volume III (1927-1929)

Applications for Enrollment of Seminole Newborn Act of 1905 Volumes I & II

North Carolina Eastern Cherokee Indian Census 1898-1899, 1904, 1906, 1909-1912, 1914 Revised and Expanded Edition

1932 Hopi and Navajo Native American Census with Birth & Death Rolls (1925-1931) Volume 1 - Hopi
1932 Hopi and Navajo Native American Census with Birth & Death Rolls (1930-1932) Volume 2 - Navajo

Western Navajo Reservation Navajo, Hopi and Paiute 1933 Census with Birth & Death Rolls 1925-1933

Cherokee Citizenship Commission Dockets 1880-1884 and 1887-1889 Volumes I thru V

Copyright © 2013
by Jeff Bowen

ALL RIGHTS RESERVED
No part of this publication may be reproduced
or used in any form or manner whatsoever
without previous written permission from the
copyright holder or publisher.

Originally published:
Baltimore, Maryland
2012

Reprinted by:

Native Study LLC
Gallipolis, OH
www.nativestudy.com
2020

Library of Congress Control Number: 2020918113

ISBN: 978-1-64968-097-6

Made in the United States of America.

This series is dedicated to the descendants of the Choctaw newborn listed in these applications.

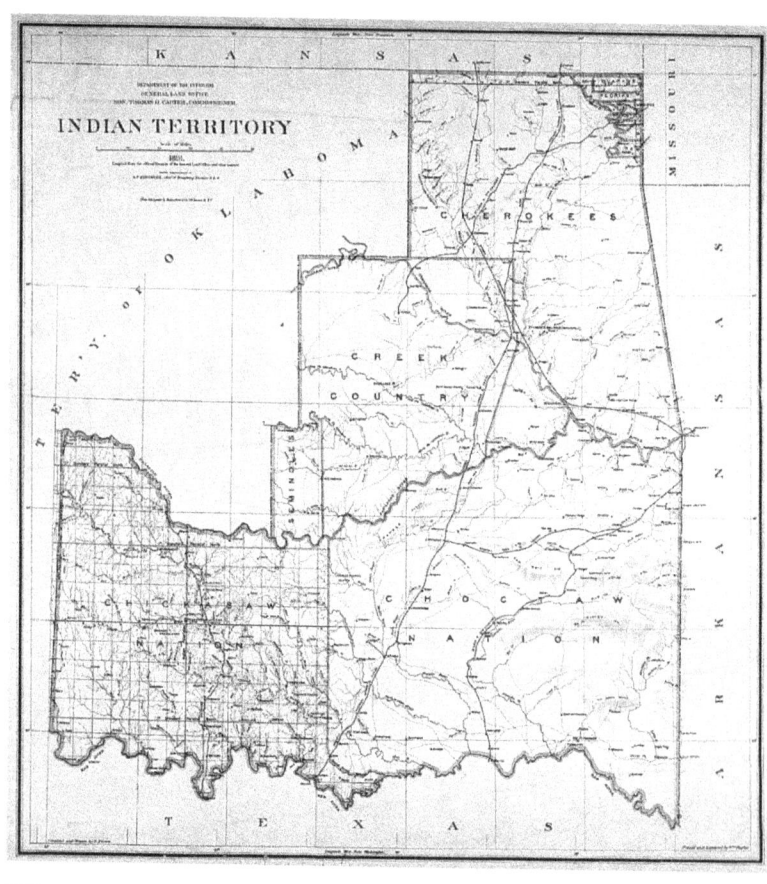

This map of Indian Territory shows how large the Choctaw and Chickasaw Nations' land base was that contained huge deposits of asphalt and coal. Just the size and territory involved was flooded with the "Grafters".

DEPARTMENT OF THE INTERIOR.
Commissioner to the Five Civilized Tribes.

NOTICE.

Opening of Land Office at Wewoka,
IN THE SEMINOLE NATION, INDIAN TERRITORY.

Notice is hereby given that on Monday, September 4, 1905, the Commissioner to the Five Civilized Tribes will establish a land office at Wewoka, in the Seminole Nation, Indian Territory, for the purpose of allowing citizens and freedmen of the Seminole Nation to select allotments of land for their minor children enrolled under the Act of Congress approved March 3, 1905 (33 Stat. L. 1060), and for the further purpose of allowing citizens and freedmen of the Seminole Nation, whose allotments are incomplete, to select additional land in order to bring the value of their allotments up to the standard of $309.09, as nearly as may be practicable.

Each child whose enrollment in accordance with the Act of March 3, 1905, has been duly approved by the Secretary of the Interior, is entitled to receive an alllotment of forty acres without regard to the character or value of the land selected.

Selection of allotments for minor children must be made by their citizen or freedmen parents or by a duly appointed guardian, or curator, or by a duly appointed administrator.

TAMS BIXBY,
Commissioner.

Muskogee, Indian Territory,
July 29, 1905.

This particular notice for the Seminole and Creek Newborn makes mention of the Act of 1905. It is likely that a similar notice was posted in the Choctaw and Chickasaw Nations for the registration of newborn children.

DEPARTMENT OF THE INTERIOR,
Commission to the Five Civilized Tribes.

Rules and Regulations Governing the Selection of Allotments and the Designation of Homesteads in the Choctaw and Chickasaw Nations.

1. Selections of allotments and designations of homesteads for adult citizens and selections of allotments for adult freedmen must be made in person except as herein otherwise provided.
2. Applications to have land set apart and homesteads designated for duly identified Mississippi Choctaws must be made personally before the Commission to the Five Civilized Tribes. Fathers may apply for their minor children and if the father be dead the mother may apply. Husbands may apply for wives. Applications for orphans, insane persons and persons of unsound mind may be made by duly appointed guardian or curator, and for aged and infirm persons and prisoners by agents duly authorized thereunto by power of attorney, in the discretion of said Commission.
3. At the time of the selection of allotment each citizen and duly identified Mississippi Choctaw shall designate as a homestead out of said selection land equal in value to one hundred and sixty acres of the average allottable land of the Choctaw and Chickasaw Nations, as nearly as may be.
4. Each Choctaw and Chickasaw freedman, at the time of selection shall designate as his or her allotment of the lands of the Choctaw and Chickasaw Nations, land equal in value to forty acres of the average allottable land of the Choctaw and Chickasaw Nations.
5. Citizens, freedmen and identified Mississippi Choctaws who are married, whether they have attained their majority or not, will be regarded as of age for the purpose of making selections.
6. Selections may be made by citizen and freedman parents for unmarried male children under twenty-one years of age and for unmarried female children under eighteen years of age, and a male citizen or freedman may make selection for his wife, if she is entitled to make selection, unless she shall, at the time or previously thereto, protest in writing.
7. Where the father of an unmarried minor citizen, freedman or identified Mississippi Choctaw is a non-citizen, the citizen, freedman or identified Mississippi Choctaw mother of such children must make selection in person in behalf of said children.
8. Selections of allotments and designations of homesteads for minor citizens and selections of allotments for minor freedmen may be made by the citizen father or mother or freedman father or mother, as the case may be, or by a guardian, curator, or an administrator having charge of their estate, in the order named
9. Selections of allotments and designations of homesteads for citizen, and selections of allotment for freedmen, prisoners, convicts, aged and infirm persons and soldiers and sailors of the United States on duty outside of Indian Territory, may be made by duly appointed agents under power of attorney, and for incompetents by guardians, curators, or other suitable person akin to them.
10. Selections may be made and homesteads designated by duly identified Mississippi Choctaws, who have, within one year after the date of their identification as such, made satisfactory proof of bona fide settlement within the Choctaw-Chickasaw country, at any time within six months after the date of their said identification.
11. Persons authorized to make selections by power of attorney, as provided in rules 2 and 9 hereof, must be the husband or wife, or a relative not further removed than a cousin of the first degree of the person for whom such selection is made.
12. It shall be the duty of the Commission to the Five Civilized Tribes to see that selections of allotments and designations of homesteads for the classes of persons mentioned in rules 2, 6, 7, 8 and 9 hereof, are made for the best interests of such persons.
13. Selections of allotments for citizens, freedmen and identified Mississippi Choctaws who have died subsequent to September 25, 1902, and before making a selection of allotment, shall be made by a duly appointed administrator or executor. If, however, such administrator or executor be not duly and expeditiously appointed, or fails to act promptly when appointed, or for any other cause such selections be not so made within a reasonable and practicable time, the Commission to the Five Civilized Tribes shall designate the lands thus to be allotted.
14. In determining the value of a selection the appraised value of the land selected shall be increased by the appraised value of such pine timber on such land as has heretofore been estimated by the Commission to the Five Civilized Tribes.
15. Selections of allotments may be made only by citizens and freedmen whose enrollment has been approved by the Secretary of the Interior, and by persons duly identified by the Commission to the Five Civilized Tribes as Mississippi Choctaws, and by none others.
16. When a selection of land has been made by a citizen, freedman or identified Mississippi Choctaw, and the land so selected is claimed by a person whose rights as a citizen or freedman have not been finally determined, contest for the land so selected may be instituted by the person claiming the land, formal application for the land being first made as is required by the Rules of Practice in Choctaw and Chickasaw allotment contest cases.

THE COMMISSION TO THE FIVE CIVILIZED TRIBES.

TAMS BIXBY, Chairman.

Muskogee, Indian Territory, March 24, 1903.

The above statement published prior to 1905, was established for what was supposed to be a set of guidelines when it came to allotments. But with supplemental agreements and Congressional legislation, time frames as well as rules and regulations often changed and were not the same for every tribe.

INTRODUCTION

The *Applications for Enrollment of Choctaw Newborn Act of 1905*, National Archive film M-1301, Rolls 50-57, are found under the heading of Applications for Enrollment of the Commission to the Five Civilized Tribes. For this series, I have transcribed the application forms filled out by individuals applying for enrollment in the Five Civilized Tribes under the Dawes Commission. These applications contain considerably more information than stated on the census cards found in series M-1186. M-1301 possesses its own numerical sequence, separate from M-1186. To find each party's roll number you would have to reference M-1186.

The Choctaw as well as the Chickasaw allotments were likely some of the most sought after properties in Indian Territory. There was supposed to be a 25-year restriction on the sale or lease of any Indian lands so as to insure that the owners wouldn't be swindled, but that isn't what happened. This fact is borne out in the Dawes Commission General Allotment Act, of February 8, 1887, Section 5, which "Provides that after an Indian person is allotted land, the United States will hold the land 'in trust [1] for the sole use and benefit of the Indian' (or his heirs if the Indian landowner dies) for a period of 25 years. (Land held in trust by the United States government cannot be sold or in anyway alienated by the Indian landowner, since the United States government considers the underlying ownership of the land held by itself and not the tribe. After the period of trust ends, the Indian landowner is free to sell the land and is free from any encumbrance from the United States.)"[1] Instead, Native Americans were exploited by the devious. The Choctaw and Chickasaw Districts both had huge asphalt and coal deposits, so there was pressure from outsiders to acquire them from the minute they were discovered. After repeated attacks throughout the years and many legislative changes, President "Roosevelt finally signed the Five Tribes Bill at noon on April 26, 1906, the forces seeking to end all restrictions were disappointed. Section 19 removed restrictions from the sale of all inherited land but directed that no full-bloods could sell their land for twenty-five years. The Act also prohibited leases for more than one year without the approval of the Secretary of the Interior."[2]

Angie Debo described the opportunists that wanted these Native American allotments as, "Grafters". The parents of the newborns enumerated within this series would no sooner receive the approval for their child's allotment than there would be someone there with cash in hand holding a new deed or lease for the parents to sign their child's birthright away. Angie Debo said it best, "As the business incapacity of the allottees became apparent, a horde of despoilers fastened themselves upon their property." According to Debo, "The term 'grafter' was applied as a matter of course to dealers in Indian land, and was frankly accepted by them. The speculative fever also affected Government employees so that it was almost impossible to prevent them from making personal investments."[3]

---

[1] General Allotment Act, Act of Feb. 8, 1887 (24 Stat. 388, ch. 119, 25 USCA 331)
[2] The Dawes Commission and the Allotment of the Five Civilized Tribes, 1893-1914 by Kent Carter, pg. 173
[3] And Still the Waters Run, Angie Debo, p. 92.

INTRODUCTION

According to the Department of Interior in 1905, "It is estimated that there will be added to the final rolls of the citizens and freedmen of the Choctaw and Chickasaw nations the names of 2,000 persons, including 1,500 new-born children to be enrolled under the provisions of the act of Congress approved March 3, 1905."[4]

The quote below explains, in detail, the requirements for qualifying as a newborn Choctaw, "By the act of Congress approved March 3, 1905 (H.R. 17474), entitled 'An act making appropriations for the current and contingent expenses of the Indian Department and for fulfilling treaty stipulations with various Indian tribes for the fiscal year ending June 30, 1906, and for other purposes,' it was provided as follows:

'That the Commission to the Five Civilized Tribes is hereby authorized for sixty days after the date of the approval of this act to receive and consider applications for enrollment of infant children born prior to September twenty-fifth, nineteen hundred and two, and who were living on said date, to citizens by blood of the Choctaw and Chickasaw tribes of Indians whose enrollment has been approved by the Secretary of the Interior prior to the date of the approval of this act; and to enroll and make allotments to such children.'

'That the Commission to the Five Civilized Tribes is authorized for sixty days after the date of the approval of this act to receive and consider applications for enrollment of children born subsequent to September twenty-fifth, nineteen hundred and two, and prior to March fourth, nineteen hundred and five, and who were living on said latter date, to citizens by blood of the Choctaw and Chickasaw tribes of Indians whose enrollment has been approved by the Secretary of the Interior prior to the date of the approval of this act; and to enroll and make allotments to such children.'

"Notice is hereby given that the Commission to the Five Civilized Tribes will, up to and inclusive of midnight, May 2, 1905, receive applications for the enrollment of infant children born prior to September 25, 1902, and who were living on said date, to citizens by blood of the Choctaw and Chickasaw tribes of Indians whose enrollment has been approved by the Secretary of the Interior prior to March 3, 1905."[5]

Following is the scope of these transcriptions: Besides the applications themselves, researchers will find the identities of other individuals within these applications -- doctors, lawyers, mid-wives, and other relatives -- that may help with you genealogical research.

Jeff Bowen
Gallipolis, Ohio
NativeStudy.com

---

[4] Annual Reports of the Department of the Interior For the Fiscal Year Ended June 30, 1905, p. 609.
[5] Annual Reports of the Department of the Interior For the Fiscal Year Ended June 30, 1905, p. 593.

Applications for Enrollment of Choctaw Newborn
Act of 1905 Volume IV

Choc New Born 186
    Benjamin C Merryman
    (Born March 12, 1903)

BIRTH AFFIDAVIT.

DEPARTMENT OF THE INTERIOR,
COMMISSION TO THE FIVE CIVILIZED TRIBES.

In Re Application for Enrollment, as a citizen of the Choctaw Nation, of Benjamin C. Merryman, born on the 12 day of March, 1903

Name of Father: Walter Merryman   a citizen of the Choctaw Nation.
Name of Mother: Mary Merryman   a citizen of the By Marriage Nation.
                                                                   Choctaw
                        Post-office   Bengal, I.T.

AFFIDAVIT OF MOTHER.

UNITED STATES OF AMERICA,
  INDIAN TERRITORY,
Central   District.

    I, Mary Merryman, on oath state that I am 28 years of age and a citizen by Marriage, of the Choctaw Nation; that I am the lawful wife of Walter Merryman, who is a citizen, by blood of the Choctaw Nation; that a male child was born to me on 12 day of March, 1903, that said child has been named Benjamin C. Merryman, and is now living.

                                                          Mary Merryman
WITNESSES TO MARK:

    Subscribed and sworn to before me this 11th day of April, 1903.

                                                          B F Johnson
                                                               NOTARY PUBLIC.

Applications for Enrollment of Choctaw Newborn
Act of 1905   Volume IV

AFFIDAVIT OF ATTENDING PHYSICIAN OR MID-WIFE.

UNITED STATES OF AMERICA,
INDIAN TERRITORY,
Central   District.

I,   Ruth Millus   , a   mid Wife   , on oath state that I attended on Mrs. Mary Merryman , wife of Walter Merryman on the 12th day of March , 1903 ; that there was born to her on said date a   male   child; that said child is now living and is said to have been named Benjamin C Merryman

Ruth Millus

WITNESSES TO MARK:

Subscribed and sworn to before me this 11th day of April   , 1903.

B.F. Johnson
NOTARY PUBLIC.

[The above affidavit given again.]

NEW BORN AFFIDAVIT

No

CHOCTAW ENROLLING COMMISSION

IN THE MATTER OF THE APPLICATION FOR ENROLLMENT as a citizen of the Choctaw Nation, of   Benjamin Colbert Merryman   born on the 12   day of   March   190 3

Name of father   Walter G. Merryman   a citizen of   Choctaw   Nation, final enrollment No. 8460
Name of mother   Mary Merryman   a citizen of   Choctaw   Nation, final enrollment No.   824

Leflore I.T.   Postoffice.

2

Applications for Enrollment of Choctaw Newborn
Act of 1905   Volume IV

AFFIDAVIT OF MOTHER

UNITED STATES OF AMERICA
INDIAN TERRITORY
DISTRICT   Central

I Mary Merryman , on oath state that I am   33   years of age and a citizen by   marriage   of the   Choctaw   Nation, and as such have been placed upon the final roll of the   Choctaw   Nation, by the Honorable Secretary of the Interior my final enrollment number being   824 ; that I am the lawful wife of   Walter G Merryman , who is a citizen of the   Choctaw   Nation, and as such has been placed upon the final roll of said Nation by the Honorable Secretary of the Interior, his final enrollment number being   8460   and that a   Male   child was born to me on the   12   day of   March   190 3; that said child has been named   Benjamin Colbert Merryman , and is now living.

her
Mary Merryman   x
mark

WITNESSETH:
Must be two witnesses { Thomas McCurtain
who are citizens   { Watson Wright

Subscribed and sworn to before me this, the   25   day of   February   , 190 5

B.F. Johnson
Notary Public.

My Commission Expires: January 28=1909

Affidavit of Attending Physician or Midwife

UNITED STATES OF AMERICA,
INDIAN TERRITORY,
Central   DISTRICT

I,   Rutha Millus   a   Midwife on oath state that I attended on Mrs. Mary Merryman   wife of   Walter G. Merryman on the   12   day of   March , 190 3, that there was born to her on said date a   male   child, that said child is now living, and is said to have been named   Benjamin Colbert Merryman

Midwife
Rutha Millus   M. D.

Subscribed and sworn to before me this the   25   day of   February   1905

B.F. Johnson
Notary Public.

Applications for Enrollment of Choctaw Newborn
Act of 1905   Volume IV

WITNESSETH:
Must be two witnesses who are citizens and know the child.
{ Thomas McCurtain
  Watson Wright

We hereby certify that we are well acquainted with   Rutha Millus   a   midwife   and know   her   to be reputable and of good standing in the community.

Must be two citizen witnesses.
{ Watson Wright
  [Illegible] Young

NEW BORN 7-186

In the matter of the application for the enrollment of Benjamin Colbert Merryman as a citizen by blood of the Choctaw Nation

Born Mch 12, 1903

BIRTH AFFIDAVIT.

DEPARTMENT OF THE INTERIOR.
COMMISSION TO THE FIVE CIVILIZED TRIBES.

IN RE APPLICATION FOR ENROLLMENT, as a citizen of the   Choctaw   Nation, of   Benjamin Colbert Merryman   , born on the 12   day of   March   , 1903

Name of Father: Walter Merryman   a citizen of the   Choctaw   Nation.
Name of Mother: Mary Merryman   a citizen of the   Choctaw   Nation.

Postoffice   LeFlore, Ind. Ter.

AFFIDAVIT OF MOTHER.

UNITED STATES OF AMERICA, Indian Territory, }
Central   DISTRICT. }

I,   Mary Merryman   , on oath state that I am   32   years of age and a citizen by   Marriage   , of the   Choctaw   Nation; that I am the lawful wife of   Walter Merryman   , who is a citizen, by blood   of the   Choctaw   Nation; that a   male   child was born to me on 12   day of March   , 1903; that said child has been named Benjamin Colbert Merryman   , and was living March 4, 1905.

her
Mary x Merryman
mark

Applications for Enrollment of Choctaw Newborn
Act of 1905 Volume IV

Witnesses To Mark:
  { Logan Harlin
    Ben Jones

Subscribed and sworn to before me this 30 day of March , 1905

My com. expires Jan. 11-1906

Robert E. Lee
Notary Public.

AFFIDAVIT OF ATTENDING PHYSICIAN OR MID-WIFE.

UNITED STATES OF AMERICA, Indian Territory,
  Central DISTRICT.

I, Ruth Millus , a midwife , on oath state that I attended on Mrs. Mary Merryman , wife of Walter Merryman on the 12 day of March , 1903; that there was born to her on said date a male child; that said child was living March 4, 1905, and is said to have been named Benjamin Colbert Merryman

Mrs. Ruth Millus

Witnesses To Mark:
  { H. E. Claborn
    John B. Millus

Subscribed and sworn to before me this 30 day of March , 1905

Robert E. Lee
Notary Public.

My com. expires Jan. 11-1906
    Enrollment of Mary Merryman being 824

BIRTH AFFIDAVIT.

DEPARTMENT OF THE INTERIOR.
COMMISSION TO THE FIVE CIVILIZED TRIBES.

IN RE APPLICATION FOR ENROLLMENT, as a citizen of the Choctaw Nation, of Benjamin C. Merryman , born on the 12 day of March , 1903

Name of Father: Walter G. Merryman   a citizen of the Choctaw Nation.
Name of Mother: Mary Merryman   a citizen of the U.S. Nation.

Postoffice Bengal I.T.

Applications for Enrollment of Choctaw Newborn
Act of 1905   Volume IV

AFFIDAVIT OF MOTHER.

UNITED STATES OF AMERICA, Indian Territory, }
Central   DISTRICT. }

I, Mary Merryman , on oath state that I am 32 years of age and a citizen by , of the U.S. Nation; that I am the lawful wife of Walter G. Merryman , who is a citizen, by blood of the Choctaw Nation; that a male child was born to me on 12 day of March , 1903; that said child has been named Benjamin C. Merryman , and was living March 4, 1905.

                                                her
                                      Mary Merryman x
                                                mark

Witnesses To Mark:
  { Lulie Loring
    C. R. Isaacs

Subscribed and sworn to before me this 17 day of April , 1905

                                      B.F. Johnson
                                      Notary Public.

AFFIDAVIT OF ATTENDING PHYSICIAN OR MID-WIFE.

UNITED STATES OF AMERICA, Indian Territory, }
Central   DISTRICT. }

I, Rutha Millus , a midwife , on oath state that I attended on Mrs. Mary Merryman , wife of Walter G. Merryman on the 12 day of March , 1903; that there was born to her on said date a male child; that said child was living March 4, 1905, and is said to have been named Benjamin C. Merryman

                                              her
                                      Rutha Millus x
Witnesses To Mark: mark
  { Lulie Loring
    C. R. Isaacs

Subscribed and sworn to before me this 17 day of April , 1905

                                      B.F. Johnson
                                      Notary Public.

My Commission Expires Jan. 28-1909

Applications for Enrollment of Choctaw Newborn
Act of 1905 Volume IV

COPY

7 NB 186

Muskogee, Indian Territory, April 20, 1905.

Walter G. Merryman,
    Bengal, Indian Territory.

Dear Sir:

    Receipt is hereby acknowledged of the affidavits of Mary Merryman and Rutha Millens[sic] to the birth of Benjamin C. Merryman, son of Walter G. and Mary Merryman, March 12, 1903, and the same have been filed with our records as an application for the enrollment of said child.

Respectively,
SIGNED
Tams Bixby
Chairman.

Choctaw 2880.

Muskogee, Indian Territory, April 12, 1905.

Walter Merryman,
    Leflore, Indian Territory.

Dear Sir:

    Receipt is hereby acknowledged of the affidavit of Mary Merryman and Mrs. Ruth Millus to the birth of Benjiman[sic] Colbert Merryman, March 12, 1903, and the same have been filed with our records as an application for the enrollment of said child.

Respectfully,

Commissioner in Charge.

Applications for Enrollment of Choctaw Newborn
Act of 1905   Volume IV

COPY

N. B. 186

Muskogee, Indian Territory, April 5, 1905.

Walter J[sic] Merryman,
    Bengal, Indian Territory.

Dear Sir:

    There is inclosed you herewith for execution application for the enrollment of your infant child, Benjamin C. Merryman, born March 12, 1903.

    The affidavits heretofore filed with the Commission show the child living on April 11, 1903. It is necessary, for the child to be enrolled, that he was living on March 4, 1905. You will please insert the age of the mother in space provided for the purpose.

    In having these affidavits executed care should be exercised to see that all the names are written in full as they appear in the body of the affidavit, and in the event that either of the persons signing the affidavit are unable to write, signatures by mark must be attested by two witnesses. Each affidavit must be executed before a Notary Public and the notarial seal and signature of the officer attached to each affidavit.

    Respectfully,
    SIGNED

T. B. Needles
Commissioner in Charge.

LM 5-7

Applications for Enrollment of Choctaw Newborn
Act of 1905   Volume IV

Choc New Born 187
    John Wesley LeFlore
    (Born Oct. 4, 1904)

BIRTH AFFIDAVIT.

DEPARTMENT OF THE INTERIOR,
COMMISSION TO THE FIVE CIVILIZED TRIBES.

IN RE Application for Enrollment, as a citizen of the Choctaw Nation, of John Wesley, born on the 4 day of October, 1904

Name of Father: Jno. Wesley Leflore   a citizen of the Choctaw Nation.
Name of Mother: Laura E.   "   a citizen by marriage of the Choctaw Nation.

Post-Office: Milton, I.T.

AFFIDAVIT OF MOTHER.

UNITED STATES OF AMERICA,
  INDIAN TERRITORY.
Central District.

    I, Laura E. Leflore, on oath state that I am 33 years of age and a citizen by Marriage, of the Choctaw Nation; that I am the lawful wife of Jno. Wesley Leflore, who is a citizen, by Blood of the Choctaw Nation; that a male child was born to me on 4th day of October, 1904, that said child has been named John Wesley Leflore, and is now living.

                                      her
                              Laura E. x Leflore
WITNESSES TO MARK: mark
    D.D. Daugherty
    G.W. Adams

    Subscribed and sworn to before me this 3rd day of Dec, 1904.

                                  J. L. Lewis
                                    NOTARY PUBLIC.

Applications for Enrollment of Choctaw Newborn
Act of 1905   Volume IV

AFFIDAVIT OF ATTENDING PHYSICIAN OR MID-WIFE.

UNITED STATES OF AMERICA,
    INDIAN TERRITORY.
  Central   District.

    I, T L Hedgecock, a physician, on oath state that I attended on Mrs. Laura E. Leflore, wife of Jno. W. Leflore on the 4 day of Oct, 1904 ; that there was born to her on said date a male child; that said child is now living and is said to have been named John Wesley Leflore

                            T L Hedgecock M.D.

WITNESSES TO MARK:

Subscribed and sworn to before me this 2 *day of* Dec , 1904.

                          J. L. Lewis
    My commission expires Mar. 15, 1905   **NOTARY PUBLIC.**
                          Milton, I.T.

NEW-BORN AFFIDAVIT.

    Number..........

...Choctaw Enrolling Commission...

    IN THE MATTER OF THE APPLICATION FOR ENROLLMENT, as a citizen of the Choctaw Nation, of John Wesley Leflore

born on the 4th day of October 190 4

Name of father Jno. W. Leflore   a citizen of Choctaw
Nation final enrollment No. 7622
Name of mother Laura Leflore   a citizen of Choctaw
Nation final enrollment No. Interm 255

                        Postoffice Milton, I.T.

Applications for Enrollment of Choctaw Newborn
Act of 1905   Volume IV

AFFIDAVIT OF MOTHER.

UNITED STATES OF AMERICA
INDIAN TERRITORY
Central   DISTRICT

I   Laura Leflore   , on oath state that I am   33   years of age and a citizen by   Marriage   of the   Choctaw   Nation, and as such have been placed upon the final roll of the   Choctaw   Nation, by the Honorable Secretary of the Interior my final enrollment number being   Intermarriage 255 ; that I am the lawful wife of   Jno. W. Leflore   , who is a citizen of the   Choctaw   Nation, and as such has been placed upon the final roll of said Nation by the Honorable Secretary of the Interior, his final enrollment number being   7622   and that a   Boy   child was born to me on the   4   day of   October 190 4; that said child has been named   John Wesley Leflore   , and is now living.

                        her
              Laura E.   x   Leflore
Witnesseth.   mark

Must be two Witnesses who are Citizens.
- J P Burns
- T.L. Leflore

Subscribed and sworn to before me this   20   day of   Feb   190 5

                      J. L. Lewis
                      Notary Public.

My commission expires:
My commission expires Mar. 15, 1905

AFFIDAVIT OF ATTENDING PHYSICIAN OR MIDWIFE

UNITED STATES OF AMERICA
INDIAN TERRITORY
Central   DISTRICT

I,   T. L. Hedgecock   a   physician on oath state that I attended on Mrs.   Laura Leflore   wife of   Jno. W. Leflore   on the   4   day of   October , 190 4, that there was born to her on said date a   boy   child, that said child is now living, and is said to have been named   John Wesley

              T.L. Hedgecock   M.D.
WITNESSETH:

Must be two witnesses who are citizens and know the child.
- J P Burns
- T L Leflore

Subscribed and sworn to before me this, the   20   day of   Feb   190 5

              J.L. Lewis   Notary Public.

Applications for Enrollment of Choctaw Newborn
Act of 1905 Volume IV

We hereby certify that we are well acquainted with ~~J.P Burns~~ T.L. Hedgecock a physician ~~T.L. Leflore~~ and know him to be reputable and of good standing in the community.

{ J P Burns
  T L Leflore

BIRTH AFFIDAVIT.

DEPARTMENT OF THE INTERIOR.
COMMISSION TO THE FIVE CIVILIZED TRIBES.

IN RE APPLICATION FOR ENROLLMENT, as a citizen of the Choctaw Nation, of John Wesley Leflore, born on the 4 day of Oct, 1904

Name of Father: Jno. W. Leflore   a citizen of the Choctaw Nation.
Name of Mother: Laure E. Leflore   a citizen of the Choctaw Nation.

Postoffice Milton, I.T.

AFFIDAVIT OF MOTHER.

UNITED STATES OF AMERICA, Indian Territory,
Central DISTRICT.

I, Laura E. Leflore, on oath state that I am 33 years of age and a citizen by Marriage, of the Choctaw Nation; that I am the lawful wife of Jno. W. Leflore, who is a citizen, by blood of the Choctaw Nation; that a boy child was born to me on 4 day of October, 1905[sic]; that said child has been named John Wesley Leflore, Jr., and was living March 4, 1905.

                         her
                 Laura E. x Leflore
Witnesses To Mark: mark
{ Mrs. N.D. Abernathy
  G.W. Adams

Subscribed and sworn to before me this 10 day of April, 1905

                 J. L. Lewis
                    Notary Public.

Applications for Enrollment of Choctaw Newborn
Act of 1905 Volume IV

AFFIDAVIT OF ATTENDING PHYSICIAN OR MID-WIFE.

UNITED STATES OF AMERICA, Indian Territory, }
Central   DISTRICT. }

I, T.L. Hedgecock, a Physician, on oath state that I attended on Mrs. Laura E. Leflore, wife of Jno. W. Leflore on the 4 day of Oct, 1904; that there was born to her on said date a boy child; that said child was living March 4, 1905, and is said to have been named John Wesley Leflore, Jr

T. L. Hedgecock M.D.

Witnesses To Mark:
{

Subscribed and sworn to before me this 10 day of April, 1905

J. L. Lewis
Notary Public.

My commission expires Mar. 15, 1905

COPY

N. B. 187

Muskogee, Indian Territory, April 10, 1905.

John W. Leflore,
    Milton, Indian Territory.

Dear Sir:

    There is inclosed you herewith for execution application for the enrollment of your infant child, John Wesley LeFlore, born October 4, 1904.

    The affidavits heretofore filed with the Commission show the child was living on December 3, 1904. It is necessary, for the child to be enrolled, that he was living on March 4, 1905. You will please insert the mother's age in the place left blank for that purpose.

    In having these affidavits executed care should be exercised to see that all the names are written in full as they appear in the body of the affidavit, and in the event that either of the persons signing the affidavit are unable to write, signatures by mark must be attested by two witnesses. Each affidavit must be executed before a Notary Public and the notarial seal and signature of the officer must be attached to each separate affidavit.

Applications for Enrollment of Choctaw Newborn
Act of 1905   Volume IV

Respectfully,
SIGNED

T. B. Needles

SEV 16-10.   Commissioner in Charge.

7-2624

Muskogee, Indian Territory, April 17, 1905.

John W. Leflore,
    Milton, Indian Territory.

Dear Sir:

    Receipt is hereby acknowledged of your letter of April 26, 1905, enclosing affidavits of Laura E. Leflore and T. L. Hedgecock to the birth of John Wesley Leflore, son of John W. and Laura E. Leflore, October 4, 1904, and the same have been filed with our records as an application for the enrollment of said child.

    Replying to that portion of your letter in which you ask if you can go to the land office and file on land for your child, you are advised that no selection of allotment can be permitted for children for whom application was made under the provision of the act of Congress approved March 3, 1905, until their enrollment has been approved by the Secretary of the Interior.

Respectfully,

Chairman.

Applications for Enrollment of Choctaw Newborn
Act of 1905   Volume IV

Choc New Born 188
    Virginia Garland
    (Born Oct. 7, 1902)

BIRTH AFFIDAVIT.

DEPARTMENT OF THE INTERIOR.
COMMISSION TO THE FIVE CIVILIZED TRIBES.

IN RE APPLICATION FOR ENROLLMENT, as a citizen of the   Choctaw   Nation, of   Virginia Garland , born on the 7   day of   October , 1902

Name of Father: William G. Garland   a citizen of the Choctaw Nation.
Name of Mother: Mary L. Garland   a citizen of the " by marriage Nation.

        Postoffice   Garland, I.T.

AFFIDAVIT OF ~~MOTHER~~.
    father

UNITED STATES OF AMERICA, Indian Territory, }
   Central   DISTRICT.

    I, William G Garland , on oath state that I am 37   years of age and a citizen by blood , of the   Choctaw   Nation; that I am the lawful ~~wife~~ husband of Mary L. Garland , who is a citizen, by marriage of the Choctaw   Nation; that a Female child was born to ~~me~~ her on 7   day of October , 1902 , that said child has been named Virginia Garland   , and is now living.

                           W. G. Garland

Witnesses To Mark:
{

    Subscribed and sworn to before me this 15   day of December , 1902.

                           H.C. Risteen
                           Notary Public.

Applications for Enrollment of Choctaw Newborn
Act of 1905   Volume IV

NEW-BORN AFFIDAVIT.

Number..............

...Choctaw Enrolling Commission...

IN THE MATTER OF THE APPLICATION FOR ENROLLMENT, as a citizen of the Choctaw Nation, of   Virginia Garland

born on the 7 day of __October__ 190 2

Name of father   W^m G Garland   a citizen of   Choctaw
Nation final enrollment No. 7592
Name of mother   Mary L Garland   a citizen of   Choctaw
Nation final enrollment No. 253

Postoffice   Garland I.T.

AFFIDAVIT OF MOTHER.

UNITED STATES OF AMERICA
INDIAN TERRITORY
..............................DISTRICT

I   Mary L Garland   , on oath state that I am 35 years of age and a citizen by Marriage of the   Choctaw   Nation, and as such have been placed upon the final roll of the   Choctaw   Nation, by the Honorable Secretary of the Interior my final enrollment number being   253 ; that I am the lawful wife of   William G Garland , who is a citizen of the   Choctaw   Nation, and as such has been placed upon the final roll of said Nation by the Honorable Secretary of the Interior, his final enrollment number being   7592   and that a   Female   child was born to me on the   7   day of October   190 2; that said child has been named   Virginia , and is now living.

Mary L Garland

Witnesseth.
　Must be two　⎱ Osborne N Cass
　Witnesses who ⎰
　are Citizens.　 C C Garland

Subscribed and sworn to before me this 30   day of Jan   190 5

C. C. Jones
Notary Public.

My commission expires: 3/3/1905

Applications for Enrollment of Choctaw Newborn
Act of 1905   Volume IV

AFFIDAVIT OF ATTENDING PHYSICIAN OR MIDWIFE

UNITED STATES OF AMERICA
INDIAN TERRITORY
..............................DISTRICT

I, C C Jones a Physician on oath state that I attended on Mrs. Mary L. Garland wife of W. G. Garland on the 7th day of October , 190 2 , that there was born to her on said date a Female child, that said child is now living, and is said to have been named Virginia

C.C. Jones

Subscribed and sworn to before me this, the 30 day of January 190 5

WITNESSETH: J.N. Jones Notary Public.

Must be two witnesses who are citizens { Osborne N Cass

C C Garland

We hereby certify that we are well acquainted with C C Jones a Physician and know................to be reputable and of good standing in the community.

Osborne N Cass

C C Garland

BIRTH AFFIDAVIT.

DEPARTMENT OF THE INTERIOR.
COMMISSION TO THE FIVE CIVILIZED TRIBES.

Choctaw

IN RE APPLICATION FOR ENROLLMENT, as a citizen of the CREEK Nation, of Virginnia[sic] Garland , born on the 7 day of October , 1902

Name of Father: William G Garland   a citizen of the Choctaw Nation.
Name of Mother: Mary L Garland   a citizen of the Choctaw Nation.

Postoffice   Garland Indian Territory

Applications for Enrollment of Choctaw Newborn
Act of 1905 Volume IV

AFFIDAVIT OF MOTHER.

UNITED STATES OF AMERICA, Indian Territory, }
Central ~~WESTERN~~ DISTRICT.

    I, Mary L Garland, on oath state that I am 36 years of age and a citizen by intermarriage, of the Choctaw Nation; that I am the lawful wife of William G Garland, who is a citizen, by blood of the Choctaw Nation; that a Female child was born to me on 7th day of October, 1902, that said child has been named Virginnia, and is now living.

                                                         Mary L Garland

Witnesses To Mark:
{

    Subscribed and sworn to before me this 25th day of March, 1905.

                                  C C Jones
                                  Notary Public.

AFFIDAVIT OF ATTENDING PHYSICIAN OR MID-WIFE.

UNITED STATES OF AMERICA, Indian Territory, }
Central DISTRICT.

    I, C C Jones, a Physician, on oath state that I attended on Mrs. Mary L Garland, wife of W G Garland on the 7th day of October, 1902; that there was born to her on said date a Female child; that said child is now living and is said to have been named Virginia

                                                  C C Jones

Witnesses To Mark:
{

    Subscribed and sworn to before me this 25 day of March, 1905.

                                  J N Jones
                                  Notary Public.

Applications for Enrollment of Choctaw Newborn
Act of 1905 Volume IV

BIRTH AFFIDAVIT.

DEPARTMENT OF THE INTERIOR.
COMMISSION TO THE FIVE CIVILIZED TRIBES.

IN RE APPLICATION FOR ENROLLMENT, as a citizen of the Choctaw Nation, of Virginia Garland, born on the 7 day of October, 1902

Name of Father: William G Garland a citizen of the Choctaw Nation.
Name of Mother: Mary L Garland   a citizen of the Choctaw Nation.

Postoffice   Garland Ind. Ter.

AFFIDAVIT OF MOTHER.

UNITED STATES OF AMERICA, Indian Territory,
Central DISTRICT.

I, Mary L Garland, on oath state that I am 36 years of age and a citizen by Intermarriage, of the Choctaw Nation; that I am the lawful wife of William G Garland, who is a citizen, by Blood of the Choctaw Nation; that a Female child was born to me on 7" day of October, 1902; that said child has been named Virginia Garland, and was living March 4, 1905.

Mary L Garland

Witnesses To Mark:

Subscribed and sworn to before me this 11 day of April, 1905

C C Jones
Notary Public.

AFFIDAVIT OF ATTENDING PHYSICIAN OR MID-WIFE.

UNITED STATES OF AMERICA, Indian Territory,
Central DISTRICT.

I, C C Jones, a physician, on oath state that I attended on Mrs. Mary L Garland, wife of William G Garland on the 7" day of October, 1902; that there was born to her on said date a Female child; that said child was living March 4, 1905, and is said to have been named Virginia Garland

Witnesses To Mark: C C Jones

Applications for Enrollment of Choctaw Newborn
Act of 1905   Volume IV

Subscribed and sworn to before me this 11 day of April   , 1905

J N Jones
Notary Public.

7-2615.

Muskogee, Indian Territory, January 6, 1903.

William G. Garland,
    Garland, Indian Territory.

Dear Sir:

    Referring to the application for enrollment as a citizen of the Choctaw Nation of Virginia Garland, infant daughter of William G. and Mary L. Garland, born October 7, 1902; you are advised that the Commission is without authority to enroll this child as a citizen of the Choctaw Nation, it appearing that said child was born October 7, 1902, subsequent to the ratification by the citizens of the Choctaw and Chickasaw Nations September 25, 1902 of an act of Congress approved July 1, 1902 (32 Stats., 641).

    Section twenty-eight thereof provides as follows:

"The names of all persons living on the date of the final ratification of this agreement entitled to be enrolled as provided in section 27 hereof shall be placed upon the rolls made by said Commission; and no child born thereafter to a citizen or freedman and no person intermarried thereafter to a citizen shall be entitled to enrollment or to participate in the distribution of the tribal property of the Choctaws and Chickasaws."

Respectfully,

Acting Chairman.

Applications for Enrollment of Choctaw Newborn
Act of 1905   Volume IV

COPY.

N. B. 188

Muskogee, Indian Territory, April 6, 1905.

William G. Garland,
    Garland, Indian Territory.

Dear Sir:

    There is inclosed you herewith for execution application for the enrollment of your infant child, Virginia Garland, born October 7, 1902.

    The papers heretofore filed with the Commission were incomplete in that they contained neither the affidavit of the mother nor that of the attending physician or midwife. Your affidavit which is on file in this office shows that the applicant was living on December 15, 1902. It is necessary, for the child to be enrolled, that she was living on March 4, 1905.

    In the event that the mother is dead, or that there was no physician or midwife in attendance, it will be necessary that you procure the affidavits of two persons who have actual knowledge of the fact, that the child was born, was living on March 4, 1905, and that Mary L. Garland was her mother.

    In having these affidavits execute care should be exercised to see that all the names are written in full as they appear in the body of the affidavit, and in the event that either of the persons signing the affidavit are unable to write, signatures by mark must be attested by two witnesses. Each affidavit must be executed before a Notary Public and the notarial seal and signature of the officer must be attached to each separate affidavit.

                     Respectfully,
                       SIGNED

                       T.B. Needles
LM 6-6   Commissioner in Charge.

Applications for Enrollment of Choctaw Newborn
Act of 1905   Volume IV

7-2615

Muskogee, Indian Territory, April 8, 1905.

William J[sic] Garland,
    Garland, Indian Territory.

Dear Sir:

    Receipt is hereby acknowledged of the affidavits of Mary L. Garland and C. C. Jones to the birth of Virginnia[sic] Garland daughter of William G. and Marcy[sic] L. Garland, October 7, 1902, and the same have been filed with our records as an application for the enrollment of said child.

Respectfully,

Commissioner in Charge.

Choctaw N.B. 188.

Muskogee, Indian Territory, April 16, 1905.

William G. Garland,
    Garland, Indian Territory.

Dear Sir:

    Receipt is hereby acknowledged of the affidavits of Mary L. Garland and C. C. Jones to the birth of Virginia Garland, daughter of William G. and Mary L. Garland, October 7, 1902, and the same have been filed with our records in the matter of the enrollment of said child.

Respectfully,

Chairman.

Applications for Enrollment of Choctaw Newborn
Act of 1905   Volume IV

Choc New Born 189
    [Lee O. Bench]
    [Born November 19, 1902]
    [Alton Brooks Bench]
    [Born September 11, 1904]

BIRTH AFFIDAVIT.
DEPARTMENT OF THE INTERIOR.
COMMISSION TO THE FIVE CIVILIZED TRIBES.

IN RE APPLICATION FOR ENROLLMENT, as a citizen of the Choctaw Nation, of Lee O. Bench, born on the 19 day of November, 1902

Name of Father: John D Bench   a citizen of the Choctaw Nation.
Name of Mother: Bettie Bench   a citizen of the Choctaw Nation.

    Postoffice   Enterprise, I.T.

AFFIDAVIT OF MOTHER.

UNITED STATES OF AMERICA, Indian Territory,
  Western   DISTRICT.

    I, Bettie Bench, on oath state that I am Twenty Five years of age and a citizen by Blood, of the Choctaw Nation; that I am the lawful wife of John D. Bench, who is a citizen, by Marriage of the Choctaw Nation; that a male child was born to me on 19 day of November, 1902, that said child has been named Lee O. Bench, and is now living.

                                                Bettie Bench
Witnesses To Mark:

    Subscribed and sworn to before me this 4 day of December, 1902.

                                         A. J. Rodden
                                       Notary Public Notary Public.

Applications for Enrollment of Choctaw Newborn
Act of 1905   Volume IV

AFFIDAVIT OF ATTENDING PHYSICIAN OR MID-WIFE.

UNITED STATES OF AMERICA, Indian Territory, }
Western   DISTRICT.

    I, T. B. Turner, a Physician, on oath state that I attended on Mrs. Bettie Bench, wife of John D Bench on the 19 day of December, 1902; that there was born to her on said date a   male   child; that said child is now living and is said to have been named Lee O Bench

                                              T.B. Turner M.D.

Witnesses To Mark:
{

    Subscribed and sworn to before me this 4 day of December, 1902.

                                        A.J. Rodden
                                        Notary Public Notary Public.

NEW-BORN AFFIDAVIT.

        Number..............

...Choctaw Enrolling Commission...

    IN THE MATTER OF THE APPLICATION FOR ENROLLMENT, as a citizen of the Choctaw   Nation, of   Alton Brooks Bench

born on the 11" day of __September__ 190 4

Name of father   John D. Bench   a citizen of   Choctaw
Nation final enrollment No.   909
Name of mother   Bettie Bench   a citizen of   Choctaw
Nation final enrollment No.   ~~909~~ 7048

                                        Postoffice   Hoyte[sic] I.T.

AFFIDAVIT OF MOTHER.

UNITED STATES OF AMERICA
INDIAN TERRITORY
............................DISTRICT

               I   Bettie Bench, on oath state that I am 27   years of age and a citizen by   Blood   of the   Choctaw   Nation, and as such have been placed upon the final roll of the   Choctaw   Nation, by the Honorable Secretary of the Interior my final enrollment number being   7048 ; that I am the lawful wife

Applications for Enrollment of Choctaw Newborn
Act of 1905   Volume IV

of   John D Bench   , who is a citizen of the   Choctaw   Nation, and as such has been placed upon the final roll of said Nation by the Honorable Secretary of the Interior, his final enrollment number being................and that a   Male   child was born to me on the   11th day of September   1904 ; that said child has been named   Alton Brooks Bench , and is now living.

Bettie Bench

Witnesseth.
Must be two Witnesses who are Citizens.   }   James Cooper
Minnie Farret

Subscribed and sworn to before me this 3   day of   Jan   190 5

James Bower
My commission expires: Notary Public.
Sept 23-1907

AFFIDAVIT OF ATTENDING PHYSICIAN OR MIDWIFE

UNITED STATES OF AMERICA
INDIAN TERRITORY
Central   DISTRICT

I,   T B Turner   a   Physician on oath state that I attended on Mrs.   Bettie Bench   wife of   John D Bench on the 11th day of   September , 190 4, that there was born to her on said date a   Male   child, that said child is now living, and is said to have been named   Alton Brooks Bench

T B Turner   M.D.

Subscribed and sworn to before me this, the   3   day of Jan   190 5

WITNESSETH: James Bower   Notary Public.
Must be two witnesses who are citizens and know the child.   {   James Cooper
Cathrine[sic] Holder

We hereby certify that we are well acquainted with_____
a_____and know_____to be reputable and of good standing in the community.

J. S. Stigler   _____

James Cooper   _____

Applications for Enrollment of Choctaw Newborn
Act of 1905   Volume IV

NEW-BORN AFFIDAVIT.

Number............

...Choctaw Enrolling Commission...

IN THE MATTER OF THE APPLICATION FOR ENROLLMENT, as a citizen of the Chocktaw[sic]   Nation, of   Lee O. Bench

born on the   19"   day of   November   190 2

Name of father   John D Bench   a citizen of   Choctaw
Nation final enrollment No.   909
Name of mother   Bettie Bench   a citizen of   Choctaw
Nation final enrollment No.   7048

Postoffice   Hoyt I.T.

AFFIDAVIT OF MOTHER.

UNITED STATES OF AMERICA
INDIAN TERRITORY
   Central   DISTRICT

I   Bettie Bench   , on oath state that I am 27 years of age and a citizen by   Blood   of the   Chotaw[sic]   Nation, and as such have been placed upon the final roll of the   Choctaw   Nation, by the Honorable Secretary of the Interior my final enrollment number being 7048 ; that I am the lawful wife of John D. Bench   , who is a citizen of the   Choctaw   Nation, and as such has been placed upon the final roll of said Nation by the Honorable Secretary of the Interior, his final enrollment number being_____ and that a   Male   child was born to me on the 19th day of   November   190 2; that said child has been named   Lee O. Bench   , and is now living.

Bettie Bench

Witnesseth.
   Must be two
   Witnesses who   } James Cooper
   are Citizens.   Minnie Farret

Subscribed and sworn to before me this   3   day of   Jan   190 5

James Bower
Notary Public.

My commission expires:
   Sept 23-1907

26

Applications for Enrollment of Choctaw Newborn
Act of 1905   Volume IV

AFFIDAVIT OF ATTENDING PHYSICIAN OR MIDWIFE

UNITED STATES OF AMERICA
INDIAN TERRITORY
Central   DISTRICT

I, T.B. Turner   a   Physician on oath state that I attended on Mrs. Bettie Bench   wife of   John D. Bench on the 19" day of November , 190 2 , that there was born to her on said date a   male child, that said child is now living, and is said to have been named Lee O. Bench

T. B. Turner M.D.

Subscribed and sworn to before me this, the   3   day of January   190 5

WITNESSETH: James Bower   Notary Public.

Must be two witnesses who are citizens { James Cooper

Henry Cooper

We hereby certify that we are well acquainted with _____
a_____ and know_____to be reputable and of good standing in the community.

J.S. Stigler

James Cooper

BIRTH AFFIDAVIT.

DEPARTMENT OF THE INTERIOR.
COMMISSION TO THE FIVE CIVILIZED TRIBES.

IN RE APPLICATION FOR ENROLLMENT, as a citizen of the   Choctaw   Nation, of   Alton Brooks Bench   , born on the 11th day of September , 1904

Name of Father: a citizen of the   Choctaw Nation.
Name of Mother: a citizen of the   Choctaw Nation.

Postoffice

Applications for Enrollment of Choctaw Newborn
Act of 1905 Volume IV

AFFIDAVIT OF MOTHER.

UNITED STATES OF AMERICA, Indian Territory,
Western DISTRICT.

I, Bettie Bench, on oath state that I a 28 years of age and a citizen by Blood, of the Choctaw Nation; that I am the lawful wife of John D Bench, who is a citizen, by Marriage of the Choctaw Nation; that a male child was born to me on the 11th day of September, 1904; that said child has been named Alton Brooks Bench, and was living March 4, 1905.

Bettie Bench

Witnesses To Mark:
 B F Grace

Subscribed and sworn to before me this 30 day of March, 1905

John M Lantz
Notary Public.

AFFIDAVIT OF ATTENDING PHYSICIAN OR MID-WIFE.

UNITED STATES OF AMERICA, Indian Territory,
Western DISTRICT.

I, T B Turner, a M.D., on oath state that I attended on Mrs. Bettie Bench, wife of John D Bench on the 11th day of September, 1904; that there was born to her on said date a male child; that said child was living March 4, 1905, and is said to have been named Alton Brooks Bench

T B Turner MD

Witnesses To Mark:

Subscribed and sworn to before me this 30 day of March, 1905

My Commission
Expires Nov 27 1909

John M. Lantz
Notary Public.

Applications for Enrollment of Choctaw Newborn
Act of 1905   Volume IV

BIRTH AFFIDAVIT.

DEPARTMENT OF THE INTERIOR.
COMMISSION TO THE FIVE CIVILIZED TRIBES.

IN RE APPLICATION FOR ENROLLMENT, as a citizen of the Choctaw Nation, of Lee O. Bench, born on the 19 day of November, 1902

Name of Father: John D. Bench   a citizen of the Choctaw Nation.
Name of Mother: Bettie Bench   a citizen of the Choctaw Nation.

Postoffice   Hoyt Ind. Ter.

AFFIDAVIT OF MOTHER.

UNITED STATES OF AMERICA, Indian Territory,
Western   DISTRICT.

I, Bettie Bench, on oath state that I am 28 years of age and a citizen by blood, of the Choctaw Nation; that I am the lawful wife of John D Bench, who is a citizen, by marriage of the Choctaw Nation; that a male child was born to me 19th day of November, 1902; that said child has been named Lee O. Bench, and was living March 4, 1905.

Bettie Bench

Witnesses To Mark:
   B F Grace

Subscribed and sworn to before me this 30 day of March, 1905.

John M. Lantz
Notary Public.

AFFIDAVIT OF ATTENDING PHYSICIAN OR MID-WIFE.

UNITED STATES OF AMERICA, Indian Territory,
Western   DISTRICT.

I, T B Turner, a M.D., on oath state that I attended on Mrs. Bettie Bench, wife of John D Bench on the 19th day of November, 1902; that there was born to her on said date a male child; that said child was living March 4, 1905, and is said to have been named Lee O. Bench.

T B Turner M D

Applications for Enrollment of Choctaw Newborn
Act of 1905   Volume IV

Witnesses To Mark:
{

Subscribed and sworn to before me this 30   day of March   , 1905
My commission
Expires Nov. 27 1907   John M. Lantz
                                                   Notary Public.

COPY.

N. B. 189

Muskogee, Indian Territory, April 6, 1905.

John D. Bench,
   Enterprise, Indian Territory.

Dear Sir:

   There is inclosed you herewith for execution application for the enrollment of your infant child, Lee O. Bench, born November 19, 1902.

   The affidavits heretofore filed with the Commission show the child was living on December 4, 1902. It is necessary, for the child to be enrolled, that he was living on March 4, 1905. You will please insert the mother's age in the place left blank for that purpose.

   In having these affidavits executed, care should be exercised to see that all the names are written in full as they appear in the body of the affidavit, and in the event that either of the persons signing the affidavit are unable to write, signatures by mark must be attested by two witnesses. Each affidavit must be executed before a Notary Public and the notorial[sic] seal and signature of the officer must be attached to each separate affidavit.

                           Respectfully,
                           SIGNED

                           T.B. Needles
SEV 6-6   Commissioner in Charge.

Applications for Enrollment of Choctaw Newborn
Act of 1905   Volume IV

COPY.

7 NB 189

Muskogee, Indian Territory, April 25, 1905.

John D. Bench,
    Hoyt, Indian Territory.

Dear Sir:

    Receipt is hereby acknowledged of the affidavits of Bettie Bench and T. B. Turner to the birth of Alton Brooks Bench, son of John D. and Bettie Bench, September 11, 1904. Receipt is also acknowledged of your letter of April 17, 1905, referring to affidavits recently left by you at the Choctaw Land Office in the matter of the enrollment of Lee O. Bench.

    In reply to your letter you are informed that the affidavits of Bettie Bench and T. B. Turner to the birth of Lee O. Bench have been filed with our records as an application for the enrollment of said child.

Respectfully,
SIGNED
Tams Bixby
Chairman.

7-N.B.189.

Muskogee, Indian Territory, June 5, 1905.

John D. Bench,
    Hoyt, Indian Territory.

Dear Sir:

    Receipt is hereby acknowledged of your letter of May 27, asking to be notified when you may file for your children, Lee O. Bench and Alton B. Bench.

    In reply to your letter you are advised that the names of your children, Lee O. Bench and Alton Brooks Bench, have been placed upon a schedule of citizens by blood of the Choctaw Nation prepared for forwarding to the Secretary of the Interior, and you will be notified when their enrollment is approved. Pending their approval, however, no selection of allotment can be made for your children.

Respectfully,

Commissioner in Charge.

Applications for Enrollment of Choctaw Newborn
Act of 1905   Volume IV

Choc New Born 190
    Losera Matthews
    (Born Nov. 20, 1903)

BIRTH AFFIDAVIT.

DEPARTMENT OF THE INTERIOR,
COMMISSION TO THE FIVE CIVILIZED TRIBES.

In Re Application for Enrollment, as a citizen of the Choctaw Nation, of Indian Territory, born on the 20 day of November, 1908[sic]

Name of Father: John W Matthews   a citizen of the Choctaw Nation.
Name of Mother: Rosa Matthews   a citizen of the Choctaw Nation.

Post-office

AFFIDAVIT OF MOTHER.

UNITED STATES OF AMERICA,
   INDIAN TERRITORY,
Central District.

    I, Rosa Matthews, on oath state that I am 26 years of age and a citizen by birth, of the Choctaw Nation; that I am the lawful wife of John W Matthews, who is a citizen, by Marriage of the Choctaw Nation; that a girl female child was born to me on 20 day of November, 1903, that said child has been named Losera Matthews, and is now living.

                                          Rosa Matthews

WITNESSES TO MARK:
  W R Stafford
  R B Stafford

    Subscribed and sworn to before me this 12 day of January, 1904.

                                    A. F. M. Keener
                                        NOTARY PUBLIC.

Applications for Enrollment of Choctaw Newborn
Act of 1905   Volume IV

AFFIDAVIT OF ATTENDING PHYSICIAN OR MID-WIFE.

UNITED STATES OF AMERICA,
    INDIAN TERRITORY,
                District.

I, Anna Stafford, a Midwife, on oath state that I attended on Mrs. Rosa Matthews, wife of John W Matthews on the 20 day of November, 1903 ; that there was born to her on said date a girl or female child; that said child is now living and is said to have been named Losera Matthews

                                      Anna Stafford

WITNESSES TO MARK:
- W R Stafford
- R B Stafford

Subscribed and sworn to before me this 12 day of January, 1904.

                                      A.F.M. Keener
                                            NOTARY PUBLIC.

BIRTH AFFIDAVIT.

DEPARTMENT OF THE INTERIOR.
COMMISSION TO THE FIVE CIVILIZED TRIBES.

IN RE APPLICATION FOR ENROLLMENT, as a citizen of the Choctaw Nation, of Losera Matthews, born on the 20 day of November, 1903

Name of Father: John W. Matthews   a citizen of the Choctaw Nation.
Name of Mother: Rosa Matthews   a citizen of the Choctaw Nation.

                              Postoffice   Farris   Indian Territory

AFFIDAVIT OF MOTHER.

UNITED STATES OF AMERICA, Indian Territory,
    Central   DISTRICT.

I, Rosa Matthews, on oath state that I am 26 years of age and a citizen by birth, of the Choctaw Nation; that I am the lawful wife of John W. Matthews, who is a citizen, by marriage of the Choctaw Nation; that a female child was born to me on 20 day of November, 1903; that said child has been named Losera Matthews, and was living March 4, 1905.

Applications for Enrollment of Choctaw Newborn
Act of 1905   Volume IV

Rosa Matthews

Witnesses To Mark:
 { Ben V. Hampton
   Anna Crabtree

Subscribed and sworn to before me this 8th day of May, 1905

C.B. Prather
Notary Public.

AFFIDAVIT OF ATTENDING PHYSICIAN OR MID-WIFE.

UNITED STATES OF AMERICA, Indian Territory, }
Central   DISTRICT. }

I, Anna Stafford, a midwife, on oath state that I attended on Mrs. Rosa Matthews, wife of John W. Matthews on the 20 day of November, 1903; that there was born to her on said date a female child; that said child was living March 4, 1905, and is said to have been named Losera Matthews

Anna Stafford

Witnesses To Mark:
 { Ben V. Hampton
   Anna Crabtree

Subscribed and sworn to before me this 8th day of May, 1905

C.B. Prather
Notary Public.

COPY.

N. B. 190

Muskogee, Indian Territory, April 7, 1905.

John W. Mathews[sic],
    Lloyd, Indian Territory.

Dear Sir:

There is inclosed you herewith for execution application for the enrollment of your infant child, Lorena[sic] Mathews, born November 20, 1903.

Applications for Enrollment of Choctaw Newborn
Act of 1905   Volume IV

The affidavits heretofore filed with the Commission show the child was living on January 12, 1904. It is necessary, for the child to be enrolled, that she was living on March 4, 1905.

In having these affidavits executed care should be exercised to see that all the names are written in full as they appear in the body of the affidavit, and in the event that either of the persons signing the affidavit are unable to write, signatures by mark must be attested by two witnesses. Each affidavit must be executed before a Notary Public and the notorial[sic] seal and signature of the officer must be attached to each separate affidavit.

Respectfully,
SIGNED

LM 7-4

T.B. Needles
Commissioner in Charge.

Choctaw 2186.

Muskogee, Indian Territory, April 15, 1905.

John W. Matthews,
  Farris, Indian Territory.

Dear Sir:

Receipt is hereby acknowledged of the affidavits of Rosa Matthews and Anna Stafford to the birth of Losera Matthews, daughter of John W. and Rosa Matthews, November 20, 1903, and the same have been filed with our records as an application for the enrollment of said child.

Respectfully,

Chairman.

7-N.B. 190 .

Muskogee, Indian Territory, May 15, 1905.

John W. Mathews[sic],
  Farris, Indian Territory.

Dear Sir:

Receipt is hereby acknowledged of the affidavits of Rosa Matthews and Anna Stafford to the birth of Losera Matthews, daughter of John W. and Rosa Matthews,

Applications for Enrollment of Choctaw Newborn
Act of 1905   Volume IV

November 20, 1903, and the same have been filed with our records as an application for the enrollment of said child.

Respectfully,

Chairman.

7-NB-190

Muskogee, Indian Territory, June 7, 1905.

John W. Matthews,
Farris, Indian Territory.

Dear Sir:

Receipt is hereby acknowledged of your letter of May 30, 1905, asking when the enrollment of your child for whom application was recently made will be approved so that you can select allotment.

In reply to your letter you are advised that the name of your child Losera Matthews has been placed upon a schedule of citizens by blood of the Choctaw Nation which has been forwarded the Secretary of the Interior for approval, but the Commission has not yet been advised of Departmental action thereon. You will be notified when this action is approved by the Department.

Replying to that portion of your letter in which you ask if your child born March 27, 1905, can be enrolled you are advised that under the provisions of the act of Congress approved March 3, 1905, the Commission to the Five Civilized Tribes was authorized for a period of sixty days from that date to receive applications for the enrollment of children born to enrolled citizens by blood of the Choctaw and Chickasaw Nations between September 25, 1902 and March 4, 1905, and living on the latter date. You will therefore see that the Commission is without authority to enroll children born subsequent to March 4, 1905.

Respectfully,

Chairman.

Applications for Enrollment of Choctaw Newborn
Act of 1905   Volume IV

Choc New Born 191
    Clarence Bond
    (Born Sep. 20, 1904)

NEW-BORN AFFIDAVIT.

Number..............

Choctaw Enrolling Commission.

IN THE MATTER OF THE APPLICATION FOR ENROLLMENT, as a citizen of the Choctaw   Nation, of   Clarence Bond

born on the 20   day of   September   1904

Name of father   Henry J Bond   a citizen of   Choctaw
Nation final enrollment No   13687
Name of mother   Lizzie Bond   a citizen of   Choctaw
Nation final enrollment No 621

Postoffice

AFFIDAVIT OF MOTHER.

UNITED STATES OF AMERICA,
    INDIAN TERRITORY,
    Central   DISTRICT

I   Lizzie Bond   on oath state that I am   31   years of age and a citizen by   blood   of the   Choctaw   Nation, and as such have been placed upon the final roll of the   Choctaw   Nation, by the Honorable Secretary of the Interior my final enrollment number being   621   ; that I am the lawful wife of   Henry J Bond   , who is a citizen of the   Choctaw   Nation, and as such has been placed upon the final roll of said Nation by the Honorable Secretary of the Interior, his final enrollment number being 13,687   and that a   male   child was born to me on the   20   day of September   1904 ; that said child has been named   Clarence Bond   , and is now living.

                                    Lizzie Bond

WITNESSETH:
    Must be two   Silas Byington
    Witnesses who
    are Citizens.   Jno H Self

Applications for Enrollment of Choctaw Newborn
Act of 1905 Volume IV

Subscribed and sworn to before me this 4th day of Feby   190 5

                             D S Kennedy
                                           Notary Public.

My commission expires
         Nov. 1st 1905

AFFIDAVIT OF ATTENDING PHYSICIAN OR MIDWIFE

UNITED STATES OF AMERICA
INDIAN TERRITORY
   Central   DISTRICT

     I,   J. A. Dabney   a   Practicing Physician on oath state that I attended on Mrs.   Lizzie Bond   wife of   Henry J Bond on the   20   day of   September , 190 4, that there was born to her on said date a   male child, that said child is now living, and is said to have been named   Clarence Bond

                         J. A. Dabney   M.D.

WITNESSETH:
Must be two witnesses who are citizens and know the child.
     { Silas Byington
       Jno H Self

         Subscribed and sworn to before me this, the   6th day of   Feby   190 5

                    D S Kennedy   Notary Public.

    We hereby certify that we are well acquainted with   Dr. J.A. Dabney   a   Physician   and know   him   to be reputable and of good standing in the community.

                 { O.C. Elkins
                 { E J Vaughan

BIRTH AFFIDAVIT.

DEPARTMENT OF THE INTERIOR.
COMMISSION TO THE FIVE CIVILIZED TRIBES.

    IN RE APPLICATION FOR ENROLLMENT, as a citizen of the   Choctaw   Nation, of   Clarence Bond   , born on the 20th day of Sept.   , 1904

Name of Father: Henry J Bond   a citizen of the   Choctaw   Nation.
Name of Mother: Lizzie Bond   a citizen of the   Choctaw   Nation.

Applications for Enrollment of Choctaw Newborn
Act of 1905   Volume IV

Postoffice   Stringtown, I.T.

AFFIDAVIT OF MOTHER.

UNITED STATES OF AMERICA, Indian Territory,
Central Judicial   DISTRICT.

I, Lizzie Bond, on oath state that I am 31 years of age and a citizen by blood, of the Choctaw Nation; that I am the lawful wife of Henry J Bond, who is a citizen, by blood of the Choctaw Nation; that a male child was born to me on 20th day of Sept, 1904; that said child has been named Clarence Bond, and was living March 4, 1905.

Lizzie Bond

Witnesses To Mark:

Subscribed and sworn to before me this 20th day of Mch, 1905

D.S. Kennedy
Notary Public.

AFFIDAVIT OF ATTENDING PHYSICIAN OR MID-WIFE.

UNITED STATES OF AMERICA, Indian Territory,
Central Judicial   DISTRICT.

I, J.A. Dabney, a Physician, on oath state that I attended on Mrs. Lizzie Bond, wife of Henry J Bond on the 20th day of Sept., 1904; that there was born to her on said date a male child; that said child was living March 4, 1905, and is said to have been named Clarence Bond

J.A. Dabney M.D.

Witnesses To Mark:

Subscribed and sworn to before me this 20th day of Mch, 1905

D.S. Kennedy
Notary Public.

Applications for Enrollment of Choctaw Newborn
Act of 1905   Volume IV

7-291

Muskogee, Indian Territory, March 23, 1905.

Henry J. Bond,
    Stringtown, Indian Territory.

Dear Sir:

    Receipt is hereby acknowledged of the affidavits of Lizzie Bond and J. A. Gadney[sic] to the birth of Clarance[sic] Bond, son of Henry J. and Lizzie Bond, September 20, 1904, and the same have been filed with our records as an application for the enrollment of said child.

    Respectfully,

    Chairman.

Substitute.

7-NB-191

Muskogee, Indian Territory, July 22, 1905.

Henry J. Bond,
    Stringtown, Indian Territory.

Dear Sir:

    Receipt if hereby acknowledged of your letter of July 8, 1905, asking if parents will be allowed to file for their new born children in the Choctaw and Chickasaw Nations; that as soon as your child is approved you want to file on his homestead and a part of his surplus land in the Chickasaw Nation and the remainder in the Choctaw Nation; you therefore ask to be advised the ruling in regard to this matter.

    In reply to your letter you are advised that on June 30, 1905, the Secretary of the Interior approved the enrollment of your son Clarence Bond as a citizen by blood of the Choctaw Nation and selection of allotment may now be made in his behalf.

    You are further advised that when it is the desire of the representation of an allottee who has been enrolled under the provisions of the act of Congress approved March 3, 1905, to take the allotment in both nations, the initial selection shall include at least a complete homestead as nearly as may be according to the valuation of the land and at the second appearance the balance of the allotment [the file ends here].

Applications for Enrollment of Choctaw Newborn
Act of 1905   Volume IV

Choc New Born 192
　　George Ewing Hartshorne
　　(Born Sep. 18, 1903)

NEW BORN AFFIDAVIT

No ....

CHOCTAW ENROLLING COMMISSION

IN THE MATTER OF THE APPLICATION FOR ENROLLMENT as a citizen of the Choctaw Nation, of   George Ewing Hartshorne   born on the 18th   day of September   190 3

Name of father G. E. Hartshorne   a citizen of   Choctaw   Nation,
final enrollment No. Intermarriage No. 51
Name of mother David C. Hartshorne   a citizen of   Choctaw   Nation,
final enrollment No. 8123

　　　　　　　　　　　　　　　　　　South McAlester, I.T.   Postoffice.

AFFIDAVIT OF MOTHER

UNITED STATES OF AMERICA
　　INDIAN TERRITORY
DISTRICT   Central

　　I David C. Hartshorne   , on oath state that I am 30   years of age and a citizen by   Blood   of the   Choctaw   Nation, and as such have been placed upon the final roll of the   Choctaw   Nation, by the Honorable Secretary of the Interior my final enrollment number being   8123   ; that I am the lawful wife of   G.E. Hartshorne   , who is a citizen of the   Choctaw   Nation, and as such has been placed upon the final roll of said Nation by the Honorable Secretary of the Interior, his final enrollment number being 51   and that a   Male   child was born to me on the   18th   day of   September   190 3; that said child has been named George Ewing Hartshorne   , and is now living.

　　　　　　　　　　　　　　　　　　David C Hartshorne

WITNESSETH:
　Must be two witnesses { N.B. Ainsworth
　who are citizens   { Lee Silmon

Applications for Enrollment of Choctaw Newborn
Act of 1905 Volume IV

Subscribed and sworn to before me this, the 15 day of   March , 190 5

                               James Bower
                                         Notary Public.

My Commission Expires:
         Sept 23, 1907

Affidavit of Attending Physician or Midwife

UNITED STATES OF AMERICA,
    INDIAN TERRITORY,
 Central   DISTRICT

     I, G. E. Hartshorne   a   Practicing Physician
on oath state that I attended on Mrs. David C Hartshorne   wife of G.E. Hartshorne
on the 18th   day of September , 190 3, that there was born to her on said date a   male
child, that said child is now living, and is said to have been named George Ewing Hartshorne

                               G.E. Hartshorne   M. D.

Subscribed and sworn to before me this the 15   day of March   1905

                               James Bower
                                  Notary Public.

WITNESSETH:
Must be two witnesses { N.B. Ainsworth
who are citizens and
know the child.   Lee Silmon

     We hereby certify that we are well acquainted with   G. E. Hartshorne
a Practicing Physician   and know   him   to be reputable and of good
standing in the community.

                       Must be two citizen { Eli E Mitchell
                       witnesses.   W H Ansley

Applications for Enrollment of Choctaw Newborn
Act of 1905   Volume IV

Affidavits

United States of America
Indian Territory
Central District.

I, Mary Spears, on oath state that I am 36 years old and am personally acquainted with Mrs. David C. Hartshorne, wife of G. E. Hartshorne, that I was present on the 18th day of September, 1903, when there was born to said Mrs. David C Hartshorne a male child, and that said child is now living and has been named George Ewing Hartshorne.

Mary Spears

Subscribed and sworn to before me this 17th day of March, 1905.

Wirt Franklin
Notary Public.

BIRTH AFFIDAVIT.

DEPARTMENT OF THE INTERIOR.
COMMISSION TO THE FIVE CIVILIZED TRIBES.

IN RE APPLICATION FOR ENROLLMENT, as a citizen of the Choctaw Nation, of George Ewing Hartshorne, born on the 18th day of September, 1903

Name of Father: G. E. Hartshorne   a citizen of the Choctaw Nation.
Name of Mother: David C Hartshorne   a citizen of the Choctaw Nation.

Postoffice   South McAlester, I.T.

AFFIDAVIT OF MOTHER.

UNITED STATES OF AMERICA, Indian Territory,
Central DISTRICT.

I, David C Hartshorne, on oath state that I am 30 years of age and a citizen by blood, of the Choctaw Nation; that I am the lawful wife of G. E. Hartshorne, who is a citizen, by marriage of the Choctaw Nation; that a male child was born to me on 18th day of September, 1903; that said child has been named George Ewing Hartshorne, and was living March 4, 1905.

David C Hartshorne

Witnesses To Mark:

Applications for Enrollment of Choctaw Newborn
Act of 1905 Volume IV

Subscribed and sworn to before me this 17th day of March, 1905

Wirt Franklin
Notary Public.

AFFIDAVIT OF ATTENDING PHYSICIAN OR MID-WIFE.

UNITED STATES OF AMERICA, Indian Territory,
Central DISTRICT.

I, G. E. Hartshorne, a physician, on oath state that I attended on Mrs. David C Hartshorne my, wife ~~of~~ on the 18th day of September, 1903; that there was born to her on said date a male child; that said child was living March 4, 1905, and is said to have been named George Ewing Hartshorne

G.E. Hartshorne

Witnesses To Mark:

Subscribed and sworn to before me this 17th day of March, 1905

Wirt Franklin
Notary Public.

Choc New Born 193
    John Lawson [Barbour]
    (Born Jan. 3, 1903)

BIRTH AFFIDAVIT.

DEPARTMENT OF THE INTERIOR,
COMMISSION TO THE FIVE CIVILIZED TRIBES.

In Re Application for Enrollment, as a citizen of the Choctaw Nation, of John Lawson Barbour, born on the 3 day of January, 1903

Name of Father: David P Barbour   a citizen of the Choctaw Nation.
Name of Mother: Hester A. Barbour   a citizen of the Choctaw Nation.

Post-office   Tamaha I.T.

Applications for Enrollment of Choctaw Newborn
Act of 1905   Volume IV

AFFIDAVIT OF MOTHER.

UNITED STATES OF AMERICA, }
   INDIAN TERRITORY,
_____District.

I, Hester A. Barbour , on oath state that I am   years of age and a citizen by blood , of the   Choctaw   Nation; that I am the lawful wife of David P Barbour , who is a citizen, by Intermarriage of the   Choctaw   Nation; that a male   child was born to me on   3   day of   January   , 1903 , that said child has been named John Lawson Barbour   , and is now living.

                                            Hester A. Barbour

WITNESSES TO MARK:

{ My Commission
Subscribed and sworn to before me this   21   day of   November   , 1904.
expires 11th May 1907

                                          W^m B Davidson
                                          NOTARY PUBLIC.

AFFIDAVIT OF ATTENDING PHYSICIAN OR MID-WIFE.

UNITED STATES OF AMERICA, }
   INDIAN TERRITORY,
Central   District.

I,   S.M. Smith   , a   physician   , on oath state that I attended on Mrs. Hester A. Barbour , wife of   David P Barbour   on the   3   day of January   , 1903 ; that there was born to her on said date a   male   child; that said child is now living and is said to have been named   John Lawson Barbour

WITNESSES TO MARK: S. M. Smith M.D.

{

Subscribed and sworn to before me this   21   day of November   , 1904.

                                        W^m B Davidson
                                        NOTARY PUBLIC.

Applications for Enrollment of Choctaw Newborn
Act of 1905   Volume IV

NEW-BORN AFFIDAVIT.

Number..................

...Choctaw Enrolling Commission...

IN THE MATTER OF THE APPLICATION FOR ENROLLMENT, as a citizen of the Choctaw Nation, of John Lawson Barbour

born on the 3 day of ___January___ 190 4

Name of father David P Barbour   a citizen of Choctaw Nation final enrollment No.
Name of mother Hester A Barbour   a citizen of Choctaw Nation final enrollment No. 8126

                                       Postoffice   Tamaha

AFFIDAVIT OF MOTHER.

UNITED STATES OF AMERICA
INDIAN TERRITORY
  Central   DISTRICT

I Hester A Barbour , on oath state that I am 24 years of age and a citizen by Blood of the Choctaw Nation, and as such have been placed upon the final roll of the Choctaw Nation, by the Honorable Secretary of the Interior my final enrollment number being 8126 ; that I am the lawful wife of David P Barbour , who is a citizen of the Choctaw Nation, and as such has been placed upon the final roll of said Nation by the Honorable Secretary of the Interior, his final enrollment number being _____ and that a Male child was born to me on the 3 day of January 190 4; that said child has been named John Lawson Barbour , and is now living.

                               Hester A Barbour

Witnesseth.
  Must be two } George L Wadley
  Witnesses who
  are Citizens.   J M Scantler

Subscribed and sworn to before me this 28 day of Jany 190 5

                               W^m B Davidson
                                    Notary Public.

My commission expires: 11th May 1907

Applications for Enrollment of Choctaw Newborn
Act of 1905 Volume IV

AFFIDAVIT OF ATTENDING PHYSICIAN OR MIDWIFE

UNITED STATES OF AMERICA
INDIAN TERRITORY
Central   DISTRICT

I, Ella Hall a Midwife Nurse on oath state that I attended on Mrs. Hester A. Barbour wife of David P. Barbour, on the 3 day of January, 190 4, that there was born to her on said date a Male child, that said child is now living, and is said to have been named John Lawson Barbour

Ella Hall

Subscribed and sworn to before me this, the 28 day of January 190 5

WITNESSETH: Wm B. Davidson Notary Public.
Must be two witnesses { George W. Wadley
who are citizens   { J. M. Scantler

We hereby certify that we are well acquainted with Ella Hall a nurse and know she to be reputable and of good standing in the community.

_____   George L. Wadley

_____   J.M. Scantler

DEPARTMENT OF THE INTERIOR,
COMMISSION TO THE FIVE CIVILIZED TRIBES.
BOKOSHE, INDIAN TERRITORY APRIL 5, 1905.

In the matter of the application for the enrollment of John Lawson Barbour as a citizen by blood of the Choctaw Nation.

Hester A. Barbour being first duly sworn testifies as follows:

EXAMINATION BY THE COMMISSION:

Q What is your name? A Hester A. Barbour.
Q What is your age? A Twenty-three.
Q What is your post office address? A Tamaha.
Q You have this day made application for the enrollment of your minor child John Lawson Barbour: A Yes, sir.
Q Who attended you when this child was born? A Dr. Smith.

Applications for Enrollment of Choctaw Newborn
Act of 1905   Volume IV

Q Where was he located   A At Sailor, four miles below Tamaha.
Q Is he living at this time?   A No, sir.
Q Have you heretofore forwarded to the Commission at Muskogee a doctor's certificate?
A Yes, sir, at one time.
Q Signed by Dr. Smith?   A Yes, sir.
Q When did this Dr. Smith die?   A It was in January 1905 some time.

Witness excused.

Chas. T. Difendafer being first duly sworn states that the above and foregoing is a full, true and correct transcript of his stenographic notes taken in said cause on said date.

Chas. T. Difendafer

Subscribed and sworn to before me this 5th day of April 1905.

OL Johnson
Notary Public.

BIRTH AFFIDAVIT.
DEPARTMENT OF THE INTERIOR.
COMMISSION TO THE FIVE CIVILIZED TRIBES.

IN RE APPLICATION FOR ENROLLMENT, as a citizen of the   Choctaw   Nation, of   John Lawson Barbour   , born on the 3rd   day of   January   , 1904

Name of Father: D. P. Barbour   a citizen of the United States ~~Nation~~.
Name of Mother: Hester A. Barbour   a citizen of the   Choctaw   Nation.

Postoffice   Tamaha, Ind. Ter.

AFFIDAVIT OF MOTHER.

UNITED STATES OF AMERICA, Indian Territory,
  Central   DISTRICT.

I,   Hester A. Barbour   , on oath state that I am   23   years of age and a citizen by   blood   , of the   Choctaw   Nation; that I am the lawful wife of D. P. Barbour   , who is a citizen, ~~by~~ .... of the   Unites States   Nation; that a   male   child was born to me on   3rd   day of   January   , 1904; that said child has been named   John Lawson Barbour   , and was living March 4, 1905.

Hester A. Barbour

Witnesses To Mark:

Applications for Enrollment of Choctaw Newborn
Act of 1905   Volume IV

Subscribed and sworn to before me this 5th day of April, 1905

OL Johnson
Notary Public.

BIRTH AFFIDAVIT.

DEPARTMENT OF THE INTERIOR.
COMMISSION TO THE FIVE CIVILIZED TRIBES.

IN RE APPLICATION FOR ENROLLMENT, as a citizen of the Choctaw Nation, of John Lawson Barbour, born on the 3 day of January, 1903

Name of Father: David P. Barbour   a citizen of the Choctaw Nation.
Name of Mother: Hester A Barbour   a citizen of the Choctaw Nation.

Postoffice   Tamaha, Indian Territory

AFFIDAVIT OF MOTHER.

UNITED STATES OF AMERICA, Indian Territory, } DISTRICT.

I, Hester A. Barbour, on oath state that I am 23 years of age and a citizen by blood, of the Choctaw Nation; that I am the lawful wife of David P. Barbour, who is a citizen, by intermarriage of the Choctaw Nation; that a male child was born to me on 3 day of January, 1903; that said child has been named John Lawson Barbour, and was living March 4, 1905.

Hester A. Barbour

Witnesses To Mark:

Subscribed and sworn to before me this 17 day of April, 1905

My Commission Expires } Wm B. Davidson
11th May 1907   Notary Public.

AFFIDAVIT OF ATTENDING PHYSICIAN OR MID-WIFE.

UNITED STATES OF AMERICA, Indian Territory, } Central   DISTRICT.

I, Ella Hall, attending nurse, on oath state that I attended on Mrs. Hester A Barbour, wife of David P Barbour on the 3 day of

Applications for Enrollment of Choctaw Newborn
Act of 1905   Volume IV

January   , 1903; that there was born to her on said date a   male   child; that said child was living March 4, 1905, and is said to have been named John Lawson Barbour

Ella Hall

Witnesses To Mark:
{

Subscribed and sworn to before me this 17 day of   April   , 1905

My Commission Expires   } Wm B. Davidson
11th May 1907   Notary Public.

(Blank 731.)
CHOCTAW ROLL, CITIZENS BY BLOOD.

NEW BORN.

Act of Congress Approved March 3rd, 1905. (Public No. 212).

Number.	Name.	Age.	Sex.	Blood.	Card
195	Barbour, John Lawson	2	M	1/16	193

7-2772

Muskogee, Indian Territory, November 28, 1904.

David P. Barbour,
    Tamaha, Indian Territory.

Dear Sir:

Receipt is hereby acknowledged of the affidavits of Hester Barbour and S. M. Smith relative to the birth of your infant son John Lawson Barbour January 3, 1903, which it is presumed have been forwarded to this office as an application for the enrollment of said child as a citizen by blood of the Choctaw Nation.

Applications for Enrollment of Choctaw Newborn
Act of 1905   Volume IV

The Act of Congress approved July 1, 1902, which was ratified by the citizens of the Choctaw and Chickasaw Nations September 25, 1902, among other things provides that no child born to a citizen of the Choctaw or Chickasaw Nation subsequent to the date of said ratification shall be entitled to enrollment or to participate in the distribution of the tribal property of the Choctaws and Chickasaws.

Respectfully,

Commissioner in Charge.

COPY.

Choc. N. B. 193

Muskogee, Indian Territory, April 6, 1905.

David P. Barbour,
Tamaha, Indian Territory.

Dear Sir:

There is inclosed you herewith for execution application for the enrollment of your infant child, John Lawson Barbour, born January 3, 1903.

The affidavits heretofore filed with the Commission show the child was living on November 21, 1904. It is necessary, for the child to be enrolled, that he was living on March 4, 1905. You will please insert the mother's age in the place left blank for that purpose.

In having these affidavits executed, care should be exercised to see that all the names are written in full as they appear in the body of the affidavit, and in the event that either of the persons signing the affidavit are unable to write, signatures by mark must be attested by two witnesses. Each affidavit must be executed before a Notary Public and the notorial[sic] seal and signature of the officer must be attached to each separate affidavit.

Respectfully,
SIGNED

T.B. Needles

SEV 2-6.
Commissioner in Charge.

Applications for Enrollment of Choctaw Newborn
Act of 1905   Volume IV

Choctaw N.B. 193.

Muskogee, Indian Territory, April 22, 1905.

David P. Barbour,
    Tamaha, Indian Territory.

Dear Sir:

    Receipt is hereby acknowledged of the affidavits of Hester A. Barbour and Ella Hall to the birth of John Lawson Barbour, son of David P. and Hester A. Barbour, January 3, 1903, and the same have been filed with our records in the matter of the enrollment of said child.

Respectfully,

Chairman.

Blank 734.

DEPARTMENT OF THE INTERIOR.
UNITED STATES INDIAN SERVICE.
Office of
SUPERINTENDENT FOR THE FIVE CIVILIZED TRIBES.
MUSKOGEE, INDIAN TERRITORY, OKLAHOMA.

    This is to certify that I am the officer having the custody of the records pertaining to the enrollment of the members of the Choctaw, Chickasaw, Cherokee, Creek and Seminole Tribes of Indians, and the disposition of the land of said tribes, and that the copies of the following papers, attached hereto, are true and correct copies of that portion of the enrollment record on file in this office in connection with the application of __John Lawson Barbour__. Roll No. __195__, for enrollment as a __New Born citizen by blood__ of the Choctaw Nation, so far as same relates to the age of said citizen.

Choctaw New Born Census Care No. 193. Five (5) Birth Affidavits.
Testimony dated 4/5/1905. Two (2) Office Letters dated 4/6/1905 & 4/22/1905.
Approved roll as to No. 195.

GABE E. PARKER, Superintendent,
By __W.H. Angell__ CLERK
IN CHARGE __CHOCTAW__ RECORDS
DATE __OCT 2 - 1916__ 191__

Applications for Enrollment of Choctaw Newborn
Act of 1905 Volume IV

Choc New Born 194
        Martha B. Merryman

Dismissed June 15, 1905.
Died on Dec. 1, 1904.

DEPARTMENT OF THE INTERIOR,
COMMISSION TO THE FIVE CIVILIZED TRIBES.

      Record in the matter of the application for enrollment as a citizen by blood of the Choctaw Nation of:

        MARTHA B. MERRYMAN   7-NB-194.

COPY.

N. B. 194.

William B. Merryman,
    Oak Lodge, Indian Territory.

Dear Sir:

      There is inclosed you herewith for execution application for the enrollment of your infant child, Martha B. Merryman, born November 12, 1903.

      The affidavits heretofore filed with the Commission show the child was living on June 23, 1904. It is necessary, for the child to be enrolled, that she was living on March 4, 1905.

      In having these affidavits executed, care should be exercised to see that all the names are written in full as they appear in the body of the affidavit, and in the event that either of the persons signing the affidavit are unable to write, signatures by mark must be attested by two witnesses. Each affidavit must be executed before a Notary Public and the notarial seal and signature of the officer must be attached to each separate affidavit.

                      Respectfully,
                      SIGNED

                      T.B. Needles
SEV-1-6   Commissioner in Charge.

Applications for Enrollment of Choctaw Newborn
Act of 1905 Volume IV

COPY.

7-2782

Muskogee, Indian Territory, March 27, 1905.

William B. Merryman,
    Oaklodge, Indian Territory.

Dear Sir:

    Receipt is hereby acknowledged of your letter of March 22, 1905, asking if the affidavits heretofore forwarded to the birth of your child Martha B. Merryman in 1903 are not good that you be furnished other blanks for the enrolment of said child; you further state that this child died December 1, 1904, and for the purpose of making the death of this child a matter of record there is inclosed herewith blank form which you are requested to have executed and returned to this office as early as practicable.

                  Respectfully,
                  SIGNED

                  Tams Bixby
D.C.   Chairman.

Muskogee, Indian Territory, April 12, 1905.

William B. Merryman,
    Oaklodge, Indian Territory.

Dear Sir:

    Receipt is hereby acknowledged of the affidavits of William B. Merryman and Felix Leflore to the death of Martha B. Merryman, December 1, 1904.

    Referring to the application heretofore forwarded for the enrollment of Martha B. Merryman, you are advised that the act of Congress approved March 3, 1905, authorizes the Commission for a period of sixty days from that date to receive applications for the enrollment of children born to enrolled citizens by blood of the Choctaw and Chickasaw Nations between September 25, 1902 and March 4, 1905, and living on said latter date.

                  Respectfully,

              SIGNED   *T.B. Needles*
              Commissioner in Charge.

Applications for Enrollment of Choctaw Newborn
Act of 1905 Volume IV

Choctaw N.B. 194.

Muskogee, Indian Territory, April 12, 1905.

William B. Merryman,
    Oak Lodge, Indian Territory.

Dear Sir:

    Receipt is hereby acknowledged of your affidavit and the affidavit of Felix Leflore to the death of your daughter, Martha B. Merryman, December 1, 1904, and the same have been filed with our records as evidence of the death of the above named child.

    Referring to the affidavits heretofore forwarded to the birth of this child, you are advised that under the provisions of the Act of Congress approved March 3, 1905, the Commission is authorized for a period of sixty days from that date to receive applications for the enrollment of children born to enrolled citizens by blood of the Choctaw and Chickasaw Nations between September 25, 1902 and March 4, 1905, and living on said latter date.

    You will, therefore see that the Commission is without authority to enroll your child.

        Respectfully,

SIGNED *T.B. Needles*
Commissioner in Charge.

BIRTH AFFIDAVIT.

DEPARTMENT OF THE INTERIOR,
COMMISSION TO THE FIVE CIVILIZED TRIBES.

IN RE Application for Enrollment, as a citizen of the Choctaw Nation, of Martha B. Merryman, born on the 12th day of November, 1903

Name of Father: W^m. B. Merryman   a citizen of the Choctaw Nation.
Name of Mother: F. A. Merryman   a citizen of the Choctaw Nation.

    Post-Office: Oak Lodge

Applications for Enrollment of Choctaw Newborn
Act of 1905   Volume IV

AFFIDAVIT OF MOTHER.

UNITED STATES OF AMERICA,
　INDIAN TERRITORY.
Central　　District.

I, Florence A. Merryman, on oath state that I am 32 years of age and a citizen by Marriage, of the Choctaw Nation; that I am the lawful wife of William B. Merryman, who is a citizen, by Blood of the Choctaw Nation; that a Female child was born to me on 12th day of November, 1903, that said child has been named Martha B. Merryman, and is now living.

　　　　　　　　　　　　　　　　　　　Florence A. Merryman
WITNESSES TO MARK:

Subscribed and sworn to before me this 23 day of June, 1904.

　　　　　　　　　　　　　　　　　　　J. H. Bowman
　　　　　　　　　　　　　　　　　　　NOTARY PUBLIC.
　　　　　　　　　　Commission Expires March 3rd 1916

AFFIDAVIT OF ATTENDING PHYSICIAN OR MID-WIFE.

UNITED STATES OF AMERICA,
　INDIAN TERRITORY.
　　　　　　　　　　District.

I, N. J. Willkitt, a Midwife, on oath state that I attended on Mrs. Florence A. Merryman, wife of William B. Merryman on the 12th day of November, 1903; that there was born to her on said date a Female child; that said child is now living and is said to have been named Martha B. Merryman

　　　　　　　　　　　　　　　　　　　N. J. Willkitt
WITNESSES TO MARK:

Subscribed and sworn to before me this 23 day of June, 1904.

　　　　　　　　　　　　　　　　　　　J. H. Bowman
　　　　　　　　　　　　　　　　　　　NOTARY PUBLIC.
　　　　　　　　　　Commission Expires March 3rd 1916

Applications for Enrollment of Choctaw Newborn
Act of 1905   Volume IV

DEPARTMENT OF THE INTERIOR.
COMMISSION TO THE FIVE CIVILIZED TRIBES.

In the matter of the death of   Martha B. Merryman   a citizen of the Choctaw   Nation, who formerly resided at or near   Oak Lodge   , Ind. Ter., and died on the   1   day of   December   , 1904

AFFIDAVIT OF RELATIVE.

UNITED STATES OF AMERICA, Indian Territory,
Central   DISTRICT.

I,   William B. Merryman   , on oath state that I am   32   years of age and a citizen by   blood   , of the Choctaw   Nation; that my postoffice address is   Oak Lodge   , Ind. Ter.; that I am   father   of   Martha B. Merryman   who was a citizen, by   blood   , of the   Choctaw   Nation and that said   Martha B Merryman   died on the   1   day of   December   , 1904

William B. Merryman

Witnesses To Mark:

Subscribed and sworn to before me   30   day of   March   , 1905.

James Bower
Notary Public.

AFFIDAVIT OF ACQUAINTANCE.

UNITED STATES OF AMERICA, Indian Territory,
Central   DISTRICT.

I,   Felix Leflore   , on oath state that I am   40   years of age, and a citizen by   blood   of the   Choctaw   Nation; that my postoffice address is   Oak Lodge   , Ind. Ter.; that I was personally acquainted with   Martha B. Merryman   who was a citizen, by   blood   , of the   Choctaw   Nation; and that said   Martha B. Merryman   died on the   1   day of   December   , 1904

Felix Leflore

Witnesses To Mark:

Subscribed and sworn to before me this   30   day of   March   , 1905.

James Bower
Notary Public.

Applications for Enrollment of Choctaw Newborn
Act of 1905   Volume IV

𝓌.𝟊.
7-NB-194.

DEPARTMENT OF THE INTERIOR,
COMMISSION TO THE FIVE CIVILIZED TRIBES.

In the matter of the application for the enrollment of Martha B. Merryman as a citizen by blood of the Choctaw Nation.

---oOo---

It appears from the record herein that on March 4, 1905 there was filed with the Commission applicationfor[sic] the enrollment of Martha B. Merryman as a citizen by blood of the Choctaw Nation.

It further appears from the record in this case and the records of the Commission that the applicant was born on November 12, 1903; that she is a daughter of William B. Merryman, a recognized and enrolled citizen by blood of the Choctaw Nation whose name appears as number 8168 upon the final roll of citizens by blood of the Choctaw Nation, approved by the Secretary of the Interior January 17, 1903, and Florence A. Merryman, a recognized and enrolled citizen by intermarriage of the Choctaw Nation whose name appears as number 270 upon the final roll of citizens by intermarriage of the Choctaw Nation, approved by the Secretary of the Interior September 12, 1903; and that said applicant died on December 1, 1904.

The Act of Congress approved March 3, 1905 (Public No. 212) among other things provides:

"That the Commission to the Five Civilized Tribes is authorized for sixty days after the date of the approval of this act to receive and consider applications for enrollment of children born subsequent to September twenty-fifth, nineteen hundred and two, and prior to March fourth, nineteen hundred and five, and who were living on said latter date, to citizens by blood of the Choctaw and Chickasaw tribes of Indians whose enrollment has been approved by the Secretary of the Interior prior to the date of the approval of this act; and to enroll and make allotments to such children."

It is, therefore, hereby ordered that the application for the enrollment of Martha B. Merryman as a citizen by blood of the Choctaw Nation be dismissed in accordance with the order of the Commission of March 31, 1905.

COMMISSION TO THE FIVE CIVILIZED TRIBES,

Muskogee, Ind. Ter.

<u>   Tams Bixby   </u>
Chairman.

<u>JUN 15 1905</u>

Applications for Enrollment of Choctaw Newborn
Act of 1905   Volume IV

7 NB 194

Muskogee, Indian Territory, June 15, 1905.

William B. Merryman,
    Oaklodge, Indian Territory.   COPY.

Dear Sir:

    Inclosed herewith you will find a copy of the decision of this Commission, dated June 15, 1905, dismissing the application for the enrollment of your infant child, Martha B. Merryman, as a citizen by blood of the Choctaw Nation.

Respectfully,
SIGNED
Tams Bixby
Chairman.

Registered.
Incl. 7- NB-194

---

7 NB 194

Muskogee, Indian Territory, June 15, 1905.

Mansfield, McMurry & Cornish,
    Attorneys for Choctaw and Chickasaw Nations,
        South McAlester, Indian Territory.   COPY.

Gentlemen:

    Inclosed herewith you will find a copy of the order of this Commission, dated June 15, 1905, dismissing the application for the enrollment of Martha B. Merryman as a citizen by blood of the Choctaw Nation.

Respectfully,

SIGNED *Tams Bixby*
Chairman.

Incl. 7-NB-194

Applications for Enrollment of Choctaw Newborn
Act of 1905 Volume IV

Choc New Born 195
    Maud Folsom
    (Born Dec. 10, 1902)

BIRTH AFFIDAVIT.

DEPARTMENT OF THE INTERIOR,
COMMISSION TO THE FIVE CIVILIZED TRIBES.

IN RE Application for Enrollment, as a citizen of the Choctaw Nation, of Maud Folsom, born on the 10 day of Dec., 1902

Name of Father: Robert Folsom   a citizen of the Choctaw Nation.
Name of Mother: Alice Folsom   a citizen of the Choctaw Nation.

Post-Office: Garland

AFFIDAVIT OF ~~MOTHER~~. father

UNITED STATES OF AMERICA, }
    INDIAN TERRITORY.
  Central   District.

I, Robert Folsom, on oath state that I am 29 years of age and a citizen by blood, of the Choctaw Nation; that I am the lawful ~~wife~~ husband of Alice Folsom, who is a citizen, by marriage of the Choctaw Nation; that a female child was born to me on 10 day of Dec, 1902, that said child has been named Maud Folsom, and is now living.

                                        Robert Folsom

WITNESSES TO MARK:

Subscribed and sworn to before me this 23 day of Dec, 1902.

                            T. C. Humphrey
                                  NOTARY PUBLIC.

Applications for Enrollment of Choctaw Newborn
Act of 1905 Volume IV

BIRTH AFFIDAVIT.

DEPARTMENT OF THE INTERIOR.
COMMISSION TO THE FIVE CIVILIZED TRIBES.

IN RE APPLICATION FOR ENROLLMENT, as a citizen of the Choctaw Nation, of Maud Folsom, born on the 10 day of December, 1902

Name of Father: Robert Folsom   a citizen of the Choctaw Nation.
Name of Mother: Alice Folsom   a citizen of the Choctaw Nation.

Postoffice   Garland, Indian Territory

AFFIDAVIT OF MOTHER.

UNITED STATES OF AMERICA, Indian Territory,
Central   DISTRICT.

I, Alice Folsom, on oath state that I am 31 years of age and a citizen by marriage, of the Choctaw Nation; that I am the lawful wife of Robert Folsom, who is a citizen, by blood of the Choctaw Nation; that a female child was born to me on 10 day of December, 1902; that said child has been named Maud Folsom, and was living March 4, 1905.

           Alice Folsom

Witnesses To Mark:

Subscribed and sworn to before me this 17 day of March, 1905.

           C.C. Jones
           Notary Public.

AFFIDAVIT OF ATTENDING PHYSICIAN OR MID-WIFE.

UNITED STATES OF AMERICA, Indian Territory,
Central   DISTRICT.

I, C. C. Jones, a Physician, on oath state that I attended on Mrs. Alice Folsom, wife of Robert Folsom on the 10 day of December, 1902; that there was born to her on said date a female child; that said child was living March 4, 1905, and is said to have been named Maud Folsom

           C.C. Jones

Witnesses To Mark:

Applications for Enrollment of Choctaw Newborn
Act of 1905   Volume IV

Subscribed and sworn to before me this 17 day of   March   , 1905

J N Jones
Notary Public.

BIRTH AFFIDAVIT.

DEPARTMENT OF THE INTERIOR.
COMMISSION TO THE FIVE CIVILIZED TRIBES.

IN RE APPLICATION FOR ENROLLMENT, as a citizen of the   Choctaw   Nation, of   Maud Folsom   , born on the   10   day of December   , 1902

Name of Father: Robert Folsom   a citizen of the   Choctaw   Nation.
Name of Mother: Allice[sic] Folsom   a citizen of the   Choctaw   Nation.

Postoffice   Garland I.T.

AFFIDAVIT OF MOTHER.

UNITED STATES OF AMERICA, Indian Territory,
Central   DISTRICT.

I, Alice Folsom   , on oath state that I am   31   years of age and a citizen by Intermarriage   , of the   Choctaw   Nation; that I am the lawful wife of   Robert Folsom   , who is a citizen, by blood   of the   Choctaw   Nation; that a female   child was born to me on   10th day of December   , 1902; that said child has been named   Maud Folsom   , and was living March 4, 1905.

Alice Folsom

Witnesses To Mark:

Subscribed and sworn to before me this   1st day of   April   , 1905

C. C. Jones
Notary Public.

AFFIDAVIT OF ATTENDING PHYSICIAN OR MID-WIFE.

UNITED STATES OF AMERICA, Indian Territory,
Central   DISTRICT.

I, C. C. Jones   , a Physician   , on oath state that I attended on Mrs. Alice Folsom   , wife of Robert Folsom   on the 10 day of December ,

Applications for Enrollment of Choctaw Newborn
Act of 1905   Volume IV

1902; that there was born to her on said date a   female   child; that said child was living March 4, 1905, and is said to have been named Maud

C.C. Jones

Witnesses To Mark:
{

Subscribed and sworn to before me this 1st day of April   , 1905

J N Jones
Notary Public.

COPY.

N. B. 195

Muskogee, Indian Territory, April 6, 1905.

Robert Folsom,
    Garland, Indian Territory.

Dear Sir:

    There is inclosed you herewith for execution application for the enrollment of your infant child, Maud Folsom, born December 10, 1902.

    The affidavit heretofore filed with the Commission show the child was living on December 23, 1902. It is necessary, for the child to be enrolled, that she was living on March 4, 1905. You will please insert the mother's age in the place left blank for that purpose.

    In having these affidavits executed, care should be exercised to see that all the names are written in full as they appear in the body of the affidavit, and in the event that either of the persons signing the affidavit are unable to write, signatures by mark must be attested by two witnesses. Each affidavit must be executed before a Notary Public and the notorial[sic] seal and signature of the officer must be attached to each separate affidavit.

    In case there was no physician or midwife in attendance upon your wife at the time of the birth of the applicant, it will be necessary that you submit the affidavits of two persons who know the child was born, stating date of birth, that she was living on March 4, 1905 and that Alice Folsom is her mother.

Respectfully,
SIGNED

T.B. Needles
Commissioner in Charge.

SEV 3-6

Applications for Enrollment of Choctaw Newborn
Act of 1905   Volume IV

7-2788

Muskogee, Indian Territory, April 20, 1905.

Robert Folsom,
    Garland, Indian Territory.

Dear Sir:

    Receipt is hereby acknowledged of the affidavits of Alice Folsom and C. C. Jones to the birth of Maud Folsom, daughter of Robert and Allice[sic] Folsom, December 10, 1902, and the same have been filed with our records as an application for the enrollment of said child.

        Respectfully,

            Chairman.

COPY.

Choctaw N.B. 195

Muskogee, Indian Territory, April 22, 1905.

Robert Folsom,
    Garland, Indian Territory.

Dear Sir:

    Receipt is hereby acknowledged of the affidavits of Alice Folsom and C. C. Jones to the birth of Maud Folson[sic], daughter of Robert and Alice Folsom, December 10, 1902, and the same have been filed with our records in the matter of the enrollment of said child.

        Respectfully,
        SIGNED

          Tams Bixby
            Chairman.

Applications for Enrollment of Choctaw Newborn
Act of 1905 Volume IV

Choc New Born 196
  Susan Myrtle Nessmith
  (Born Dec. 20, 1903)

BIRTH AFFIDAVIT.

DEPARTMENT OF THE INTERIOR.
COMMISSION TO THE FIVE CIVILIZED TRIBES.

IN RE APPLICATION FOR ENROLLMENT, as a citizen of the Choctaw Nation, of Suzan[sic] Myrtle Nessmith, born on the 20th day of December, 1903

Name of Father: David Nessmith   a citizen of the Choctaw Nation.
Name of Mother: Mary V Nessmith   a citizen of the Choctaw Nation.

Postoffice Ft. Smith, Ark

AFFIDAVIT OF MOTHER.

UNITED STATES OF AMERICA, Indian Territory,
  Ft. Smith   DISTRICT.

I, Mary V Nessmith, on oath state that I am 26 years of age and a citizen by birth, of the Choctaw Nation; that I am the lawful wife of David Nessmith, who is a citizen, by intermarriage of the Choctaw Nation; that a female child was born to me on 20th day of December, 1903, that said child has been named Suzan Myrtle Nessmith, and is now living.

                                        Mary V Nessmith
Witnesses To Mark:
  { Jno W Jasper
  { Earl Harley

Subscribed and sworn to before me this 22 day of October, 1904

                                        H P Leveridge
                                          Notary Public.

Applications for Enrollment of Choctaw Newborn
Act of 1905 Volume IV

AFFIDAVIT OF ATTENDING PHYSICIAN OR MID-WIFE.

UNITED STATES OF AMERICA, Indian Territory,
Ft Smith   **DISTRICT.**

    I, H. C. King, a Physician & Surgeon, on oath state that I attended on Mrs. Nessmith, wife of David Nessmith on the 20 day of December, 1903; that there was born to her on said date a Female child; that said child is now living and is said to have been named Suzan Myrtle Nessmith

                                             H.C. King, M.D.

Witnesses To Mark:
{ Ira M Shuler
{ A Billingsley

    Subscribed and sworn to before me this 22 day of October, 1904

                        H P Leveridge
                            Notary Public.

BIRTH AFFIDAVIT.

DEPARTMENT OF THE INTERIOR.
COMMISSION TO THE FIVE CIVILIZED TRIBES.

    IN RE APPLICATION FOR ENROLLMENT, as a citizen of the Choctaw Nation, of Susan Myrtle Nessmith, born on the 20th day of Dec, 1903

Name of Father: David Nessmith   a citizen of the Choctaw Nation.
Name of Mother: Mary V. Nessmith   a citizen of the Choctaw Nation.

                Postoffice   Ft Smith, Arkansas
                                 R.F.D. Route No. 3

AFFIDAVIT OF MOTHER.

UNITED STATES OF AMERICA, Indian Territory,
Central   **DISTRICT.**

    I, Mary V. Nessmith, on oath state that I am 26 years of age and a citizen by blood, of the Choctaw Nation; that I am the lawful wife of David Nessmith, who is a citizen, by marriage of the Choctaw Nation; that a female child was born to me on 20th day of December, 1903; that said child has been named Susan Myrtle Nessmith, and was living March 4, 1905.

                                      Mary V Nessmith

Applications for Enrollment of Choctaw Newborn
Act of 1905 Volume IV

Witnesses To Mark:
{

    Subscribed and sworn to before me this 30th day of March , 1905

                      Wirt Franklin
                      Notary Public.

AFFIDAVIT OF ATTENDING PHYSICIAN OR MID-WIFE.

UNITED STATES OF AMERICA, Indian Territory, }
....DISTRICT. }

    I, H.C. King , a Physician , on oath state that I attended on Mrs. Mary V Nessmith , wife of David Nessmith on the 20th day of December , 1903; that there was born to her on said date a Female child; that said child was living March 4, 1905, and is said to have been named Susan Myrtle Nessmith

                      H.C. King, M.D.

Witnesses To Mark:
{

    Subscribed and sworn to before me this 29 day of March , 1905

                      H.P. Leveridge
                      Notary Public.

                      7-2795

            Muskogee, Indian Territory, October 27, 1904.

David Nessmith,
    R.F.D. Route Number 3,
        Fort Smith, Arkansas.

Dear Sir:-

    Receipt is hereby acknowledged of the affidavits of Mary V. Nessmith and H. C. King, relative to the birth of your infant daughter Suzan Myrtle Nessmith December 20, 1903, which it is presumed have been forwarded to this office as an application for the enrollment of said child as a citizen by blood of the Choctaw Nation.

    The Act of Congress approved July 1, 1902, which was ratified by the citizens of the Choctaw and Chickasaw Nations September 25, 1902, among other things provides that no child born to a citizen of the Choctaw and Chickasaw Nation subsequent to the

Applications for Enrollment of Choctaw Newborn
Act of 1905 Volume IV

date of said ratification shall be entitled to enrollment or to participate in the distribution of the tribal property of the Choctaws and Chickasaws.

Respectfully,

Chairman.

Choc New Born 197
    Viola Collins
    (Born Nov. 20[sic], 1902)

DEPARTMENT OF THE INTERIOR,
COMMISSION TO THE FIVE CIVILIZED TRIBES.

Record in the matter of the application for enrollment as a citizen by blood of the Choctaw Nation of:

    VIOLA COLLINS   7-NB-197.

BIRTH AFFIDAVIT.

DEPARTMENT OF THE INTERIOR,
COMMISSION TO THE FIVE CIVILIZED TRIBES.

IN RE APPLICATION FOR ENROLLMENT, as a citizen of the Choctaw Nation, of Viola Collins, born on the 30 day of November, 1902

Name of Father: John F. Collins   a citizen of the Choctaw Nation.
Name of Mother: Daisy Lee Collins   a citizen of the Choctaw Nation.

                                Post-Office :   Ft. Smith Ark

AFFIDAVIT OF MOTHER.

UNITED STATES OF AMERICA,
    INDIAN TERRITORY,
    Central   District.

    I, Daisy Lee Collins, on oath state that I am 25 years of age and a citizen by Marriage, of the Choctaw Nation; that I am the lawful wife of John Foley Collins, who is a citizen, by blood of the Choctaw Nation; that a Female child

Applications for Enrollment of Choctaw Newborn
Act of 1905   Volume IV

was born to me on the   30   day of November   , 190 2, that said child has been named Viola Collins   , and is now living.

Daisy Lee Collins

WITNESSES TO MARK:

{

Subscribed and sworn to before me this 30   day of   December   , 1902

C. E. Field

NOTARY PUBLIC.

AFFIDAVIT OF ATTENDING PHYSICIAN OR MID-WIFE.

UNITED STATES OF AMERICA,
~~INDIAN TERRITORY,~~
State of Arkansas   ~~District~~.
County of Sebastian

I, E. G. Epler   , a   Physician   , on oath state that I attended on Mrs. Daisy Lee Collins   , wife of John F Collins   on the   30th   day of November   , 190 2; that there was born to her on said date a   Female   child; that said child is now living and is said to have been named Viola Collins

E. G. Epler M.D.

WITNESSES TO MARK:

{

Subscribed and sworn to before me this   31st   day of   December   , 1902.
My commission
expires Jany 20-1906   T. J. Greenstreet

NOTARY PUBLIC.

N. B. 197

Muskogee, Indian Territory, April 5, 1905.

John F. Collins,
        Fort Smith, Arkansas.

Dear Sir:

        There is inclosed you herewith for execution application for the enrollment of your infant child, Viola Collins, born November 30, 1902.

Applications for Enrollment of Choctaw Newborn
Act of 1905 Volume IV

The affidavit heretofore filed with the Commission show the child was living on 31st day of December 1902. It is necessary, for the child to be enrolled, that she was living on March 4, 1905.

In having these affidavits executed care should be exercised to see that all the names are written in full as they appear in the body of the affidavit, and in the event that either of the persons signing the affidavit are unable to write, signatures by mark must be attested by two witnesses. Each affidavit must be executed before a Notary Public and the notarial seal and signature of the officer must be attached to each separate affidavit.

Respectfully,

SIGNED T.B. Needles
Commissioner in Charge.

LM 5-10

7-NB-197.

Muskogee, Indian Territory, May 12, 1905.

John F. Collins,
    Fort Smith, Arkansas,

Dear Sir:

There is enclosed you herewith for execution application for the enrollment of your infant child, Viola Collins, born November 30, 1902.

The affidavits heretofore filed with the Commission show that the child was living December 30, 1902. It is necessary, for the child to be enrolled, that she was living on March 4, 1905.

In having these affidavits executed care should be exercised to see that all the names are written in full, as they appear in the body of the affidavit and in the event that either of the persons signing the affidavit are unable to write, signatures by mark must be attested by two witnesses. Each affidavit must be executed before a Notary Public and the notarial seal and signature of the officer must be attached to each separate affidavit.

Respectfully,

SIGNED Tams Bixby
Chairman.

V 12/3.

Applications for Enrollment of Choctaw Newborn
Act of 1905 Volume IV

Choctaw N B 197

Muskogee, Indian Territory, May 20, 1905.

John F. Collins,
    Spiro, Indian Territory, (Box 85)

Dear Sir:

    Receipt is hereby acknowledged of your letter of May 15, referring to the application for the enrollment of your child recently forwarded you, and stating that she was born November 30, 1902, and died November 24, 1903. You ask if this child is entitled to enrollment.

    In reply to your letter you are advised that by the provisions of the act of Congress approved March 3, 1905, the Commission was authorized, for a period of sixty days from that date, to receive applications for the enrollment of children born to enrolled citizens by blood of the Choctaw and Chickasaw Nations between September 25, 1902, and March 4, 1905, and living on the latter date. You will therefore see that the Commission is without authority to enroll children born subsequent to September 25, 1902, who were not living on March 4, 1905.

    For the purpose of making the death of your child a matter of record there is inclosed herewith blank form for proof of death which please have executed and returned to this office at the earliest practicable date. Be careful to see that all blanks are properly filled, all names written in full, and that the Notary Public before whom the affidavits are acknowledged affixes his name and seal to each affidavit. Signatures by mark must be attested by two witnesses who can write.

    Respectfully,

SIGNED *Tams Bixby*
Chairman.

D C
Env.

DEPARTMENT OF THE INTERIOR.
COMMISSION TO THE FIVE CIVILIZED TRIBES.

In the matter of the death of Viola Collins a citizen of the Choctaw Nation, who formerly resided at or near Spiro , Ind. Ter., and died on the 24th day of November , 1903

Applications for Enrollment of Choctaw Newborn
Act of 1905   Volume IV

AFFIDAVIT OF RELATIVE.

UNITED STATES OF AMERICA, Indian Territory,
Central   DISTRICT.

I, John F. Collins, on oath state that I am 30 years of age and a citizen by Blood, of the Choctaw Nation; that my postoffice address is Spiro, Ind. Ter.; that I am the Father of Viola Collins who was a citizen, by Blood, of the Choctaw Nation and that said Viola Collins died on the 24th day of November, 1903

Witnesses To Mark: John F. Collins

Subscribed and sworn to before me this 30th day of May, 1905.

J Wesley Smith
Notary Public.

AFFIDAVIT OF ACQUAINTANCE.

UNITED STATES OF AMERICA, Indian Territory,
Central   DISTRICT.

I, John H Hinton, on oath state that I am 50 years of age, and a citizen by --------- of the United States Nation; that my postoffice address is Spiro, Ind. Ter.; that I was personally acquainted with Viola Collins who was a citizen, by Blood, of the Choctaw Nation; and that said Viola Collins died on the 24th day of November, 1903

John H Hinton
Witnesses To Mark:

Subscribed and sworn to before me this 30th day of May, 1905.

J Wesley Smith
My Com Ex Oct 29 1905   Notary Public.

Applications for Enrollment of Choctaw Newborn
Act of 1905   Volume IV

W.F.
7-NB-197.

DEPARTMENT OF THE INTERIOR,
COMMISSION TO THE FIVE CIVILIZED TRIBES.

In the matter of the application for the enrollment of Viola Collins as a citizen by blood of the Choctaw Nation.

---oOo---

It appears from the record herein that on March 4, 1905 there was filed with the Commission application for the enrollment of Viola Collins as a citizen by blood of the Choctaw Nation.

It further appears from the record in this case and the records of the Commission that the applicant was born on November 30, 1902; that she is a daughter of John F. Collins, a recognized and enrolled citizen by blood of the Choctaw Nation whose name appears as number 8230 upon the final roll of citizens by blood of the Choctaw Nation, approved by the Secretary of the Interior January 17, 1903, and Daisy Collins, a recognized and enrolled citizen by intermarriage of the Choctaw Nation whose name appears as number 731 upon the final roll of citizens by intermarriage of the Choctaw Nation, approved by the Secretary of the Interior May 7, 1904, and that said applicant died November 24, 1903.

The Act of Congress approved March 3, 1905 (Public No. 212) among other things provides:

"That the Commission to the Five Civilized Tribes is authorized for sixty days after the date of the approval of this act to receive and consider applications for enrollment of children born subsequent to September twenty-fifth, nineteen hundred and two, and prior to March fourth, nineteen hundred and five, and who were living on said latter date, to citizens by blood of the Choctaw and Chickasaw tribes of Indians whose enrollment has been approved by the Secretary of the Interior prior to the date of the approval of this act; and to enroll and make allotments to such children."

It is, therefore, hereby ordered that the application for the enrollment of Viola Collins as a citizen by blood of the Choctaw Nation be dismissed in accordance with the order of the Commission of March 31, 1905.

COMMISSION TO THE FIVE CIVILIZED TRIBES,

                              Tams Bixby
                                   Chairman.

Muskogee, Indian Territory,

    JUN 15 1905

Applications for Enrollment of Choctaw Newborn
Act of 1905   Volume IV

7 NB 107

Muskogee, Indian Territory, June 15, 1905.

John F. Collins,
    Spiro, Indian Territory,

COPY.

Dear Sir:

    Inclosed herewith you will find a copy of the order of this Commission, dated June 15, 1905, dismissing the application for the enrollment of your infant child, Viola Collins, as a citizen by blood of the Choctaw Nation.

    Respectfully,

SIGNED   *Tams Bixby*

Registered.   Chairman.
Incl. 7- NB-197

---

7 NB 197

Muskogee, Indian Territory, June 15, 1905.

Mansfield, McMurray & Cornish,
    Attorneys for Choctaw and Chickasaw Nations,
        South McAlester, Indian Territory.

Gentlemen:

    Inclosed herewith you will find a copy of the order of this Commission, dated June 15, 1905, dismissing the application for the enrollment of Viola Collins as a citizen by blood of the Choctaw Nation.

    Respectfully,

SIGNED   *Tams Bixby*

Incl. 7- NB 197.   Chairman.

Applications for Enrollment of Choctaw Newborn
Act of 1905 Volume IV

7-2806.

Muskogee, Indian Territory, January 15, 1903.

John F. Collins,
      Fort Smith, Arkansas.

Dear Sir:

    Receipt is hereby acknowledged of your letter of December 31, 1902, enclosing the application for enrollment as a citizen of the Choctaw Nation of Viola Collins, infant daughter of John F. and Daisy Lee Collins, born November 30, 1902.

    You are advised that the Commission is now without authority to enroll this child as a citizen of the Choctaw Nation, said child having been born November 30, 1902, subsequent to the ratification by the citizens of the Choctaw and Chickasaw Nations September 25, 1902, of the act of Congress approved July 1, 1903 (32 Stats., 641).

    Section twenty-eight thereof provides as follows:

    "The names of all persons living on the date of the final ratification of this agreement entitled to be enrolled as provided in section 27 hereof shall be placed upon the rolls made by said Commission; and no child born thereafter to a citizen or freedman and no person intermarried thereafter to a citizen shall be entitled to enrollment or to participate in the distribution of the tribal property of the Choctaws and Chickasaws."

                      Respectfully,

                                     Commissioner in Charge.

---

7 NB 197

Muskogee, Indian Territory, June 6, 1905.

John F. Collins,
      Spiro, Indian Territory.

Dear Sir:

    Receipt is hereby acknowledged of your affidavit and the affidavit of John H. Hinton to the death of your child Viola Collins which occurred November 24, 1903.

    You are advised that under the provisions of the act of Congress approved March 3, 1905, the Commission was authorized for a period of sixty days from that date to receive applications for the enrollment of children born to enrolled citizens by blood of

Applications for Enrollment of Choctaw Newborn
Act of 1905 Volume IV

the Choctaw and Chickasaw Nations between September 25, 1902 and March 4, 1905, and living on the latter date. You will therefore see that the Commission is without authority to enroll your child.

Respectfully,

Chairman.

Choc New Born 198
    Frank Alfred Bolling
    (Born March 1, 1903)

    Louis Layfayett[sic] Bolling
    (Born Sep. 16, 1904)

BIRTH AFFIDAVIT.

DEPARTMENT OF THE INTERIOR,
COMMISSION TO THE FIVE CIVILIZED TRIBES.

In Re Application for Enrollment, as a citizen of the Choctaw Nation, of Frank Alfred Bolling , born on the 1st day of March , 1903

Name of Father: John F Bolling   a citizen of the Choctaw Nation.
Name of Mother: Nancy I Bolling   a citizen of the Choctaw Nation.

Post-office   Canadian Ind Tery

AFFIDAVIT OF MOTHER.

UNITED STATES OF AMERICA, }
    INDIAN TERRITORY,
................................District.

I, Nancy I Bolling , on oath state that I am 23 years of age and a citizen by blood , of the Choctaw Nation; that I am the lawful wife of John F Bolling , who is a citizen, by blood of the Choctaw Nation; that a male child was born to me on first day of March , 190 3, that said child has been named Frank Alfred Bolling , and is now living.

                            Nancy I Bolling

WITNESSES TO MARK:

Applications for Enrollment of Choctaw Newborn
Act of 1905   Volume IV

Subscribed and sworn to before me this 23 day of March , 19053

W C Bolling

NOTARY PUBLIC.

AFFIDAVIT OF ATTENDING PHYSICIAN OR MID-WIFE.

UNITED STATES OF AMERICA,
INDIAN TERRITORY,
Western   District.

I, Eliza Ann Smith , a midwife , on oath state that I attended on Mrs. Nancy I Bolling , wife of John F Bolling on the 1st day of March , 190 3; that there was born to her on said date a male child; that said child is now living and is said to have been named Frank Alfred Bolling

WITNESSES TO MARK: Eliza Ann Smith

Subscribed and sworn to before me this 23 day of March , 19053

W C Bolling

NOTARY PUBLIC.

NEW-BORN AFFIDAVIT.

Number

Choctaw Enrolling Commission.

IN THE MATTER OF THE APPLICATION FOR ENROLLMENT, as a citizen of the Choctaw   Nation, of   Frank Alfred Bolling

born on the 1 day of   March   190 3

Name of father   John F Bolling   a citizen of   Choctaw
Nation final enrollment No   11466
Name of mother   Nancy I Bolling   a citizen of   Choctaw
Nation final enrollment No 8290

Postoffice   Crowder, I. T.

Applications for Enrollment of Choctaw Newborn
Act of 1905 Volume IV

AFFIDAVIT OF MOTHER.

UNITED STATES OF AMERICA,
    INDIAN TERRITORY,
Western   DISTRICT

I   Nancy I Bolling   on oath state that I am   25   years of age and a citizen by   Blood   of the   Choctaw   Nation, and as such have been placed upon the final roll of the   Choctaw   Nation, by the Honorable Secretary of the Interior my final enrollment number being   8290   ; that I am the lawful wife of   John F Bolling   , who is a citizen of the   Choctaw   Nation, and as such has been placed upon the final roll of said Nation by the Honorable Secretary of the Interior, his final enrollment number being   11466   and that a   male   child was born to me on the   1   day of   March   190 3; that said child has been named   Frank Alfred Bolling   , and is now living.

                                                   Nancy I Bolling

WITNESSETH:
Must be two Witnesses who are Citizens.   M W Priddy
                         J Y Toole

Subscribed and sworn to before me this   25   day of   Febr   190 5

                                                 J D Tignor
                                                      Notary Public.

My commission expires
     Dec 22, 1907

AFFIDAVIT OF ATTENDING PHYSICIAN OR MIDWIFE

UNITED STATES OF AMERICA
INDIAN TERRITORY
Western   DISTRICT

I,   P. S. Johnston   a   Physician on oath state that I attended on Mrs.   Nancy I Bolling wife of   John F. Bolling on the   1st day of   March   , 190 3, that there was born to her on said date a   Male   child, that said child is now living, and is said to have been named   Frank Alfred Bolling

                                             P. S. Johnston   M.D.

WITNESSETH:
Must be two witnesses who are citizens and know the child.   RS [Illegible]
                                 L. H. Perkins

Subscribed and sworn to before me this, the   23^{d} day of   February   190 5

                                             S.M. Gold   Notary Public.

Applications for Enrollment of Choctaw Newborn
Act of 1905 Volume IV

We hereby certify that we are well acquainted with P. S. Johnston a Physician and know him to be reputable and of good standing in the community.

{ RS [Illegible]
{ L. H. Perkins

BIRTH AFFIDAVIT.

DEPARTMENT OF THE INTERIOR.
COMMISSION TO THE FIVE CIVILIZED TRIBES.

IN RE APPLICATION FOR ENROLLMENT, as a citizen of the Choctaw Nation, of Frank Alfred Bolling, born on the first day of March, 1903

Name of Father: John F Bolling a citizen of the Choctaw Nation.
Name of Mother: Nancy I Bolling a citizen of the Choctaw Nation.

Postoffice Crowder Indian Ty

AFFIDAVIT OF MOTHER.

UNITED STATES OF AMERICA, Indian Territory, }
Western DISTRICT. }

I, Nancy I Bolling, on oath state that I am 24 years of age and a citizen by Blood, of the Choctaw Nation; that I am the lawful wife of John F Bolling, who is a citizen, by Blood of the Choctaw Nation; that a Male child was born to me on first day of March, 1903; that said child has been named Frank Alfred Bolling, and was living March 4, 1905.

Nancy I Bolling

Witnesses To Mark:
{ William J. Bunch
{ William H Brown

Subscribed and sworn to before me this 5th day of April, 1905

Jos B Henderson
Notary Public.

Applications for Enrollment of Choctaw Newborn
Act of 1905 Volume IV

AFFIDAVIT OF ATTENDING PHYSICIAN OR MID-WIFE.

UNITED STATES OF AMERICA, Indian Territory,
Western DISTRICT.

I, P. S. Johnston, a Physician, on oath state that I attended on Mrs. Nancy I Bolling, wife of John F Bolling on the first day of March, 1903; that there was born to her on said date a Male child; that said child was living March 4, 1905, and is said to have been named Frank Alfred Bolling

Witnesses To Mark:

P.S. Johnston M.D.

Subscribed and sworn to before me this 4th day of April, 1905.

S.M. Gold
MY COMMISSION EXPIRES FEB. 19, 1908   Notary Public.

BIRTH AFFIDAVIT.

DEPARTMENT OF THE INTERIOR.
COMMISSION TO THE FIVE CIVILIZED TRIBES.

IN RE APPLICATION FOR ENROLLMENT, as a citizen of the Choctaw Nation, of Frank Alfred Bolling, born on the 1st day of March, 1903

Name of Father: John F Bolling   a citizen of the Choctaw Nation.
Name of Mother: Nancy I Bolling (Denton)   a citizen of the Choctaw Nation.

Postoffice   Canadian Ind Ter

AFFIDAVIT OF MOTHER.

UNITED STATES OF AMERICA, Indian Territory,
Western DISTRICT.

I, Nancy I Bolling, on oath state that I am 24 years of age and a citizen by blood, of the Choctaw Nation; that I am the lawful wife of John F Bolling, who is a citizen, by blood of the Choctaw Nation; that a male child was born to me on 1st day of March, 1903; that said child has been named Frank Alfred Bolling, and was living March 4, 1905.

Nancy I Bolling

Witnesses To Mark:

Applications for Enrollment of Choctaw Newborn
Act of 1905 Volume IV

Subscribed and sworn to before me this 11 day of April , 1905

My commission expires Jos. B. Henderson
Dec 19-1908 Notary Public.

AFFIDAVIT OF ATTENDING PHYSICIAN OR MID-WIFE.

UNITED STATES OF AMERICA, Indian Territory,
Western DISTRICT.

I, P.S. Johnston , a Physician , on oath state that I attended on Mrs. Nancy I Bolling (Denton) , wife of John F. Bolling on the 1st day of March , 1903; that there was born to her on said date a Male child; that said child was living March 4, 1905, and is said to have been named Frank Alfred Bolling

Witnesses To Mark: P.S. Johnston M.D.
{

Subscribed and sworn to before me this 8th day of April , 1905

S.M. Gold
MY COMMISSION EXPIRES FEB. 19, 1908 Notary Public.

BIRTH AFFIDAVIT.

DEPARTMENT OF THE INTERIOR,
COMMISSION TO THE FIVE CIVILIZED TRIBES.

In Re Application for Enrollment, as a citizen of the Choctaw Nation, of Louis Layfayett Bolling , born on the 16 day of September , 1904

Name of Father: John F Bolling a citizen of the Choctaw Nation.
Name of Mother: Nancy I Bolling a citizen of the Choctaw Nation.

Post-office Juanita I.T.

AFFIDAVIT OF MOTHER.

UNITED STATES OF AMERICA,
INDIAN TERRITORY,
Western District.

I, Nancy I Bolling , on oath state that I am 24 years of age and a citizen by Blood , of the Choctaw Nation; that I am the lawful wife of John F

Applications for Enrollment of Choctaw Newborn
Act of 1905 Volume IV

Bolling   , who is a citizen, by Blood of the   Choctaw   Nation; that a   male child was born to me on   16   day of September   , 1904 , that said child has been named   Louis Layfayett Bolling   , and is now living.

Nancy I Bolling

WITNESSES TO MARK:
{ A. C. Wilson
{ Geo Adams

Subscribed and sworn to before me this   12   day of   Oct   , 1904

T.J. Rice

NOTARY PUBLIC.

AFFIDAVIT OF ATTENDING PHYSICIAN OR MID-WIFE.

UNITED STATES OF AMERICA, }
INDIAN TERRITORY,
Western   District.

I,   P. S. Johnston   , a   Physician   , on oath state that I attended on Mrs.   Nancy I Bolling   , wife of   John F Bolling   on the 16 day of September , 1904 ; that there was born to her on said date a   male   child; that said child is now living and is said to have been named   Louis Layfayett Bolling

P.S. Johnston M.D.

WITNESSES TO MARK:
{ D S Cornelison[sic]
{ J N Bynum

Subscribed and sworn to before me this   12   day of   Oct   , 1904

T. J. Rice

NOTARY PUBLIC.

Applications for Enrollment of Choctaw Newborn
Act of 1905 Volume IV

NEW-BORN AFFIDAVIT.

Number..................

...Choctaw Enrolling Commission...

IN THE MATTER OF THE APPLICATION FOR ENROLLMENT, as a citizen of the Choctaw Nation, of Louis Lafayett[sic] Bolling

born on the 16 day of September 190 4

Name of father John F Bolling   a citizen of   Choctaw
Nation final enrollment No. 11466
Name of mother Nancy I Bolling   a citizen of   Choctaw
Nation final enrollment No. 8290

Postoffice   Crowder, I.T.

AFFIDAVIT OF MOTHER.

UNITED STATES OF AMERICA
INDIAN TERRITORY
    Western   DISTRICT

I Nancy I Bolling, on oath state that I am 25 years of age and a citizen by Blood of the Choctaw Nation, and as such have been placed upon the final roll of the Choctaw Nation, by the Honorable Secretary of the Interior my final enrollment number being 8290 ; that I am the lawful wife of John F Bolling , who is a citizen of the Choctaw Nation, and as such has been placed upon the final roll of said Nation by the Honorable Secretary of the Interior, his final enrollment number being 11466 and that a Male child was born to me on the 16 day of September 190 4; that said child has been named Louis Lafayett Bolling , and is now living.

                               Nancy I Bolling

Witnesseth.
Must be two Witnesses who are Citizens.   MW Priddy
                    J Y Toole

Subscribed and sworn to before me this 25 day of Febr 190 5

                               J D Tignor
                                   Notary Public.

My commission expires:
      Dec 22, 1907

Applications for Enrollment of Choctaw Newborn
Act of 1905 Volume IV

AFFIDAVIT OF ATTENDING PHYSICIAN OR MIDWIFE

UNITED STATES OF AMERICA
INDIAN TERRITORY
Western   DISTRICT

I, P. S. Johnston   a   Physician on oath state that I attended on Mrs. Nancy I Bolling   wife of   John F Bolling on the 16th day of September, 190 4, that there was born to her on said date a male child, that said child is now living, and is said to have been named   Louis Lafayett Bolling

P.S. Johnston   M.D.

WITNESSETH:
Must be two witnesses who are citizens and know the child.
{ RS [Illegible]
  L.H. Perkins

Subscribed and sworn to before me this, the 23d day of February 190 5

S.M. Gold   Notary Public.

We hereby certify that we are well acquainted with   P.S. Johnston   a Physician   and know   him   to be reputable and of good standing in the community.

{ RS [Illegible]
  L.H. Perkins

BIRTH AFFIDAVIT.

DEPARTMENT OF THE INTERIOR.
COMMISSION TO THE FIVE CIVILIZED TRIBES.

IN RE APPLICATION FOR ENROLLMENT, as a citizen of the   Choctaw   Nation, of   Louis Layfayette Bolling   , born on the 16th day of September, 1904

Name of Father: John F Bolling   a citizen of the   Choctaw   Nation.
Name of Mother: Nancy I Bolling   a citizen of the   Choctaw   Nation.

Postoffice   Crowder Indian Ty

Applications for Enrollment of Choctaw Newborn
Act of 1905   Volume IV

AFFIDAVIT OF MOTHER.

UNITED STATES OF AMERICA, Indian Territory, }
Western   DISTRICT.

I, Nancy I Bolling, on oath state that I am 24 years of age and a citizen by blood, of the Choctaw Nation; that I am the lawful wife of John F Bolling, who is a citizen, by Blood of the Choctaw Nation; that a male child was born to me on 16th day of September, 1904; that said child has been named Louis Layfayette Bolling, and was living March 4, 1905.

Nancy I Bolling

Witnesses To Mark:
{ William J Bunch
William H Brown

Subscribed and sworn to before me this 5th day of April, 1905

Jas. B. Henderson
Notary Public.

AFFIDAVIT OF ATTENDING PHYSICIAN OR MID-WIFE.

UNITED STATES OF AMERICA, Indian Territory, }
Western   DISTRICT.

I, P.S. Johnston, a Physician, on oath state that I attended on Mrs. Nancy I Bolling, wife of John F Bolling on the 16th day of September, 1904; that there was born to her on said date a male child; that said child was living March 4, 1905, and is said to have been named Louis Layfayette Bolling

P.S. Johnston M.D.

Witnesses To Mark:
{

Subscribed and sworn to before me this 4th day of April, 1905

S.M. Gold
Notary Public.

MY COMMISSION EXPIRES FEB. 19, 1908

Applications for Enrollment of Choctaw Newborn
Act of 1905   Volume IV

BIRTH AFFIDAVIT.

DEPARTMENT OF THE INTERIOR.
COMMISSION TO THE FIVE CIVILIZED TRIBES.

IN RE APPLICATION FOR ENROLLMENT, as a citizen of the Choctaw Nation, of Louis Layfayette Bolling, born on the 16th day of September, 1904

Name of Father: John F Bolling   a citizen of the Choctaw Nation.
Name of Mother: Nancy I Bolling (Denton)   a citizen of the Choctaw Nation.

Postoffice   Juanita I.T.

AFFIDAVIT OF MOTHER.

UNITED STATES OF AMERICA, Indian Territory,
Western   DISTRICT.

I, Nancy I Bolling (Denton), on oath state that I am 24 years of age and a citizen by blood, of the Choctaw Nation; that I am the lawful wife of John F Bolling, who is a citizen, by blood of the Choctaw Nation; that a male child was born to me on 16th day of September, 1904; that said child has been named Louis Layfayette Bolling, and was living March 4, 1905.

Nancy I Bolling

Witnesses To Mark:
{

Subscribed and sworn to before me this 11 day of April, 1905

My commission expires   Jas. B. Henderson
Dec 19-1908   Notary Public.

AFFIDAVIT OF ATTENDING PHYSICIAN OR MID-WIFE.

UNITED STATES OF AMERICA, Indian Territory,
Western   DISTRICT.

I, P.S. Johnston, a Physician, on oath state that I attended on Mrs. Nancy I Bolling (Denton), wife of John F Bolling on the 16th day of September, 1904; that there was born to her on said date a male child; that said child was living March 4, 1905, and is said to have been named Louis Layfayette Bolling

P.S. Johnston M.D.

Witnesses To Mark:
{

Applications for Enrollment of Choctaw Newborn
Act of 1905   Volume IV

Subscribed and sworn to before me this 8   day of   April   , 1905

MY COMMISSION EXPIRES FEB. 19, 1908

S.M. Gold
Notary Public.

COPY.   N. B. 198

Muskogee, Indian Territory, April 5, 1905.

John F. Bolling,
    Juanita, Indian Territory.

Dear Sir:

    There is inclosed you herewith for execution applications for the enrollment of your infant children, Frank Alfred Bolling and Louis Layfayett Bolling, born March 1, 1903, and September 16, 1904, respectively.

    The affidavits heretofore filed with the Commission show the children were living on March 23, 1903, and October 12, 1904, respectively. It is necessary, for the children to be enrolled, that they were living on March 4, 1905.

    In having these affidavits executed care should be exercised to see that all the names are written in full as they appear in the body of the affidavit, and in the event that either of the persons signing the affidavit are unable to write, signatures by mark must be attested by two witnesses. Each affidavit must be executed before a Notary Public and the notarial seal and signature of the officer must be attached to each separate affidavit.

Respectfully,
SIGNED

T.B. Needles
LM 5-8   Commissioner in Charge.

7-2822

Muskogee, Indian Territory, April 10, 1905.

John F. Boling[sic],
    Crowder, Indian Territory.

Dear Sir:

    Receipt is hereby acknowledged of your letter of April 5, 1905, enclosing the affidavits of Nancy I Bolling and P.S. Johnston to the birth of Frank Alfred Bolling and Lewis Layfayette Bolling, children of John F. and Nancy I Bolling, March 1, 1903, and

Applications for Enrollment of Choctaw Newborn
Act of 1905   Volume IV

September 16, 1904, and the same have been filed with our records as an application for the enrollment of said children.

Replying to that portion of your letter in which you ask if you can select land for these children at once, you are advised that no selection of allotment can be permitted for children for whom application is made under the act of Congress approved March 4, 1905, until their enrollment is approved by the Secretary of the Interior.

Respectfully,

Commissioner in Charge.

Choctaw N.B. 198.
COPY.
Muskogee, Indian Territory, April 14, 1905.

John F. Boling,
    Crowder, Indian Territory.

Dear Sir:

Receipt is hereby acknowledged of your letter of April 10, enclosing affidavits of Nancy I. Bolling and P. S. Johnson[sic] to the birth of Frank Alfred Bolling and Louis Lafayette Bolling, sons of John F. and Nancy I. Bolling, March 1, 1903 and September 16, 1904, respectively, and the same have been filed with our records in the matter of the application for the enrollment of said children.

Replying to that portion of your letter in which you ask if you can select allotments for these children now, you are advised that no selection of allotment can be permitted for children for whom application is made under the Act of Congress approved March 3, 1905, until their enrollment has been approved by the Secretary of the Interior.

Respectfully,
SIGNED

T.B. Needles
Commissioner in Charge/[sic]

Applications for Enrollment of Choctaw Newborn
Act of 1905   Volume IV

Choc New Born 199
   Susie Davis
   (Born Feb. 26, 1904)

BIRTH AFFIDAVIT.

DEPARTMENT OF THE INTERIOR,
COMMISSION TO THE FIVE CIVILIZED TRIBES.

IN RE Application for Enrollment, as a citizen of the   Choctaw   Nation, of   Susie Davis , born on the   26   day of   February , 1904
married
Name of Father: D.E. Davis   a^ citizen of the   Choctaw   Nation.
Name of Mother: Maggie E. Davis   a citizen of the   Choctaw   Nation.

Post-Office: Milton, I.T.

AFFIDAVIT OF MOTHER.

UNITED STATES OF AMERICA,
   INDIAN TERRITORY.
Central   District.

I, Maggie E. Davis , on oath state that I am   26   years of age and a citizen by   Blood , of the   Choctaw   Nation; that I am the lawful wife of   Dave E. Davis , who is a citizen, by   marriage   of the   Choctaw   Nation; that a   girl   child was born to me on   26   day of   February , 1904 , that said child has been named   Susie Davis , and is now living.

Maggie E. Davis

WITNESSES TO MARK:
   My Roll No. is
      8295.

Subscribed and sworn to before me this 15   *day of*   March   , *1905*.

J. L. Lewis
NOTARY PUBLIC.

Applications for Enrollment of Choctaw Newborn
Act of 1905   Volume IV

AFFIDAVIT OF ATTENDING PHYSICIAN OR MID-WIFE.

UNITED STATES OF AMERICA,
    INDIAN TERRITORY.
Central District.

I, T. L. Hedgecock, a physician, on oath state that I attended on Mrs. M. E. Davis, wife of D. E. Davis on the 26 day of February, 1904; that there was born to her on said date a girl child; that said child is now living and is said to have been named Susie Davis

T. L. Hedgecock

WITNESSES TO MARK:

Subscribed and sworn to before me this 15 day of March, 1905.

J. L. Lewis
NOTARY PUBLIC.

7-2824

Muskogee, Indian Territory, March 24, 1905.

D. E. Davis,
    Milton, Indian Territory.

Dear Sir:

Receipt is hereby acknowledged of the affidavits of Maggie E. Davis and T. L. Hedgecock to the birth of Susie Davis daughter of D. E. and Maggie E. Davis, February 26, 1904, and the same have been filed with our records as an application for the enrollment of said child.

Respectfully,

Chairman.

Applications for Enrollment of Choctaw Newborn
Act of 1905 Volume IV

Choc New Born 200
    William S. Hall, Jr.
    (Born Sep. 7, 1904)
    Theodore Byron Hall
    (Born Dec. 10, 1902)

BIRTH AFFIDAVIT.

Department of the Interior,
COMMISSION TO THE FIVE CIVILIZED TRIBES.

    IN RE APPLICATION FOR ENROLLMENT, as a citizen of the Choctaw Nation, of Theodore Byron Hall, born on the 10th day of Dec, 190 2

Name of Father: W S. Hall   a citizen of the Choctaw Nation.
Name of Mother: Daisy C. Hall   a citizen of the Choctaw Nation.

Post-Office: Whitefield I.T.

AFFIDAVIT OF MOTHER.

UNITED STATES OF AMERICA,
    INDIAN TERRITORY,
Western District.

    I, Daisy C Hall, on oath state that I am 29 years of age and a citizen by Blood, of the Choctaw Nation; that I am the lawful wife of W.S. Hall, who is a citizen, by marriage of the Choctaw Nation; that a male child was born to me on 10th day of Dec, 1902, that said child has been named Theodore Byron Hall, and is now living.

                                Daisy C Hall

WITNESSES TO MARK:

{

    Subscribed and sworn to before me this 18 day of Dec, 190 .2

                                Monroe Thompson
                                  Notary Public.

Applications for Enrollment of Choctaw Newborn
Act of 1905   Volume IV

AFFIDAVIT OF ATTENDING PHYSICIAN OR MID-WIFE.

UNITED STATES OF AMERICA,
INDIAN TERRITORY,
Western District.

I, A S Thomas, a Physician, on oath state that I attended on Mrs. Daisy C Hall, wife of W S Hall on the 10th day of Dec, 190 2; that there was born to her on said date a male child; that said child is now living and is said to have been named Theodore Byron Hall

A. S. Thomas

WITNESSES TO MARK:

Subscribed and sworn to before me this 18 day of Dec, 190.2

Monroe Thompson
Notary Public.

BIRTH AFFIDAVIT.

Department of the Interior,
COMMISSION TO THE FIVE CIVILIZED TRIBES.

IN RE APPLICATION FOR ENROLLMENT, as a citizen of the Choctaw Nation, of Theodore Byron Hall, born on the 10th day of December, 190 2

Name of Father: William S Hall   a citizen of the Choctaw Nation.
Name of Mother: Daisy C Hall   a citizen of the Choctaw Nation.

Post-Office: Whitefield I.T.

AFFIDAVIT OF MOTHER.

UNITED STATES OF AMERICA,
INDIAN TERRITORY,
Central District.

I, William S Hall, on oath state that I am 47 years of age and a citizen by Marriage, of the Choctaw Nation; that I am the lawful ~~wife~~ husband of Daisy C. Hall, who is a citizen, by blood of the Choctaw Nation; that a male child was born to ~~me~~ her on 10th day of December, 190 2, that said child has been named Theodore Byron Hall, and is now living.

William S Hall

WITNESSES TO MARK:

Applications for Enrollment of Choctaw Newborn
Act of 1905   Volume IV

Subscribed and sworn to before me this 16th *day of* December , 190 2

P.C. Bolger
Notary Public.

NEW-BORN AFFIDAVIT.

Number............

...Choctaw Enrolling Commission...

IN THE MATTER OF THE APPLICATION FOR ENROLLMENT, as a citizen of the Choctaw   Nation, of   William S. Hall Jr.

born on the 7 day of __September__ 190 4

Name of father William S. Hall, Sr   a citizen of   Choctaw
Nation final enrollment No._____
Name of mother Daisy C. Hall   a citizen of   Choctaw
Nation final enrollment No. 15670

Postoffice   Whitefield I.T.

AFFIDAVIT OF MOTHER.

UNITED STATES OF AMERICA
INDIAN TERRITORY
~~Western~~ Central DISTRICT

I   Daisy C. Hall   , on oath state that I am 32   years of age and a citizen by blood   of the   Choctaw   Nation, and as such have been placed upon the final roll of the   Choctaw   Nation, by the Honorable Secretary of the Interior my final enrollment number being   15670 ; that I am the lawful wife of William S Hall, Sr.   , who is a citizen of the   Choctaw   Nation, and as such has been placed upon the final roll of said Nation by the Honorable Secretary of the Interior, his final enrollment number being_____ and that a   male   child was born to me on the 7 day of September   190 4; that said child has been named   William S Hall, Jr   , and is now living.

Daisy C. Hall

Witnesseth.
  Must be two   ⎫   John Taylor
  Witnesses who   ⎬
  are Citizens.   ⎭   Charley King

Applications for Enrollment of Choctaw Newborn
Act of 1905   Volume IV

Subscribed and sworn to before me this   13th   day of   Mch   190 5

Edwin O Clark
Notary Public.

My commission expires:
Jan. 17, 1909.

AFFIDAVIT OF ATTENDING PHYSICIAN OR MIDWIFE

UNITED STATES OF AMERICA
INDIAN TERRITORY
Central   DISTRICT

I,   A. S. Thomas   a   Physician on oath state that I attended on Mrs. Daisy C. Hall wife of   William S. Hall, Sr., on the   7   day of   September   , 190 4 , that there was born to her on said date a   male child, that said child is now living, and is said to have been named   William S. Hall, Jr.

A. S. Thomas $m.D.$

Subscribed and sworn to before me this, the   3   day of   Jan   190 5

WITNESSETH: E.M. Dalton   Notary Public.
Must be two witnesses { John Taylor   My Commission Expires Oct. 20, 1908.
who are citizens   { Charley King

We hereby certify that we are well acquainted with   A.S. Thomas   a   physician   and know   him   to be reputable and of good standing in the community.

John Taylor   _____

Charley King   _____

Applications for Enrollment of Choctaw Newborn
Act of 1905 Volume IV

NEW-BORN AFFIDAVIT.

Number................

...Choctaw Enrolling Commission...

IN THE MATTER OF THE APPLICATION FOR ENROLLMENT, as a citizen of the Choctaw Nation, of Theodore B Hall

born on the 10 day of December 190 2

Name of father William S. Hall, Sr   a citizen of _____
Nation final enrollment No._____
Name of mother Daisy C. Hall   a citizen of Choctaw
Nation final enrollment No. 15670

Postoffice Whitefield I.T.

AFFIDAVIT OF MOTHER.

UNITED STATES OF AMERICA
INDIAN TERRITORY
~~Western~~ Central DISTRICT

I Daisy C. Hall , on oath state that I am 32 years of age and a citizen by blood of the Choctaw Nation, and as such have been placed upon the final roll of the Choctaw Nation, by the Honorable Secretary of the Interior my final enrollment number being 15670 ; that I am the lawful wife of William S Hall, Sr. , who is a citizen of the Choctaw Nation, and as such has been placed upon the final roll of said Nation by the Honorable Secretary of the Interior, his final enrollment number being_____ and that a male child was born to me on the 10 day of December 190 2; that said child has been named Theodore B Hall , and is now living.

Daisy C. Hall

Witnesseth.
Must be two Witnesses who are Citizens. } John Taylor
Charley King

Subscribed and sworn to before me this 13th day of Mch 190 5

Edwin O Clark
Notary Public.

My commission expires:
     Jan. 17, 1909.

Applications for Enrollment of Choctaw Newborn
Act of 1905   Volume IV

AFFIDAVIT OF ATTENDING PHYSICIAN OR MIDWIFE

UNITED STATES OF AMERICA
INDIAN TERRITORY
~~Western~~   DISTRICT
Central

I, A. S. Thomas a Physician on oath state that I attended on Mrs. Daisy C. Hall wife of William S. Hall, Sr., on the 10 day of December, 190 2, that there was born to her on said date a male child, that said child is now living, and is said to have been named Theodore B. Hall

A. S. Thomas   M.D.

Subscribed and sworn to before me this, the 23 day of Jan 190 5

WITNESSETH: E.M. Dalton   Notary Public.
Must be two witnesses who are citizens { John Taylor   My Commission Expires Oct. 20, 1908.
Charley King

We hereby certify that we are well acquainted with A.S. Thomas a physician and know him to be reputable and of good standing in the community.

John Taylor

Charley King

BIRTH AFFIDAVIT.

DEPARTMENT OF THE INTERIOR.
COMMISSION TO THE FIVE CIVILIZED TRIBES.

IN RE APPLICATION FOR ENROLLMENT, as a citizen of the Choctaw Nation, of William S Hall, Jr, born on the 7th day of Sept, 1904

Name of Father: William S Hall   a citizen of the Choctaw Nation.
Name of Mother: Daisy C Hall   a citizen of the Choctaw Nation.

Postoffice   Whitefield, I.T.

Applications for Enrollment of Choctaw Newborn
Act of 1905   Volume IV

AFFIDAVIT OF MOTHER.

UNITED STATES OF AMERICA, Indian Territory, }
Central   DISTRICT.

    I, Daisy C. Hall   , on oath state that I am 32   years of age and a citizen by blood   , of the   Choctaw   Nation; that I am the lawful wife of William S Hall , who is a citizen, by marriage   of the   Choctaw   Nation; that a   male child was born to me on   7th   day of September   , 1904; that said child has been named   William S. Hall, Jr.   , and was living March 4, 1905.

                                         Daisy C. Hall

Witnesses To Mark:
{

    Subscribed and sworn to before me this 21st   day of   March   , 1905

                                      Wirt Franklin
                                        Notary Public.

AFFIDAVIT OF ATTENDING PHYSICIAN OR MID-WIFE.

UNITED STATES OF AMERICA, Indian Territory, }
Central   DISTRICT.

    I, A. S. Thomas   , a physician   , on oath state that I attended on Mrs. Daisy C. Hall   , wife of   W. S. Hall   on the 7th   day of September   , 1904; that there was born to her on said date a   male   child; that said child was living March 4, 1905, and is said to have been named   William S. Hall, Jr.

                                      A. S. Thomas

Witnesses To Mark:
{

    Subscribed and sworn to before me this 22nd day of   March   , 1905

                                      Edwin O. Clark
                                      Notary Public.

Applications for Enrollment of Choctaw Newborn
Act of 1905 Volume IV

BIRTH AFFIDAVIT.

DEPARTMENT OF THE INTERIOR.
COMMISSION TO THE FIVE CIVILIZED TRIBES.

IN RE APPLICATION FOR ENROLLMENT, as a citizen of the Choctaw Nation, of Theodore Byron Hall, born on the 10th day of December, 1902

Name of Father: William S. Hall   a citizen of the Choctaw Nation.
Name of Mother: Daisy C. Hall   a citizen of the Choctaw Nation.

Postoffice   Whitefield, I.T.

AFFIDAVIT OF MOTHER.

UNITED STATES OF AMERICA, Indian Territory,
Central DISTRICT.

I, Daisy C. Hall, on oath state that I am 32 years of age and a citizen by blood, of the Choctaw Nation; that I am the lawful wife of William S Hall, who is a citizen, by marriage of the Choctaw Nation; that a male child was born to me on 10th day of December, 1902; that said child has been named Theodore Byron Hall, and was living March 4, 1905.

Daisy C. Hall

Witnesses To Mark:

Subscribed and sworn to before me this 21st day of March, 1905

Wirt Franklin
Notary Public.

AFFIDAVIT OF ATTENDING PHYSICIAN OR MID-WIFE.

UNITED STATES OF AMERICA, Indian Territory,
Central DISTRICT.

I, A. S. Thomas, a physician, on oath state that I attended on Mrs. Daisy C. Hall, wife of W. S. Hall on the 10th day of December, 1902; that there was born to her on said date a male child; that said child was living March 4, 1905, and is said to have been named Theodore Byron Hall

Edwin O. Clark

Witnesses To Mark:

Applications for Enrollment of Choctaw Newborn
Act of 1905   Volume IV

Subscribed and sworn to before me this 22nd day of March, 1905

Edwin O. Clark
Notary Public.

7-2834

Muskogee, Indian Territory, March 23, 1905.

Daisy C. Hall,
   Whitefield, Indian Territory.

Dear Madam:

Receipt is hereby acknowledged of the affidavits of Daisy C. Hall and A. S. Thomas to the birth of Theodore Byron Hall and William S. Hall, Jr., children of William S. and Daisy C. Hall, December 10, 1902, and September 7, 1904, respectively, and the same have been filed with the records as an application for the enrollment of said child. the enrollment of said children.

Respectively,

Chairman.

Choc New Born 201
   Beula Thompson
   (Born Aug. 3, 1903)

BIRTH AFFIDAVIT.

DEPARTMENT OF THE INTERIOR.
COMMISSION TO THE FIVE CIVILIZED TRIBES.

IN RE APPLICATION FOR ENROLLMENT, as a citizen of the Choctaw Nation, of Beula Thompson, born on the 3rd day of August, 1903
Roll-8657
Name of Father: Nelson Thompson   a citizen of the Choctaw Nation.
Roll-8658
Name of Mother: Malinda Thompson   a citizen of the Choctaw Nation.

Postoffice   Redoak I.T.

Applications for Enrollment of Choctaw Newborn
Act of 1905   Volume IV

AFFIDAVIT OF MOTHER.

UNITED STATES OF AMERICA, Indian Territory, }
Central   DISTRICT.

I, Nelson Thompson, on oath state that I am 37 years of age, and a citizen by blood, of the Choctaw Nation; that I am the lawful ~~wife~~ husband of Malinda Thompson, who is a citizen, by blood of the Choctaw Nation; that a Female child was born ~~Malinda Thompson~~ ~~to me on~~ day of August, 1903; that said child has been named Beula Thompson, and was living March 4, 1905.

                                              Nelson Thompson

Witnesses To Mark:
{

Subscribed and sworn to before me this 20 day of March, 1905

                                              [Name Illegible]
                                              Notary Public.

AFFIDAVIT OF ATTENDING PHYSICIAN OR MID-WIFE.

UNITED STATES OF AMERICA, Indian Territory, }
Central   DISTRICT.

I, Agnes Brown, a midwife, on oath state that I attended on Mrs. Malinda Thompson, wife of Nelson Thompson on the 3rd day of August, 1903; that there was born to her on said date a Female child; that said child was living March 4, 1905, and is said to have been named Beula Thompson

                                                  her
                                         Agnes (x) Brown

Witnesses To Mark: mark
{ Joe B Williams
{ [Name Illegible]

Subscribed and sworn to before me this 20 day of March, 1905

                                            [Name Illegible]
                                            Notary Public.

Applications for Enrollment of Choctaw Newborn
Act of 1905   Volume IV

This is to certify that we the undersigned do know that there was born to Nelson Thompson on the 3rd day of August 1903 one Female Child, and that Malinda Thompson, wife of said Nelson Thompson is dead.

        Signed Siky Jefferson
        Smallwood Jefferson

Subscribed and sworn to before me this 12th day of April 1905.

        C L Stone   Notary Public

BIRTH AFFIDAVIT.

DEPARTMENT OF THE INTERIOR.
COMMISSION TO THE FIVE CIVILIZED TRIBES.

IN RE APPLICATION FOR ENROLLMENT, as a citizen of the Choctaw Nation, of Beula Thompson , born on the 3rd day of August , 1903
        Roll-8657
Name of Father: Nelson Thompson a citizen of the Choctaw Nation.
        Roll-8658
Name of Mother: Malinda Thompson a citizen of the Choctaw Nation.

        Postoffice   Redoak I.T.

AFFIDAVIT OF MOTHER.

UNITED STATES OF AMERICA, Indian Territory,
   Central   **DISTRICT.**

    I, Nelson Thompson , on oath state that I am 37 years of age, and a citizen by blood , of the Choctaw Nation; that I am the lawful ~~wife~~ husband of Malinda Thompson , who is a citizen, by blood of the Choctaw Nation; that a Female child was born ~~to me on~~ Malinda Thompson day of August , 1903; that said child has been named Beula Thompson , and was living March 4, 1905.

        Nelson Thompson

Witnesses To Mark:
  {

Subscribed and sworn to before me this 20 day of March , 1905

        [Name Illegible]
        Notary Public.

Applications for Enrollment of Choctaw Newborn
Act of 1905 Volume IV

AFFIDAVIT OF ATTENDING PHYSICIAN OR MID-WIFE.

UNITED STATES OF AMERICA, Indian Territory,
Central DISTRICT.

I, Agnes Brown , a midwife , on oath state that I attended on Mrs. Malinda Thompson , wife of Nelson Thompson on the 3rd day of August , 1903; that there was born to her on said date a Female child; that said child was living March 4, 1905, and is said to have been named Beula Thompson

                her
           Agnes (x) Brown
Witnesses To Mark: mark
{ Joe B Williams
{ [Name Illegible]

Subscribed and sworn to before me this 20 day of March , 1905

           [Name Illegible]
           Notary Public.

BIRTH AFFIDAVIT.

DEPARTMENT OF THE INTERIOR.
COMMISSION TO THE FIVE CIVILIZED TRIBES.

IN RE APPLICATION FOR ENROLLMENT, as a citizen of the Choctaw Nation, of Beula Thompson , born on the 3rd day of August , 1903

Name of Father: Nelson Thompson   a citizen of the Choctaw Nation.
Name of Mother: Malinda Thompson   citizen of the Choctaw Nation.

           Postoffice   Red Oak Ind. Ter.

AFFIDAVIT OF MOTHER.

UNITED STATES OF AMERICA, Indian Territory,
DISTRICT.

I, Malinda Thompson , on oath state that I am 30 years of age and a citizen by Blood , of the Choctaw Nation; that I am the lawful wife of Nelson Thompson , who is a citizen, by Blood of the Choctaw Nation; that a Female child was born to me on 3rd day of August , 1903; that said child has been named Beula Thompson , and was living March 4, 1905.

Applications for Enrollment of Choctaw Newborn
Act of 1905   Volume IV

Witnesses To Mark:

{

Subscribed and sworn to before me this ...... day of ...., 190....

Notary Public.

AFFIDAVIT OF ATTENDING PHYSICIAN OR MID-WIFE.

UNITED STATES OF AMERICA, Indian Territory, }
Central   DISTRICT. }

I, Agnes Brown, a midwife, on oath state that I attended on Mrs. Malinda Thompson, wife of Nelson Thompson on the 3rd day of August, 1903; that there was born to her on said date a Female child; that said child was living March 4, 1905, and is said to have been named Beula Thompson

                her
             Agnes x Brown
Witnesses To Mark: mark
{ Willis Hancock
{ Logen[sic] Harkin

Subscribed and sworn to before me this   22nd day of April , 1905

C.L. Stone
Notary Public.

7-2942

Muskogee, Indian Territory, March 25, 1905.

Nelson Thompson,
  Redoak, Indian Territory.

Dear Sir:

  Receipt is hereby acknowledged of the affidavits of Nelson Thompson and Agnes Brown to the birth of Beula Thompson, daughter of Nelson and Malinda Thompson, deceased, August 3, 1903, and the same have been filed with our records as an application for the enrollment of said child; also the affidavits of Nelson Thompson and Agnes Brown to the death of your wife Malinda Thompson a citizen by blood of the Choctaw Nation which occurred December 4, 1903, and the same have been filed with our records as evidence of the death of the above named citizen.

Applications for Enrollment of Choctaw Newborn
Act of 1905 Volume IV

Respectfully,

Chairman.

COPY.

N. B. 201

Muskogee, Indian Territory, April 7, 1905.

Nelson Thompson,
    Redoak, Indian Territory.

Dear Sir:

    There is inclosed you herewith for execution application for the enrollment of your infant child, Beula Thompson, born August 3, 1903.

    The affidavits heretofore filed with the Commission were of the physician and father. You will notice from the inclosed application that the affidavit of the mother is required. You will please insert the age of the mother in space left blank for that purpose.

    In the event that the mother is dead, it will be necessary that you procure the affidavits of two persons who have actual knowledge of the fact, that the child was born, was living on March 4, 1905, and that Malinda Thompson was her mother.

    In having these affidavits executed care should be exercised to see that all the names are written in full as they appear in the body of the affidavit, and in the event that either of the persons signing the affidavit are unable to write, signatures by mark must be attested by two witnesses. Each affidavit must be executed before a Notary Public and the notarial seal and signature of the officer must be attached to each separate affidavit.

Respectfully,

SIGNED *T.B. Needles*
Commissioner in Charge.

LER 7-11

Applications for Enrollment of Choctaw Newborn
Act of 1905   Volume IV

COPY.

7 NB 201

Muskogee, Indian Territory, April 26, 1905.

Nelson Thompson,
Redoak, Indian Territory.

Dear Sir:

Receipt is hereby acknowledged of the affidavit of Agnes Brown to the birth of Beula Thompson, daughter of Nelson and Malinda Thompson, August 3, 1903, and the same has been filed with our records in the matter of the enrollment of said child. Receipt is also acknowledged of the joint affidavits of Siky Jefferson and Smallwood Jefferson to the birth of this child.

Referring to the joint affidavit, it appears that the Notary Public before whom it was executed failed to attach his seal thereto, the same is herewith returned to you with the request to have the Notary Public affix his seal to this affidavit and return to this office at the earliest practicable date.

Respectfully,
SIGNED

Tams Bixby
Chairman.

LM 1-26

COPY.   7 N.B. 201.

Muskogee, Indian Territory, May 3, 1905.

Nelson Thompson,
Redoak, Indian Territory.

Dear Sir:

Receipt is hereby acknowledged of the joint affidavit of Sikey[sic] and Smallwood Jefferson in the matter of the enrollment of your child, Beulah[sic] Thompson, and the same has been filed with the records in the case.

Respectfully,
SIGNED

Tams Bixby
Chairman.

Applications for Enrollment of Choctaw Newborn
Act of 1905   Volume IV

Choc New Born 202
    Daisy Hicker
    (Born March 23, 1904)

BIRTH AFFIDAVIT.

DEPARTMENT OF THE INTERIOR.
COMMISSION TO THE FIVE CIVILIZED TRIBES.

IN RE APPLICATION FOR ENROLLMENT, as a citizen of the Choctaw Nation, of Daisy Hicker, born on the 23 day of March, 1904

Name of Father: Edward Hicker   a citizen of the Choctaw Nation.
(Roll Number 8756)
Name of Mother: Silaney Stallaby ^ a citizen of the Choctaw Nation.

Postoffice   Redoak I.T.

AFFIDAVIT OF MOTHER.

UNITED STATES OF AMERICA, Indian Territory, }
    Central   DISTRICT. }

    I, Silaney Stallaby, on oath state that I am 23 years of age and a citizen by blood, of the Choctaw Nation; that I am the lawful wife of Edward Hicker, who is a citizen, by blood of the Choctaw Nation; that a female child was born to me on 23 day of March, 1904; that said child has been named Daisy Hicker, and was living March 4, 1905.

                              Her
                       Silaney (x) Stallaby
Witnesses To Mark: Mark
   { Joe B Williams
   { [Name Illegible]

    Subscribed and sworn to before me this 20 day of March, 1905

                      [Name Illegible]
                         Notary Public.

Applications for Enrollment of Choctaw Newborn
Act of 1905   Volume IV

AFFIDAVIT OF ATTENDING PHYSICIAN OR MID-WIFE.

UNITED STATES OF AMERICA, Indian Territory, }
Central   DISTRICT.

I, Isham C Talley , a physician , on oath state that I attended on Mrs. Silaney Stallaby , wife of Edward Hicker on the 23 day of March , 1904; that there was born to her on said date a female child; that said child was living March 4, 1905, and is said to have been named Daisy Hicker

                                      Isham C Talley

Witnesses To Mark:
{

Subscribed and sworn to before me this 20 day of March , 1905

                                      [Name Illegible]
                                      Notary Public.

                                      7-2989

Muskogee, Indian Territory, March 25, 1905.

Edward Hicker,
    Redoak, Indian Territory.

Dear Sir:

    Receipt is hereby acknowledged of the affidavits of Silaney Stallaby and Isham C. Tally[sic] to the birth of Daisy Hicker, daughter of Edward Hicker and Silaney Stallaby, March 23, 1904, and the same have been filed with our records as an application for the enrollment of said child.

                                      Respectfully,

                                                Chairman.

Applications for Enrollment of Choctaw Newborn
Act of 1905   Volume IV

Choc New Born 203
    Earnest T. Hulsey
    (Born March 1, 1904)

BIRTH AFFIDAVIT.

DEPARTMENT OF THE INTERIOR.
COMMISSION TO THE FIVE CIVILIZED TRIBES.

IN RE APPLICATION FOR ENROLLMENT, as a citizen of the Choctaw Nation, of Earnest T. Hulsey, born on the 1st day of March, 1904

Name of Father: Marion T. Hulsey   a citizen of the US ~~Nation~~.
Name of Mother: Mary A. Hulsey   a citizen of the Choctaw Nation.

Postoffice   Pauls Valley, I.T.

AFFIDAVIT OF MOTHER.

UNITED STATES OF AMERICA, Indian Territory,
Southern DISTRICT.

    I, Mary A Hulsey, on oath state that I am 42 years of age and a citizen by blood, of the Choctaw Nation; that I am the lawful wife of Marion T. Hulsey, who is a citizen, by blood of the United States Nation; that a male child was born to me on 1st day of March, 1904; that said child has been named Earnest T. Hulsey, and was living March 4, 1905.

                        Mary A Hulsey
Witnesses To Mark: (Mary A. Hulsey)

    Subscribed and sworn to before me this 11th day of April, 1905

                        J. E. Williams
                            Notary Public.

AFFIDAVIT OF ATTENDING PHYSICIAN OR MID-WIFE.

UNITED STATES OF AMERICA, Indian Territory,
Judicial DISTRICT.

    I, H. L. Dalby, a physician, on oath state that I attended on Mrs. Mary A Hulsey, wife of Marion T Hulsey on the 1st day of

Applications for Enrollment of Choctaw Newborn
Act of 1905   Volume IV

March   , 1904; that there was born to her on said date a   male   child; that said child was living March 4, 1905, and is said to have been named Earnest T. Hulsey

                                            H. L. Dalby M.D.

Witnesses To Mark:
{

Subscribed and sworn to before me this ~~April~~ 20 day of April   , 1905

                                      T T Manning
                                      ~~Notary Public~~.
                                      Mayer[sic]

BIRTH AFFIDAVIT.

DEPARTMENT OF THE INTERIOR,
COMMISSION TO THE FIVE CIVILIZED TRIBES.

In Re Application for Enrollment, as a citizen of the   Choctaw   Nation, of   Earnest T. Hulsey , born on the 1st day of March   , 1904

Name of Father: Marion T Hulsey   a citizen of the .... Nation.
Name of Mother: Mary A Hulsey   a citizen of the   Choctaw   Nation.

                        Post-office   Wilburton

AFFIDAVIT OF MOTHER.

UNITED STATES OF AMERICA, }
   INDIAN TERRITORY,
Central   District.

I, Mary A. Hulsey , on oath state that I am   41   years of age and a citizen by blood , of the   Choctaw   Nation; that I am the lawful wife of Marion T. Hulsey   , who is a citizen, by .... of the .... Nation; that a Male   child was born to me on 1st day of March   , 1904 , that said child has been named Earnest T. , and is now living.

                                        Mary A Hulsey
WITNESSES TO MARK:
{

Subscribed and sworn to before me this 18 day of April   , 1904

                                    J N Patterson
                                      NOTARY PUBLIC.

Applications for Enrollment of Choctaw Newborn
Act of 1905   Volume IV

AFFIDAVIT OF ATTENDING PHYSICIAN OR MID-WIFE.

UNITED STATES OF AMERICA, ⎫
   INDIAN TERRITORY,   ⎬
Central   District. ⎭

I, H.L. Dalby , a Physician , on oath state that I attended on Mrs. Mary A Hulsey , wife of Marion T Hulsey on the 1st day of March , 1904 ; that there was born to her on said date a male child; that said child is now living and is said to have been named Earnest T

H.L. Dalby

WITNESSES TO MARK:

Subscribed and sworn to before me this 26 day of April , 1904

[Name Illegible]
NOTARY PUBLIC.

7-2967

Muskogee, Indian Territory, April 16, 1904.

Charles H. Hudson,
    Attorney at Law,
        Wilburton, Indian Territory.

Dear Sir:

    Receipt is hereby acknowledged of your letter of the 12th inst., enclosing a communication from the Secretary of the Interior, relative to the enrollment of an infant child born to Mary E. Hulsey, a recognized citizen of the Choctaw Nation, about six weeks ago, and you ask that a report in relation to the matter be forwarded you.

    You are informed it appears from our records that on April 12, 1904, a blank application for the enrollment of an infant child was forwarded to your address in accordance with your request of March 29, 1904.

    It does not appear, however, that any application has ever been received at this office for the enrollment of an infant child born to Mary A. Hulsey, within the time stated in your letter, and it is therefore impracticable for the Commission to make any report to you in the matter of the enrollment of said child.

Applications for Enrollment of Choctaw Newborn
Act of 1905   Volume IV

The letter from the Department is returned herewith.

Respectfully,

HG. 82

Commissioner in Charge.

7-2967

Muskogee, Indian Territory, May 5, 1904.

Marion T. Hulsey,
Wilburton, Indian Territory.

Dear Sir:

Receipt is hereby acknowledged of the affidavits of Mary A. Hulsey and H. L. Dalby relative to the birth of your infant son, Earnest T. Hulsey on March 1, 1904, which it is presumed have been forwarded to this office as an application for the enrollment of said child as a citizen by blood of the Choctaw Nation.

Under the provisions of the act of Congress approved July 1, 1902, the Commission is now without authority to receive or consider the original application for the enrollment of any person whomsoever as a citizen of the Choctaw or Chickasaw Nation.

Respectfully,

Commissioner in Charge.

N. B. 203

COPY.

Muskogee, Indian Territory, April 6, 1905.

Marion T. Hulsey,
Wilburton, Indian Territory.

Dear Sir:

There is inclosed you herewith for execution application for the enrollment of your infant child, Earnest T. Hulsey, born March 1, 1904.

The affidavits heretofore filed with the Commission show the child was living on April 26, 1904. It is necessary, for the child to be enrolled, that he was living on March 4, 1905. You will please insert the mother's age in the place left blank for that purpose.

Applications for Enrollment of Choctaw Newborn
Act of 1905   Volume IV

      In having those affidavits executed, care should be exercised to see that all the names are written in full as they appear in the body of the affidavit, and in the event that either of the persons signing the affidavit are unable to write, signatures by mark must be attested by two witnesses. Each affidavit must be executed before a Notary Public and the notorial[sic] seal and signature of the officer must be attached to each separate affidavit.

                        Respectfully,

SEV 5-6

                    SIGNED

                        T.B. Needles
                        Commissioner in Charge.

                                                  Choctaw 2967.

                      Muskogee, Indian Territory, April 26, 1905.

Marion T. Hulsey,
      Pauls Valley, Indian Territory.

Dear Sir:

      Receipt is hereby acknowledged of the affidavits of Mary A. Hulsey and H. L. Dalby to the birth of Earnest T. Hulsey, son of Marion T. and Mary A. Hulsey, March 7, 1904, and the same have been filed with our records as an application for the enrollment of said child.

                        Respectfully,

                                       Chairman.

                    COPY.   7 N.B.203.

                      Muskogee, Indian Territory, May 3, 1905.

Claude Weaver,
      Attorney at Law,
            Pauls Valley, Indian Territory.

Dear Sir:

      Receipt is hereby acknowledged of your letter of April 27, asking if application has been made for the enrollment of Earnest T. Hulsey, son of Mary A. and Marion T. Hulsey, under the act of March 3, 1905, and if the same is in proper form.

Applications for Enrollment of Choctaw Newborn
Act of 1905 Volume IV

In reply to your letter you are advised that the affidavits heretofore forwarded to the birth of Earnest T. Hulsey have been filed with our records as an application for the enrollment of said child, and in the event further evidence is necessary to enable the Commission to determine his right to enrollment, Mr. Hulsey will be duly notified.

Respectfully,
SIGNED

Tams Bixby
Chairman.

7-NB-203

Muskogee, Indian Territory, July 12, 1905.

Mary A. Hulsey,
    Pauls Valley, Indian Territory.

Dear Madam:

Receipt is hereby acknowledged of your letter of July 8, 1905, asking if the "baby rolls" have been approved.

In reply to your letter you are advised that on June 30, 1905, the Secretary of the Interior approved the enrollment of your child Earnest T. Hulsey as a citizen by blood of the Choctaw Nation and selection of allotment may now be made in his behalf in accordance with the rules and regulations governing the selection of allotments and the designation of homesteads in the Choctaw and Chickasaw Nations.

Respectfully,

Commissioner.

Applications for Enrollment of Choctaw Newborn
Act of 1905 Volume IV

Choc New Born 204
    William Joseph Lewis
    (Born Nov. 3, 1904)
    Ethel E. Lewis
    (Born Nov. 2, 1902)

BIRTH AFFIDAVIT.

Department of the Interior,
COMMISSION TO THE FIVE CIVILIZED TRIBES.

IN RE APPLICATION FOR ENROLLMENT, as a citizen of the Choctaw Nation, of Ethel Lewis, born on the 2 day of November, 190 2

Name of Father: Howard Lewis   a citizen of the Choctaw Nation.
Name of Mother: Alice Lewis   a citizen of the Choctaw Nation.

Post-Office: LeFlore, I.T.

AFFIDAVIT OF ~~MOTHER~~ father.

UNITED STATES OF AMERICA,
  INDIAN TERRITORY,
Central District.

I, Howard Lewis, on oath state that I am 31 years of age and a citizen by blood, of the Choctaw Nation; that I am the lawful ~~wife~~ husband of Alice Howard[sic], who is a citizen, by blood of the Choctaw Nation; that a Female child was born to ~~me~~ her on 2 day of November, 190 2, that said child has been named Ethel Lewis, and is now living.

                          Howard Lewis

WITNESSES TO MARK:
{

Subscribed and sworn to before me this 15 day of December, 190 2

                H.C. Risteen
                  Notary Public.

Applications for Enrollment of Choctaw Newborn
Act of 1905   Volume IV

NEW BORN AFFIDAVIT

No ....

CHOCTAW ENROLLING COMMISSION

IN THE MATTER OF THE APPLICATION FOR ENROLLMENT as a citizen of the Choctaw Nation, of   Ethel E. Lewis   born on the 2ond.[sic] day of November   190 2

Name of father   Howard E. Lewis   a citizen of   Choctaw   Nation, final enrollment No............
Name of mother   Alice J. Lewis   a citizen of   Choctaw   Nation, final enrollment No............

Wynnewood, Ind. Ter.   Postoffice.

AFFIDAVIT OF MOTHER

UNITED STATES OF AMERICA
INDIAN TERRITORY
DISTRICT   Southern

I   Alice J. Lewis   , on oath state that I am 21   years of age and a citizen by   blood   of the   Choctaw   Nation, and as such have been placed upon the final roll of the   Choctaw   Nation, by the Honorable Secretary of the Interior my final enrollment number being............; that I am the lawful wife of   Howard E. Lewis   , who is a citizen of the   Choctaw   Nation, and as such has been placed upon the final roll of said Nation by the Honorable Secretary of the Interior, his final enrollment number being............and that a   Female   child was born to me on the   2ond.   day of   Nov.   190 2; that said child has been named   Ethel Eugenia   , and is now living.

WITNESSETH: Alice Lewis

Must be two witnesses   William J Lewis
who are citizens   William Reichert

Subscribed and sworn to before me this, the   1oth[sic]   day of   March   , 190 5

[Name Illegible]
Notary Public.

My Commission Expires: 12/22/19o6[sic]

115

Applications for Enrollment of Choctaw Newborn
Act of 1905   Volume IV

Affidavit of Attending Physician or Midwife

UNITED STATES OF AMERICA,
    INDIAN TERRITORY,
Southern   DISTRICT

I, Howard E. Lewis   a   Husband
on oath state that I attended on Mrs. Alice J. Lewis   wife of Howard E. Lewis (Myself)
on the 2ond. day of Nov. 1902, 1902, that there was born to her on said date a   female child, that said child is now living, and is said to have been named Ethel Eugenia Lewis

                                                     Husband
                                     Howard E Lewis   M.D.

Subscribed and sworn to before me this, the 1oth[sic] day of March , 190 5

                                     [Name Illegible]
                                     Notary Public.

WITNESSETH:
Must be two witnesses   {   William J Lewis
who are citizens and
know the child.   William Reichert

We hereby certify that we are well acquainted with   Howard E. Lewis
a in capacity as midwife   and know   him   to be reputable and of good standing in the community.

                         Must be two citizen {   William J Lewis
                         witnesses.   William Reichert

NEW BORN AFFIDAVIT

No

CHOCTAW ENROLLING COMMISSION

IN THE MATTER OF THE APPLICATION FOR ENROLLMENT as a citizen of the Choctaw Nation, of   William Joseph Lewis   born on the   3rd.   day of   Nov.   190 4

     Name of father   Howard E. Lewis   a citizen of   Choctaw   Nation, final enrollment No
     Name of mother   Alice J. Lewis   a citizen of   Choctaw   Nation, final enrollment No

Applications for Enrollment of Choctaw Newborn
Act of 1905   Volume IV

Wynnewood, I.T.　　　　Postoffice.

AFFIDAVIT OF MOTHER

UNITED STATES OF AMERICA
　INDIAN TERRITORY
DISTRICT　Southern

I　Alice J. Lewis　　, on oath state that I am　21　years of age and a citizen by　blood　of the　Choctaw　Nation, and as such have been placed upon the final roll of the　Choctaw　Nation, by the Honorable Secretary of the Interior my final enrollment number being............; that I am the lawful wife of　Howard E. Lewis　, who is a citizen of the　Choctaw　Nation, and as such has been placed upon the final roll of said Nation by the Honorable Secretary of the Interior, his final enrollment number being............and that a　Male　child was born to me on the　3rd.　day of　Nov.　190 4; that said child has been named　William Joseph　, and is now living.

WITNESSETH:　　　　　　　　　　　　　　　　　　　　Alice Lewis
　Must be two witnesses ⎰ William J Lewis
　who are citizens　　⎱ William Reichert

Subscribed and sworn to before me this, the　1oth[sic]　day of　March　, 190 5

[Name Illegible]
Notary Public.

My Commission Expires:　12/22/19o6[sic]

Affidavit of Attending Physician or Midwife

UNITED STATES OF AMERICA,
　INDIAN TERRITORY,
Southern　　DISTRICT

I,　E. E. Norvel　a　Physician on oath state that I attended on Mrs. Alice J. Lewis wife of Howard E. Lewis on the　3rd　day of Nov.　, 190 4, that there was born to her on said date a　Male　child, that said child is now living, and is said to have been named　William Joseph Lewis

Elijah E Norvell　　M. D.

Subscribed and sworn to before me this the　16　day of　March　1905

[Name Illegible]
Notary Public.

117

Applications for Enrollment of Choctaw Newborn
Act of 1905 Volume IV

WITNESSETH:
Must be two witnesses who are citizens and know the child. { William J Lewis
William Reichert

We hereby certify that we are well acquainted with E E Norvell a Physician and know him to be reputable and of good standing in the community.

Must be two citizen witnesses. { William J Lewis
William Reichert

Affidavit of Howard E Lewis as regards Enrollment of Alice Kincade

INDIAN TERRITORY §
§
SOUTHERN DISTRICT §

Howard E. Lewis of Wynnewood, I.T. being duly sworn, upon his oath states that his wife Alice J. Lewis was listed and enrolled as Alice Kincade about six or seven years ago at Red Oak, I.T. and that her parents were named Joe and Mary Kincade, and her sister Sissie Kincade, and her grandfather Risal Winlock were enrolled at the same time. Her father and mother being dead, she was enrolled by her grand-father.

Roll Choctaw by blood No. 8798, and certificate No. 5727 issued on the 7th day of Nov. 1903, at the Chickasaw Land office.

Howard Lewis

Subscribed and sworn to before me this the 15th day of May, 1905.

JO Quigley
Notary Public, Southern District Indian Ter.

BIRTH AFFIDAVIT. 7-NB 204

DEPARTMENT OF THE INTERIOR.
COMMISSION TO THE FIVE CIVILIZED TRIBES.

IN RE APPLICATION FOR ENROLLMENT, as a citizen of the Choctaw Nation, of Ethel E. Lewis, born on the 2nd day of Nov, 1902

Name of Father: Howard Lewis   a citizen of the Choctaw Nation.
Name of Mother: Alice J Lewis   a citizen of the Choctaw Nation.

Postoffice   Wynnewood I.T.

Applications for Enrollment of Choctaw Newborn
Act of 1905   Volume IV

AFFIDAVIT OF MOTHER.

UNITED STATES OF AMERICA, Indian Territory,
So. Dist   DISTRICT.

I, Alice J Lewis, on oath state that I am 21 years of age and a citizen by blood, of the Choctaw Nation; that I am the lawful wife of Howard Lewis, who is a citizen, by blood of the Choctaw Nation; that a female child was born to me on 2nd day of November, 1902; that said child has been named Ethel Eugenia Lewis, and was living March 4, 1905.

                                                      Alice J Lewis

Witnesses To Mark:

Subscribed and sworn to before me this 19th day of Aug., 1905

                                                [Name Illegible]
                                                Notary Public.

AFFIDAVIT OF ATTENDING PHYSICIAN OR MID-WIFE.

UNITED STATES OF AMERICA, Indian Territory,
Central   DISTRICT.

I, Margret McFerrin, a midwife, on oath state that I attended on Mrs. Alice J Lewis, wife of Howard Lewis on the 2nd day of Nov, 1902; that there was born to her on said date a female child; that said child was living March 4, 1905, and is said to have been named Ethel Eugenia Lewis

                                                her
Witnesses To Mark: Margret x McFerrin
  Oscar J Baker   mark
  Sidney Amos

Subscribed and sworn to before me this 12 day of Aug, 1905

                                               W L Harris
My Com. Exp 7/8/08   Notary Public.

Applications for Enrollment of Choctaw Newborn
Act of 1905 Volume IV

7-3021.
COPY.
Muskogee, Indian Territory, January 6, 1903.

Howard Lewis,
    Leflore, Indian Territory.

Dear Sir:

    Referring to the application for enrolment as a citizen of the Choctaw Nation of Ethel Lewis, infant daughter of Howard and Alice Lewis, born November 2, 1902; you are advised that the Commission is without authority to enroll this child as a citizen of the Choctaw Nation, it appearing that said child was born November 2, 1902, subsequent to the ratification by the citizens of the Choctaw and Chickasaw Nations September 25, 1902, of an act of Congress approved July 2, 1902 (32 Stats., 641).

    Section twenty-eight thereof provides as follows:

    "The names of all persons living on the date of the final ratification of this agreement entitled to be enrolled as provided in section 27 hereof shall be placed upon the rolls made by said Commission; and no child born thereafter to a citizen or freedman and no person intermarried thereafter to a citizen shall be entitled to enrollment or to participate in the distribution of the tribal property of the Choctaws and Chickasaws."

Respectfully,
SIGNED
T.B. Needles
Acting Chairman.

7-N.B. 204.

Muskogee, Indian Territory, May 9, 1905.

Howard E. Lewis,
    Wynnewood, Indian Territory.

Dear Sir:

    Referring to the affidavits heretofore filed with the Commission, relative to the birth of your infant children, Ethel E. Lewis and William Joseph Lewis, born November 2, 1902, and November 3, 1904, respectively, it is stated in the affidavit of the mother Alice J. Lewis, that she is a citizen by blood of the Choctaw Nation.

    If this is correct you are requested to state when, where and under what name she was listed for enrollment, the names of her parents and other members of her family

Applications for Enrollment of Choctaw Newborn
Act of 1905   Volume IV

for whom application was made at the same time, and if she has selected an allotment to give her roll number as the same appears on her allotment certificate.

Respectfully,

Commissioner in Charge.

---

7 NB 204

Muskogee, Indian Territory, May 18, 1905.

H. E. Lewis,
    Wynnewood, Indian Territory.

Dear Sir:

    Receipt is hereby acknowledged of your affidavit relative to the enrollment of your wife Alcie J. Lewis which you offer in support of the application for the enrollment of your children William,[sic] Joseph and Ethel E. Lewis and the same have been filed with the records in this case.

Respectfully,

Chairman.

7-3040

Muskogee, Indian Territory, March 20, 1905.

Howard E. Lewis,
    Wynnewood, Indian Territory,

Dear Sir:

    Receipt is hereby acknowledged of the affidavits of Alice Lewis and Howard E. Lewis to the birth of Ethel E. Lewis and William Joseph Lewis, children of Howard E. and Alice Lewis, November 2, 1902 and November 3, 1905, respectively and the same have been filed with our records as an application for the enrollment of said children.

Respectfully,

Chairman.

Applications for Enrollment of Choctaw Newborn
Act of 1905   Volume IV

7-NB-204

Muskogee, Indian Territory, July 29, 1905.

Howard Lewis,
    Wynnewood, Indian Territory.

Dear Sir:

    There is inclosed you herewith for execution application for the enrollment of your infant child, born November 2, 1902.

    In the affidavits of December 15, 1902, heretofore filed in this office, the name of the child is given as Ethel Lewis, in the affidavits of March 10, 1905, the name is given as Ethel Eugenia Lewis; it also appears from said affidavits that you attended your wife at the time of the birth of the applicant.

    If there was a physician or midwife in attendance it will be necessary that you supply his or her affidavit, and the inclosed application is prepared to cover the case.

    If you were the only one present at the time of the birth of the child, it will be necessary that you furnish the affidavit of two witnesses who are disinterested and not related to the applicant, and who have actual knowledge of the facts, that the child was born, the date of her birth, that she was living March 4, 1905, and that Alice J. Lewis is her mother.

    This matter should receive your immediate attention as no further action can be taken relative to the enrollment of your said child until the evidence requested is supplied.

        Respectfully,

LM 9-29

        Commissioner.

7-NB-204

Muskogee, Indian Territory, August 23, 1905.

H. E. Lewis,
    Wynnewood, Indian Territory.

Dear Sir:

    Receipt is hereby acknowledged of your letter of August 18, 1905, enclosing affidavits of Alice J. Lewis and Margaret McFerrin to the birth of Ethel E. Lewis daughter of Howard and Alice J. Lewis, November 2, 1902, and the same have been filed with the records of this office in the matter of the enrollment of said child.

Applications for Enrollment of Choctaw Newborn
Act of 1905   Volume IV

Respectfully,

Commissioner.

7-NB-204

Muskogee, Indian Territory, December 2, 1905.

Howard E. Lewis,
    Wynnewood, Indian Territory.

Dear Sir:

    Receipt is hereby acknowledged of your letter of November 24, 1905, asking if your child Ethel E. Lewis has been approved by the Secretary of the Interior.

    In reply to your letter you are advised that the name of your child Ethel Eugenia Lewis has not been placed upon a schedule of new born citizens of the Choctaw Nation prepared for forwarding to the Secretary of the Interior for approval, but her name will probably be placed upon the next schedule of such citizens prepared for that purpose and you will be notified when her enrollment is approved by the Department.

Respectfully,

Acting Commissioner.

7-NB-204

Muskogee, Indian Territory, February 8, 1906.

Howard E. Lewis,
    Wynnewood, Indian Territory.

Dear Sir:

    Receipt is hereby acknowledged of your letter of February 3, 1906, stating that you have not received notice of the approval of your child Ethel Eugenia Lewis.

    In reply to your letter you are advised that the name of your child Ethel Eugenia Lewis was placed upon a schedule of new born citizens of the Choctaw Nation which has been forwarded the Secretary of the Interior. You will be notified when her enrollment is approved by the Department.

Respectfully,

Acting Commissioner.

Applications for Enrollment of Choctaw Newborn
Act of 1905   Volume IV

Choc New Born 205
    Harriet Colbert
    (Born Dec. 26, 1902)

BIRTH AFFIDAVIT.

Department of the Interior,
COMMISSION TO THE FIVE CIVILIZED TRIBES.

IN RE APPLICATION FOR ENROLLMENT, as a citizen of the Choctaw Nation, of Harriet Colbert, born on the 26 day of Dec, 190 2

Name of Father: Edward Colbert   a citizen of the Choctaw Nation.
Name of Mother: Lena Colbert   a citizen of the Choctaw Nation.

Post-Office: Lodi I.T.

AFFIDAVIT OF MOTHER.

UNITED STATES OF AMERICA,
   INDIAN TERRITORY,
Central   District.

I, Lena Colbert, on oath state that I am 22 years of age and a citizen by blood, of the Choctaw Nation; that I am the lawful wife of Edward Colbert, who is a citizen, by blood of the Choctaw Nation; that a female child was born to me on 26 day of Dec, 190 2, that said child has been named Harriet Colbert, and is now living.

                        Lenner[sic] Colbert

WITNESSES TO MARK:
   RL Reagan
   R.A. Welch

Subscribed and sworn to before me this 9 *day of* March, 190 .3

                        J.F. Maxey
                         Notary Public.

Applications for Enrollment of Choctaw Newborn
Act of 1905   Volume IV

AFFIDAVIT OF ATTENDING PHYSICIAN OR MID-WIFE.

UNITED STATES OF AMERICA, }
  INDIAN TERRITORY,
Central   District.

I, Salina Lewis, a midwife, on oath state that I attended on Mrs. Lena Colbert, wife of Edward Colbert on the 26 day of Dec, 1902; that there was born to her on said date a female child; that said child is now living and is said to have been named Harriet Colbert

                                                her
                                      Salina x Lewis

WITNESSES TO MARK: mark
{ RL Reagan > P.O.
  R.A. Welch   Red Oak I.T.

Subscribed and sworn to before me this 9 *day of* March, 190.3

                                J.F. Maxey
                                  Notary Public.

BIRTH AFFIDAVIT.

DEPARTMENT OF THE INTERIOR.
COMMISSION TO THE FIVE CIVILIZED TRIBES.

IN RE APPLICATION FOR ENROLLMENT, as a citizen of the Choctaw Nation, of Harriet Colbert, born on the 26th day of December, 1902

Name of Father: Edward Colbert   a citizen of the Choctaw Nation.
Name of Mother: Lena Colbert   a citizen of the Choctaw Nation.

                        Postoffice   Lodi, Ind. Ter.

AFFIDAVIT OF MOTHER.

UNITED STATES OF AMERICA, Indian Territory, }
Central   DISTRICT.

I, Lena Colbert, on oath state that I am about 24 years of age and a citizen by blood, of the Choctaw Nation; that I am the lawful wife of Edward Colbert, who is a citizen, by blood of the Choctaw Nation; that a female child was born to me on 26th day of December, 1902; that said child has been named Harriet Colbert, and was living March 4, 1905.

                                    Lena Colbert

Applications for Enrollment of Choctaw Newborn
Act of 1905   Volume IV

Witnesses To Mark:
{

Subscribed and sworn to before me this 27th day of March, 1905

Wirt Franklin
Notary Public.

AFFIDAVIT OF ATTENDING PHYSICIAN OR MID-WIFE.

UNITED STATES OF AMERICA, Indian Territory, }
   Central   DISTRICT. }

I, Salina Lewis, a midwife, on oath state that I attended on Mrs. Lena Colbert, wife of Edward Colbert on the 26 day of Dec., 1902; that there was born to her on said date a female child; that said child was living March 4, 1905, and is said to have been named Harriet Colbert

                    her
            Salina x Lewis
Witnesses To Mark: mark
{ Robert L. Reagan
  Woodson Lewis

Subscribed and sworn to before me this 31 day of March, 1905

            J. F. Maxey
My Commission Expires June 15 1907   Notary Public.

---

7 NB 205

Muskogee, Indian Territory, June 6, 1905.

Woodson Lewis,
    Lodi, Indian Territory.

Dear Sir:

    Receipt is hereby acknowledged of your letter of May 12, 1905, relative to the enrollment of Harriet Colbert, child of Lena Lewis.

    In reply to your letter you are advised that the name of Harriet Colbert has been placed upon a schedule of citizens by blood of the Choctaw Nation which has been forwarded the Secretary of the Interior for approval, but the Commission has not yet been advised of Departmental action thereon.

Applications for Enrollment of Choctaw Newborn
Act of 1905   Volume IV

Respectfully,

Chairman.

7-NB-205

Muskogee, Indian Territory, March 22, 1906.

Lena Lewis,
    Lodi, Indian Territory.

Dear Madam:

    Receipt is hereby acknowledged of your letter of February 17, 1906, asking relative to the enrollment of Harriet Colbert.

    In reply to your letter you are advised that Harriet Colbert has been enrolled as a new born citizen of the Choctaw Nation and her enrollment as such was approved by the Secretary of the Interior, June 20, 1905.

Respectfully,

Acting Commissioner.

Choc New Born 206
    Joseph Osbon Coffman
    (Born July 23, 1903)

BIRTH AFFIDAVIT.

DEPARTMENT OF THE INTERIOR,
COMMISSION TO THE FIVE CIVILIZED TRIBES.

In Re Application for Enrollment, as a citizen of the   Choctaw   Nation, of   Joseph Osbon Coffman , born on the   23   day of   July   , 1903

Name of Father: John A. Coffman   a citizen of the   Choctaw   Nation.
Name of Mother: Sarah E. Coffman   a citizen of the   Choctaw   Nation.

Post-office   Caney Ind. Ter.

Applications for Enrollment of Choctaw Newborn
Act of 1905   Volume IV

AFFIDAVIT OF MOTHER.

UNITED STATES OF AMERICA,
   INDIAN TERRITORY,
Central   District.

I, Sarah E. Coffman, on oath state that I am 30 years of age and a citizen by blood, of the Choctaw Nation; that I am the lawful wife of John A Coffman, who is a citizen, by intermarriage of the United States Nation; that a male child was born to me on 23 day of July, 1903, that said child has been named Joseph Osbon Coffman, and is now living.

                                             Sarrah[sic] E. Coffman

WITNESSES TO MARK:
{ A Denton Phillips

Subscribed and sworn to before me this 9 day of January, 1905.

                                             A Denton Phillips
                                                NOTARY PUBLIC.

AFFIDAVIT OF ATTENDING PHYSICIAN OR MID-WIFE.

UNITED STATES OF AMERICA,
   INDIAN TERRITORY,
Central   District.

I, J H Armstrong, a M.D., on oath state that I attended on Mrs. Sarah E Coffman, wife of John A Coffman on the 23 day of July, 1903; that there was born to her on said date a male child; that said child is now living and is said to have been named Joseph Osbon Coffman

                                           J H Armstrong M.D.

WITNESSES TO MARK:
{

Subscribed and sworn to before me this 10 day of January, 1905.

                                           A Denton Phillips
                                               NOTARY PUBLIC.

Applications for Enrollment of Choctaw Newborn
Act of 1905   Volume IV

NEW-BORN AFFIDAVIT.

Number............

Choctaw Enrolling Commission.

IN THE MATTER OF THE APPLICATION FOR ENROLLMENT, as a citizen of the Choctaw   Nation, of   Joseph Osbon Coffman

born on the 23   day of   July   190 3

Name of father   J. A. Coffman   a citizen of   U.S. ~~Nation final enrollment No~~
Name of mother   Sarah E. Coffman   a citizen of   Choctaw Nation final enrollment No 8965

Postoffice   Caney I.T.

AFFIDAVIT OF MOTHER.

UNITED STATES OF AMERICA,
INDIAN TERRITORY,
Central   DISTRICT

I   Sarah E. Coffman   on oath state that I am 25 years of age and a citizen by   blood   of the   Choctaw   Nation, and as such have been placed upon the final roll of the   Choctaw   Nation, by the Honorable Secretary of the Interior my final enrollment number being   8965   ; that I am the lawful wife of   J. A. Coffman   , who is a citizen of the   U.S.   ~~Nation, and as such has been placed upon the final roll~~ of said Nation by the Honorable Secretary of the Interior his final enrollment number being   and that a   male   child was born to me on the   23   day of   July   190 3 ; that said child has been named   Joseph Osbon Coffman   , and is now living.

WITNESSETH: Sarah E. Coffman

Must be two Witnesses who are Citizens.   Simeon Turnbull [illegible]
James Benton

Subscribed and sworn to before me this 31   day of   Jay   190 5

R. R. Hall
Notary Public.

My commission expires................................

Applications for Enrollment of Choctaw Newborn
Act of 1905   Volume IV

Affidavit of Attending Physician or Midwife

UNITED STATES OF AMERICA,
INDIAN TERRITORY,
Central   DISTRICT

I, J H Armstrong   a   Physician   on oath state that I attended on Mrs. Sarah E Coffman   wife of J A Coffman   on the 23rd day of July, 190 3, that there was born to her on said date a male child, that said child is now living, and is said to have been named Joseph Osbon Coffman

J H Armstrong   M. D.

Subscribed and sworn to before me this the   10   day of   Mch   1905

R. R. Hall
Notary Public.

WITNESSETH:
Must be two witnesses who are citizens and know the child.
{ N J Tolbert
  Silas Lewis }

We hereby certify that we are well acquainted with   J. H. Armstrong   a   Physician   and know him   to be reputable and of good standing in the community.

Must be two citizen witnesses.
{ N J Tolbert
  Silas Lewis }

BIRTH AFFIDAVIT.

DEPARTMENT OF THE INTERIOR.
COMMISSION TO THE FIVE CIVILIZED TRIBES.

IN RE APPLICATION FOR ENROLLMENT, as a citizen of the   Choctaw   Nation, of   Joseph Osbon Coffman , born on the 23rd day of   July , 1903

Name of Father: John A. Coffman   a citizen of the   Choctaw   Nation.
Name of Mother: Sarah E. Coffman   a citizen of the   Choctaw   Nation.

Postoffice   Caney Ind. Terr.

Applications for Enrollment of Choctaw Newborn
Act of 1905   Volume IV

AFFIDAVIT OF MOTHER.

UNITED STATES OF AMERICA, Indian Territory,
....DISTRICT.

I,   Sarah E. Coffman   , on oath state that I am   30   years of age and a citizen by   blood   , of the   Choctaw   Nation; that I am the lawful wife of   John A. Coffman   , who is a citizen, by ---------   of the   United States   Nation; that a   male   child was born to me on   23rd day of   July   , 1903; that said child has been named   Joseph Osbon Coffman   , and was living March 4, 1905.

                                                Sarah E Coffman

Witnesses To Mark:

Subscribed and sworn to before me this 29th day of   April   , 1905

                                                R. R. Hall
                                               Notary Public.

AFFIDAVIT OF ATTENDING PHYSICIAN OR MID-WIFE.

UNITED STATES OF AMERICA, Indian Territory,
....DISTRICT.

I,................................., a................................., on oath state that I attended on Mrs.   Sarah E Coffman   , wife of   John A Coffman   on the 23rd day of July   , 1903; that there was born to her on said date a   male   child; that said child was living March 4, 1905, and is said to have been named   Joseph Osbon Coffman

                                                  J H Armstrong M.D.

Witnesses To Mark:

Subscribed and sworn to before me this   29th day of   April   , 1905

                                               R. R. Hall
                                             Notary Public.

Applications for Enrollment of Choctaw Newborn
Act of 1905 Volume IV

N. B. 206
COPY.
Muskogee, Indian Territory, April 8, 1905.

John A. Coffman,
    Caney, Indian Territory.

Dear Sir:

    There is inclosed you herewith for execution application for the enrollment of your infant child, Joseph Osbon Coffman, born July 23, 1903.

    The affidavits heretofore filed with the Commission show the child was living on January 10, 1905. It is necessary for the child to be enrolled, that he was living on March 4, 1905.

    In having these affidavits executed care should be exercised to see that all the names are written in full as they appear in the body of the affidavit, and in the event that either of the persons signing the affidavit are unable to write, signatures by mark must be attested by two witnesses. Each affidavit must be executed before a Notary Public and the notarial seal and signature of the officer must be attached to each separate affidavit.

Respectfully,
SIGNED
T.B. Needles
Commissioner in Charge.

LM 8-9

COPY. 7-N.B.-206.

Muskogee, Indian Territory, May 3, 1905.

John A. Coffman,
    Caney, Indian Territory.

Dear Sir:

    Receipt is hereby acknowledged of the affidavits of Sarah E. Coffman and J. H. Armstrong to the birth of Joseph Osbon Coffman, son of John A. and Sarah E. Coffman, July 23, 1903, and the same are returned to you herewith for the reason that the Notary Public before whom the affidavit of the mother was executed has failed to affix his seal thereto.

    Please have this omission corrected and the affidavits returned to this office at the earliest practicable date.

Applications for Enrollment of Choctaw Newborn
Act of 1905   Volume IV

LMS-9

Respectfully,
SIGNED

Tams Bixby
Chairman.

7-N.B. 206.

Muskogee, Indian Territory, May 9, 1905.

John A. Coffman,
    Caney, Indian Territory.

Dear Sir:

    Receipt is hereby acknowledged of the affidavits of Sarah E. Coffman and J. H. Armstrong to the birth of Joseph Osbon Coffman, son of John A. and Sarah E. Coffman, July 23, 1903, and the same have been filed with our records in the matter of the enrollment of said child.

Respectfully,

Commissioner in Charge.

Choc New Born 207
    Oscar Anderson
    (Born Jan. 4, 1904)

BIRTH AFFIDAVIT.

DEPARTMENT OF THE INTERIOR,
COMMISSION TO THE FIVE CIVILIZED TRIBES.

IN RE Application for Enrollment, as a citizen of the Choctaw Nation, of Oscar Anderson, born on the 4th day of January, 1904

Name of Father: Rufus Anderson   a citizen of the Choctaw Nation.
                          nee Coley
Name of Mother: Silen Anderson ^   a citizen of the Choctaw Nation.

Post-Office: Sulphur I.T.

Applications for Enrollment of Choctaw Newborn
Act of 1905   Volume IV

AFFIDAVIT OF MOTHER.

UNITED STATES OF AMERICA,
    INDIAN TERRITORY.
Southern District.

I, Silen Anderson nee Coley , on oath state that I am 18 years of age and a citizen by Birth , of the Choctaw Nation; that I am the lawful wife of Rufus Anderson , who is a citizen, by Marriage of the Choctaw Nation; that a male child was born to me on 4th day of January , 1904 , that said child has been named Oscar Anderson , and is now living.

                                Silen Anderson

WITNESSES TO MARK:

Subscribed and sworn to before me this 15th day of Oct , 1904

                                T. F. Gafford
                                        NOTARY PUBLIC.

AFFIDAVIT OF ATTENDING PHYSICIAN OR MID-WIFE.

UNITED STATES OF AMERICA,
    INDIAN TERRITORY.
Southern District.

I, Josie Anderson , a midwife , on oath state that I attended on Mrs. Silen Anderson , wife of Rufus Anderson on the 4th day of January , 1904; that there was born to her on said date a male child; that said child is now living and is said to have been named Oscar Anderson

                                Josie Anderson

WITNESSES TO MARK:

Subscribed and sworn to before me this 15th day of Oct , 1904

                                T. F. Gafford
                                        NOTARY PUBLIC.

Applications for Enrollment of Choctaw Newborn
Act of 1905   Volume IV

BIRTH AFFIDAVIT.

DEPARTMENT OF THE INTERIOR.
COMMISSION TO THE FIVE CIVILIZED TRIBES.

IN RE APPLICATION FOR ENROLLMENT, as a citizen of the   Choctaw   Nation, of   Oscar Anderson   , born on the 4th   day of   January   , 1904

Name of Father: Rufus Anderson   not a citizen of the.................................Nation.
Name of Mother: Sellen Coley Anderson   a citizen of the   Choctaw   Nation.

Postoffice   Sulphur Indian Territory

AFFIDAVIT OF MOTHER.

UNITED STATES OF AMERICA, Indian Territory,
Southern   DISTRICT.

I, Sellen Coley Anderson   , on oath state that I am   years of age and a citizen by   Blood   , of the   Choctaw   Nation; that I am the lawful wife of   Rufus Anderson   , who is a citizen [not a], by.........................of the..............................Nation; that a male   child was born to me on   4th   day of   January   , 1904, that said child has been named   Oscar Anderson   , and was living March 4, 1905.

Sellen Coley Anderson

Witnesses To Mark:
{ Azalee Cathey

Subscribed and sworn to before me this   14th   day of   March   , 1905.

A D Goodenough
My Commission Expires June 27, 1907   Notary Public.

AFFIDAVIT OF ATTENDING PHYSICIAN OR MID-WIFE.

UNITED STATES OF AMERICA, Indian Territory,
Southern   DISTRICT.

I, Josie Anderson   , a   Midwife   , on oath state that I attended on Mrs. Sellen Coley   , wife of   Rufus Anderson   on the 4th   day of   January   , 1904; that there was born to her on said date a   male   child; that said child was living March 4, 1905, and is said to have been named   Oscar Anderson

Josie Anderson

Applications for Enrollment of Choctaw Newborn
Act of 1905 Volume IV

Witnesses To Mark:
{ Azalee Cathey

Subscribed and sworn to before me this 4th [sic] day of March , 1905.

My Commission Expires June 27, 1907

A D Goodenough
Notary Public.

7-3072

Muskogee, Indian Territory, March 18, 1905.

Rufus Anderson,
Sulphur, Indian Territory.

Dear Sir:

Receipt is hereby acknowledged of the affidavits of Sillan[sic] Coley Anderson and Josie Anderson to the birth of Oscar Anderson infant son of Rufus and Sillan Coley Anderson, January 4, 1904, and the same have been filed with our records as an application for the enrollment of said child.

Respectfully,

Chairman.

Choc New Born 208
Wallace Green McCurtain Dunlap
(Born Nov. 22, 1902)

AFFIDAVIT OF ATTENDING PHYSICIAN OR MIDWIFE

UNITED STATES OF AMERICA
INDIAN TERRITORY
.................................DISTRICT

I, William A Cox a Physician on oath state that I attended on Mrs. Susan L Dunlap wife of James D. Dunlap on the 22nd day of November , 190 2 , that there was born to her on said date a male child, that said child is now living, and is said to have been named Wallace Green McCurtain Dunlap

William A Cox *M.D.*

Applications for Enrollment of Choctaw Newborn
Act of 1905   Volume IV

Subscribed and sworn to before me this, the   3rd day of February   190 5

[Name Illegible]   Notary Public.

WITNESSETH:
Must be two witnesses who are citizens   { Louis Rockett
Alex Folsom

We hereby certify that we are well acquainted with   Wallace A Cox   a   Physician   and know   him   to be reputable and of good standing in the community.

Louis Rockett   _____

Alex Folsom   _____

BIRTH AFFIDAVIT.

DEPARTMENT OF THE INTERIOR.
COMMISSION TO THE FIVE CIVILIZED TRIBES.

IN RE APPLICATION FOR ENROLLMENT, as a citizen of the   Choctaw   Nation, of   Wallace Green McCurtain Dunlap , born on the 22nd day of November , 1902

Name of Father: James D. Dunlap   a citizen of the   Choctaw   Nation.
Name of Mother: Susan L Dunlap   a citizen of the   Choctaw   Nation.

Postoffice   Quinton, I.T.

AFFIDAVIT OF MOTHER.

UNITED STATES OF AMERICA, Indian Territory,
Central   DISTRICT.

I, Susan L Dunlap , on oath state that I am 32 years of age and a citizen by   blood , of the   Choctaw   Nation; that I am the lawful wife of   James D. Dunlap , who is a citizen, by   marriage   of the   Choctaw   Nation; that a male   child was born to me on   the 22nd   day of   November , 1902, that said child has been named   Wallace Green McCurtain Dunlap , and is now living.

Susan L Dunlap

Witnesses To Mark:

Applications for Enrollment of Choctaw Newborn
Act of 1905   Volume IV

Subscribed and sworn to before me this   16th day of   March   , 1905.

                                          Wirt Franklin
                                          Notary Public.

BIRTH AFFIDAVIT.

DEPARTMENT OF THE INTERIOR.
COMMISSION TO THE FIVE CIVILIZED TRIBES.

IN RE APPLICATION FOR ENROLLMENT, as a citizen of the   Choctaw   Nation, of Wallace Green McCurtain Dunlap , born on the 22nd day of November , 1902

Name of Father: James D. Dunlap   a citizen of the   Choctaw   Nation.
Name of Mother: Susan L Dunlap   a citizen of the   Choctaw   Nation.

                               Postoffice   Quinton I.T.

AFFIDAVIT OF MOTHER.

UNITED STATES OF AMERICA, Indian Territory,
   Western   DISTRICT.

    I, Susan L Dunlap   , on oath state that I am 32   years of age and a citizen by   blood   , of the   Choctaw   Nation; that I am the lawful wife of   James D. Dunlap   , who is a citizen, by intermarriage   of the   Choctaw   Nation; that a   male   child was born to me on 22nd day of November , 192; that said child has been named Wallace Green McCurtain Dunlap   , and was living March 4, 1905.

                                    Susan L Dunlap
Witnesses To Mark:

Subscribed and sworn to before me this 11th day of   April   , 1905

                                      F.J. Bonestut
                                      Notary Public.

Applications for Enrollment of Choctaw Newborn
Act of 1905   Volume IV

AFFIDAVIT OF ATTENDING PHYSICIAN OR MID-WIFE.

UNITED STATES OF AMERICA, Indian Territory,
Central   DISTRICT.

    I, William A Cox, a Physician, on oath state that I attended on Mrs. Susan L Dunlap, wife of James D Dunlap on the 22nd day of November, 1902; that there was born to her on said date a .... child; that said child was living March 4, 1905, and is said to have been named Wallace Green McCurtain Dunlap

                                              William A Cox

Witnesses To Mark:
{

    Subscribed and sworn to before me this 17th day of April, 1905

                                           Geo M Goodwin
                                               Notary Public.

                                                                7-3075

                            Muskogee, Indian Territory, March 21, 1905.

James D. Dunlap,
    Quinton, Indian Territory.

Dear Sir:

    Receipt is hereby acknowledged of the affidavits of Susan L. Dunlap and William A. Cox to the birth of Wallace Green McCurtain Dunlap, son of James D. and Susan L. Dunlap, November 22, 1902, and the same have been filed with our records as an application for the enrollment of said child.

                                          Respectfully,

                                                       Chairman.

Applications for Enrollment of Choctaw Newborn
Act of 1905 Volume IV

N. B. 208
COPY.
Muskogee, Indian Territory, April 8, 1905.

James D. Dunlap,
    Quinton, Indian Territory.

Dear Sir:

    There is inclosed you herewith for execution application for the enrollment of your infant child, Wallace Green McCurtain Dunlap, born November 22, 1902.

    In the application heretofore filed with the Commission, the affidavit of the physician shows the child was living on February 3, 1905. It will be necessary, for the child to be enrolled, that his affidavit show said child was living on March 4, 1905.

    In having these affidavits executed care should be exercised to see that all the names are written in full as they appear in the body of the affidavit, and in the event that either of the persons signing the affidavit are unable to write, signatures by mark must be attested by two witnesses. Each affidavit must be executed before a Notary Public and the notarial seal and signature of the officer must be attached to each separate affidavit.

Respectfully,
SIGNED
T.B. Needles
LM 8-7   Commissioner in Charge.

COPY.   7 NB 208

Muskogee, Indian Territory, April 20, 1905.

James D. Dunlap,
    Clinton, Indian Territory.

Dear Sir:

    Receipt is hereby acknowledged of the affidavits of Susan L. Dunlap and William A. Cox to the birth of Wallace Green McCurtain Dunlap, son of James D. and Susan L. Dunlap, November 22, 1902, and the same have been filed with our records as an application for the enrollment of said child.

Respectfully,
SIGNED
Tams Bixby
Chairman.

Applications for Enrollment of Choctaw Newborn
Act of 1905   Volume IV

Substitute

7 N B 208

Muskogee, Indian Territory, July 22, 1905.

J. D. Dunlap,
    Quinton, Indian Territory.

Dear Sir:

    Receipt is hereby acknowledged of your letter of July 13, asking if Wallace Green McCurtain Dunlap has been enrolled.

    In reply to your letter you are advised that on June 30, 1905, the Secretary of the Interior approved the enrollment of Wallace Green McCurtain Dunlap as a citizen by blood of the Choctaw Nation.

                  Respectfully,

                                Commissioner.

Choc New Born 209
    Leonard Elliott
    (Born Jan. 14, 1905)

BIRTH AFFIDAVIT.

DEPARTMENT OF THE INTERIOR.
COMMISSION TO THE FIVE CIVILIZED TRIBES.

    IN RE APPLICATION FOR ENROLLMENT, as a citizen of the Choctaw Nation, of Leonard , born on the 14th day of January , 1905

Name of Father: Richard H. Elliott   a citizen of the Choctaw Nation.
Name of Mother: Manda   a citizen of the Choctaw Nation.

                  Postoffice   Hickory Dist 16 Ind Terr

Applications for Enrollment of Choctaw Newborn
Act of 1905   Volume IV

AFFIDAVIT OF MOTHER.

UNITED STATES OF AMERICA, Indian Territory, } Ind Terr.
Southern DISTRICT.

I, Manda Elliott, on oath state that I am 38 years of age and a citizen by birth, of the Choctaw Nation; that I am the lawful wife of Richard H Elliott, who is a citizen, by intermarriage of the Choctaw Nation; that a male child was born to me on 14th day of January, 1905, that said child has been named Leonard, and is now living.

                                          her
                                Manda x Elliott
Witnesses To Mark: mark
  { E.W. Westhoff
    T. H. Cook

Subscribed and sworn to before me this 20th day of February, 1905.

                                Mrs. E. W. Westhoff
                                Notary Public.

AFFIDAVIT OF ATTENDING PHYSICIAN OR MID-WIFE.

UNITED STATES OF AMERICA, Indian Territory, }
Southern DISTRICT.

I, Elchy McCarthy, a midwife, on oath state that I attended on Mrs. Manda Elliott, wife of Richard H Elliott on the 14th day of January, 1905; that there was born to her on said date a male child; that said child is now living and is said to have been named Leonard

                                          her
                                Elciy[sic] x McCarthy
Witnesses To Mark: mark
  { E.W. Westhoff
    T. Hl. Cook

Subscribed and sworn to before me this 20th day of February, 1905.

                                Mrs. E. W. Westhoff
                                Notary Public.

Applications for Enrollment of Choctaw Newborn
Act of 1905   Volume IV

BIRTH AFFIDAVIT.

DEPARTMENT OF THE INTERIOR.
COMMISSION TO THE FIVE CIVILIZED TRIBES.

IN RE APPLICATION FOR ENROLLMENT, as a citizen of the Choctaw Nation, of Leonard Elliott, born on the 14th day of January, 1905

Name of Father: Richard H. Elliott   a citizen of the Choctaw Nation.
Name of Mother: Amanda Elliott   a citizen of the Choctaw Nation.

Postoffice   Hickory Ind. Terr.

AFFIDAVIT OF MOTHER.

UNITED STATES OF AMERICA, Indian Territory,
Southern   DISTRICT.

I, Amanda Elliott, on oath state that I am 38 years of age and a citizen by blood, of the Choctaw Nation; that I am the lawful wife of Richard H. Elliott, who is a citizen, by intermarriage of the Choctaw Nation; that a male child was born to me on 14th day of January, 1905; that said child has been named Leonard Elliott, and was living March 4, 1905.

                                        Amanda Elliott
Witnesses To Mark: my mark x
  { R.P. Cotten[sic]
  { A.F. McCarty
    Subscribed and sworn to before me this 13 day of April, 1905.

                                        J L Mentzer
                                        Notary Public.

AFFIDAVIT OF ATTENDING PHYSICIAN OR MID-WIFE.

UNITED STATES OF AMERICA, Indian Territory,
Southern   DISTRICT.

I, Mrs Elcie McCarty, a............., on oath state that I attended on Mrs. Amanda Elliott, wife of Richard H Elliott on the 14th day of January, 1905; that there was born to her on said date a male child; that said child was living March 4, 1905, and is said to have been named Leonard Elliott

                                        Mrs Elcie McCarty
                                        my mark x

Applications for Enrollment of Choctaw Newborn
Act of 1905   Volume IV

Witnesses To Mark:
{ J. V. McCarty
{ R. P. Cotten

Subscribed and sworn to before me this 13 day of April , 1905

J L Mentzer
Notary Public.

7-3086

Muskogee, Indian Territory, February 27, 1905.

Richard H. Elliott,
    Hickory, Indian Territory.

Dear Sir:

    Receipt is hereby acknowledged of the affidavits of Maude[sic] E. and Elsie McCarty to the birth of Leonard Elliot, infant son of Richard H. and Maude E. Elliott January 14, 1905, which it is presumed have been forwarded as an application for the enrollment of said child.

    You are advised that under the provisions of the act of Congress approved July 1 1902, no children born to citizens of the Choctaw and Chickasaw Nations subsequent to September 25, 1902, the date of the ratification of said act, are entitled to enrollment and allotment in the Choctaw and Chickasaw Nations.

Respectfully,

Commissioner in Charge.

COPY.   N. B. 209

Muskogee, Indian Territory, April 8, 1905.

Richard H. Elliott,
    Hickory, Indian Territory.

Dear Sir:

    There is inclosed you herewith for execution application for the enrollment of your infant child, Leonard Elliott, born January 14, 1905.

Applications for Enrollment of Choctaw Newborn
Act of 1905   Volume IV

The affidavits heretofore filed with the Commission show the child was living on February 20, 1905. It is necessary, for the child to be enrolled, that he was living on March 4, 1905.

In having these affidavits executed care should be exercised to see that all the names are written in full as they appear in the body of the affidavit, and in the event that either of the persons signing the affidavit are unable to write, signatures by mark must be attested by two witnesses. Each affidavit must be executed before a Notary Public and the notarial seal and signature of the officer must be attached to each separate affidavit.

Respectfully,
SIGNED

T.B. Needles
Commissioner in Charge.

LM 8-8

COPY.   Choctaw N.B. 209.

Muskogee, Indian Territory, April 19, 1905.

Richard H. Elliott,
 Hickory, Indian Territory.

Dear Sir:

Receipt is hereby acknowledged of the affidavits of Amanda Elliott and Mrs. Elcie McCarty to the birth of Leonard Elliott, son of Richard and Amanda Elliott, January 14, 1905, and the same have been filed with our records in the matter of the enrollment of said child.

Respectfully,
SIGNED

Tams Bixby
Chairman.

Applications for Enrollment of Choctaw Newborn
Act of 1905   Volume IV

COPY.

Choctaw N.B. 94
Choctaw N.B. 209.

Muskogee, Indian Territory, April 21, 1905.

E. O. Olds,
    Hickory, Indian Territory.

Dear Sir:

    Receipt is hereby acknowledged of your letter of April 11, in which you ask if Willie Vail will have to appear before the Commission to have his child enrolled, and the same information relative to R. H Elliott in reference to his son, Leonard Elliott.

    In reply to your letter you are informed that the affidavits heretofore filed to the birth of Minnie Vail, daughter of Willie Vail and Leonard Elliott, son of Richard H. Elliott, have been filed with our records as applications for the enrollment of said children and it will not be necessary for their parents to appear in person before the Commission in the matter of their enrollment unless they so desire.

Respectfully,
SIGNED

Tams Bixby
Chairman.

Choc New Born 210
    Ethel Wade
    (Born Dec. 11, 1903)

BIRTH AFFIDAVIT.

DEPARTMENT OF THE INTERIOR.
COMMISSION TO THE FIVE CIVILIZED TRIBES.

    IN RE APPLICATION FOR ENROLLMENT, as a citizen of the Choctaw Nation, of Ethel Wade, born on the 11 day of Dec., 1903

Name of Father: Eastman Wade   a citizen of the Choctaw Nation.
Name of Mother: Ellen Wade   a citizen of the Choctaw Nation.

Postoffice   Wilburton I.T.

Applications for Enrollment of Choctaw Newborn
Act of 1905 Volume IV

AFFIDAVIT OF MOTHER.

UNITED STATES OF AMERICA, Indian Territory, }
Central   DISTRICT.

    I, Ellen Wade, on oath state that I am 34 years of age and a citizen by blood, of the Choctaw Nation; that I am the lawful wife of Eastman Wade, who is a citizen, by blood of the Choctaw Nation; that a female child was born to me on 11 day of December, 1903; that said child has been named Ethel Wade, and was living March 4, 1905.

                                                                   her
Witnesses To Mark: Ellen x Wade
  { J Poe   mark
  { Dell Fretwell

    Subscribed and sworn to before me this 13 day of March, 1905

                                               J Poe
                                               Notary Public.

AFFIDAVIT OF ATTENDING PHYSICIAN OR MID-WIFE.

UNITED STATES OF AMERICA, Indian Territory, }
Central   DISTRICT.

    I, Selina Moore, a midwife, on oath state that I attended on Mrs. Ellen Wade, wife of Eastman Wade on the 11 day of Dec, 1903; that there was born to her on said date a female child; that said child was living March 4, 1905, and is said to have been named Ethel Wade

                                               her
                                       Selina x Moore
Witnesses To Mark: mark
  { J Poe
  { Dell Fretwell

    Subscribed and sworn to before me this 13 day of March, 1905

                                               J Poe
                                               Notary Public.

Applications for Enrollment of Choctaw Newborn
Act of 1905   Volume IV

BIRTH AFFIDAVIT.

DEPARTMENT OF THE INTERIOR.
COMMISSION TO THE FIVE CIVILIZED TRIBES.

IN RE APPLICATION FOR ENROLLMENT, as a citizen of the Choctaw Nation, of Ethel Wade, born on the 11th day of December, 1903

Name of Father: Eastman Wade   a citizen of the Choctaw Nation.
Name of Mother: Ellen Wade   a citizen of the Choctaw Nation.

Postoffice   Wilburton I.T.

AFFIDAVIT OF MOTHER.

UNITED STATES OF AMERICA, Indian Territory,
Central   DISTRICT.

I, Ellen Wade, on oath state that I am 34 years of age and a citizen by blood, of the Choctaw Nation; that I am the lawful wife of Eastman Wade, who is a citizen, by blood of the Choctaw Nation; that a female child was born to me on 11th day of December, 1903; that said child has been named Ethel Wade, and was living March 4, 1905.

                                    her
                            Ellen x Wade

Witnesses To Mark: mark
   James Culberson
   William H. Cunningham

Subscribed and sworn to before me this 1st day of May, 1905

                            W.H. Angell
                            Notary Public.

BIRTH AFFIDAVIT.

DEPARTMENT OF THE INTERIOR.
COMMISSION TO THE FIVE CIVILIZED TRIBES.

IN RE APPLICATION FOR ENROLLMENT, as a citizen of the Choctaw Nation, of Ethel Wade, born on the 11th day of December, 1903

Name of Father: Eastman Wade   a citizen of the Choctaw Nation.
Name of Mother: Ellen Wade   a citizen of the Choctaw Nation.

Postoffice   Wilburton I.T.

Applications for Enrollment of Choctaw Newborn
Act of 1905   Volume IV

AFFIDAVIT OF MOTHER.

UNITED STATES OF AMERICA, Indian Territory, }
Central   DISTRICT.

I, Ellen Wade, on oath state that I am 33 years of age and a citizen by blood, of the Choctaw Nation; that I am the lawful wife of Eastman Wade, who is a citizen, by blood of the Choctaw Nation; that a female child was born to me on 11th day of December, 1903; that said child has been named Ethel Wade, and was living March 4, 1905

her
Ellen x Wade
mark

Witnesses To Mark:
{ G W Phillips
{ Dell Fretwell

Subscribed and sworn to before me this 2 day of May, 1905

J Poe
Notary Public.

AFFIDAVIT OF ATTENDING PHYSICIAN OR MID-WIFE.

UNITED STATES OF AMERICA, Indian Territory, }
Central   DISTRICT.

I, Selina Moore, a midwife, on oath state that I attended on Mrs. Ellen Wade, wife of Eastman Wade on the 11th day of December, 1903; that there was born to her on said date a female child; that said child was living March 4, 1905, and is said to have been named Ethel Wade

her
Selina x Moore
mark

Witnesses To Mark:
{ G W Phillips
{ Dell Fretwell

Subscribed and sworn to before me this 2 day of May, 1905

J Poe
Notary Public.

Applications for Enrollment of Choctaw Newborn
Act of 1905   Volume IV

7-3099

Muskogee, Indian Territory, March 16, 1905.

Eastman Wade,
    Wilburton, Indian Territory.

Dear Sir:

    Receipt is hereby acknowledged of the affidavits of Ellen Wade and Selina Moore to the birth of Ellen W Wade, infant daughter of Eastman and Ellen Wade, December 11, 1903, and the same have been filed with our records as an application for the enrollment of said child.

Respectfully,

Chairman.

COPY.   7 NB 210

Muskogee, Indian Territory, May 5, 1905.

Eastman Wade,
    Wilburton, Indian Territory.

Dear Sir:

    Receipt is hereby acknowledged of the affidavits of Ellen Wade and Selina Moore to the birth of Ethel Wade, daughter of Eastman and Ellen Wade, December 11, 1903, and the same have been filed with our records as an application for the enrollment of said child.

Respectfully,
SIGNED

Tams Bixby
Chairman.

Applications for Enrollment of Choctaw Newborn
Act of 1905   Volume IV

Choc New Born 211
    Marie Kathleen Latimer
    (Born Jan. 22, 1903)

NEW-BORN AFFIDAVIT.

Number..........

Choctaw Enrolling Commission.

IN THE MATTER OF THE APPLICATION FOR ENROLLMENT, as a citizen of the Choctaw Nation, of Marie Kathleen Latimer

born on the 22 day of January 1903

Name of father   James S Latimer   a citizen of   Choctaw
Nation final enrollment No   657
Name of mother   Allie B Latimer   a citizen of   Choctaw
Nation final enrollment No   14345

                      Postoffice   Wilburton I.T.

AFFIDAVIT OF MOTHER.

UNITED STATES OF AMERICA,
INDIAN TERRITORY,
   Central   DISTRICT

    I   Allie B. Latimer   on oath state that I am 29 years of age and a citizen by   birth   of the   Choctaw   Nation, and as such have been placed upon the final roll of the   Choctaw   Nation, by the Honorable Secretary of the Interior my final enrollment number being 14345   ; that I am the lawful wife of James S. Latimer   , who is a citizen of the   Choctaw   Nation, and as such has been placed upon the final roll of said Nation by the Honorable Secretary of the Interior, his final enrollment number being   657   and that a   female   child was born to me on the 22 day of   January   190 3 ; that said child has been named   Marie Kathleen   , and is now living.

                                Allie B Latimer

WITNESSETH:
  Must be two
  Witnesses who   } G. W. Riddle
  are Citizens.   Eli Wade

Applications for Enrollment of Choctaw Newborn
Act of 1905   Volume IV

Subscribed and sworn to before me this   25   day of   Feb   190 5

J Poe

Notary Public.

My commission expires   Jan 23-1908

AFFIDAVIT OF ATTENDING PHYSICIAN OR MIDWIFE

UNITED STATES OF AMERICA
INDIAN TERRITORY
Central   DISTRICT

I,   Minnie Brashers   a   midwife on oath state that I attended on Mrs.   A. B. Latimer   wife of   L. S. Latimer on the 22   day of   January , 1903 , that there was born to her on said date a   female   child, that said child is now living, and is said to have been named   Marie Kathleen

Minnie Brashers   M.D.

WITNESSETH:
Must be two witnesses who are citizens and know the child.
{ G.W. Riddle
  Eli Wade

Subscribed and sworn to before me this, the   25   day of   Feb   190 5

J. Poe   Notary Public.

We hereby certify that we are well acquainted with   ~~G.W. Riddle~~   Minnie Brashears a   ~~Eli Wade~~   midwife   and know   him   to be reputable and of good standing in the community.

{ Richard R. Riddle
  Eastman Wade

BIRTH AFFIDAVIT.

DEPARTMENT OF THE INTERIOR.
COMMISSION TO THE FIVE CIVILIZED TRIBES.

IN RE APPLICATION FOR ENROLLMENT, as a citizen of the   Choctaw   Nation, of   Marie Kathleen Latimer   , born on the   22   day of   January   , 1903

Name of Father: James S. Latimer   a citizen of the   Choctaw   Nation.
Name of Mother: Allie B. Latimer   a citizen of the   Choctaw   Nation.

Applications for Enrollment of Choctaw Newborn
Act of 1905   Volume IV

Postoffice   Wilburton, I.T.

AFFIDAVIT OF MOTHER.

UNITED STATES OF AMERICA, Indian Territory, }
Central   DISTRICT. }

I, Allie B. Latimer, on oath state that I am 29 years of age and a citizen by blood, of the Choctaw Nation; that I am the lawful wife of James S. Latimer, who is a citizen, by marriage of the Choctaw Nation; that a female child was born to me on 22 day of January, 1903; that said child has been named Marie Kathleen Latimer, and was living March 4, 1905.

Allie B. Latimer

Witnesses To Mark:
{

Subscribed and sworn to before me this 23rd day of March, 1905

Wirt Franklin
Notary Public.

AFFIDAVIT OF ATTENDING PHYSICIAN OR MID-WIFE.

State of Ark
UNITED STATES OF AMERICA, Indian Territory, }
Logan County   DISTRICT. }

I, Mary E Castleberry, a............, on oath state that I attended on Mrs. Allie B. Latimer, wife of James S. Latimer on the 22 day of January, 1903; that there was born to her on said date a Female child; that said child was living March 4, 1905, and is said to have been named Marie Kathleen Latimer

Mary E. Castleberry

Witnesses To Mark:
{

Subscribed and sworn to before me this 24 day of March, 1905

My Com   J.N. Cunningham
Expires March 17, 1906   Notary Public.

Applications for Enrollment of Choctaw Newborn
Act of 1905   Volume IV

7-3112

Muskogee, Indian Territory, March 30, 1905.

James S. Latimer,
 Wilburton, Indian Territory.

Dear Sir:

Receipt is hereby acknowledged of the affidavits of Allie B. Latimer and James S. Latimer to the birth of Marie Kathleen Latimer, daughter of James S. and Allie B. Latimer, January 22, 1903, and the same have been filed with our records as an application for the enrollment of said child.

Respectfully,

Chairman.

Choc New Born 212
 Lee Ray Riddle
 (Born Sep. 11, 1903)

BIRTH AFFIDAVIT.

DEPARTMENT OF THE INTERIOR,
COMMISSION TO THE FIVE CIVILIZED TRIBES.

In Re Application for Enrollment, as a citizen of the   Choctaw   Nation, of   Lee Ray Riddle   , born on the   11"   day of   September   , 1903

Name of Father: Richard Riddle   a citizen of the   Choctaw   Nation.
Name of Mother: Florence Riddle   a citizen of the   Choctaw   Nation.

Post-office   Wilburton

Applications for Enrollment of Choctaw Newborn
Act of 1905   Volume IV

AFFIDAVIT OF MOTHER.

UNITED STATES OF AMERICA, }
~~INDIAN TERRITORY,~~
Jackson County   District.

I, Florence Riddle , on oath state that I am 24 years of age and a citizen by adoption or married , of the Choctaw Nation; that I am the lawful wife of Richard Riddle , who is a citizen, by Birth of the Choctaw Nation; that a Female child was born to me on 11" day of September 1903 that said child has been named Lee Ray Riddle , and is now living.

WITNESSES TO MARK: Florence Riddle
{ Mrs. M.E. Coyle
{ Mrs. E. E. Coyle

Subscribed and sworn to before me this 26" day of March , 1904

My Com Expires   Andrew H. Coyle
July 8" 1905   NOTARY PUBLIC.

AFFIDAVIT OF ATTENDING PHYSICIAN OR MID-WIFE.

UNITED STATES OF AMERICA, }
INDIAN TERRITORY,
................................District.

I,................................, a................................, on oath state that I attended on Mrs. Richard Riddle , wife of Richard Riddle on the 11 day of September , 1903 ; that there was born to her on said date a Living Female child; that said child is now living and is said to have been named................................

                                            Dr. W. A. Cox
WITNESSES TO MARK:
{

Subscribed and sworn to before me this 6 day of April , 1904.

                                            J. N. Patterson
                                            NOTARY PUBLIC.

Applications for Enrollment of Choctaw Newborn
Act of 1905 Volume IV

BIRTH AFFIDAVIT.

DEPARTMENT OF THE INTERIOR.
COMMISSION TO THE FIVE CIVILIZED TRIBES.

IN RE APPLICATION FOR ENROLLMENT, as a citizen of the Choctaw Nation, of Lee Ray Riddle, born on the day of , 190

Name of Father: Richard R. Riddle a citizen of the Choctaw Nation.
Name of Mother: Florence Riddle a citizen of the Choctaw Nation.

Postoffice Wilburton, I.T.

AFFIDAVIT OF MOTHER.

UNITED STATES OF AMERICA, Indian Territory, }
Central DISTRICT.

I, Florence Riddle, on oath state that I am 25 years of age and a citizen by marriage, of the Choctaw Nation; that I am the lawful wife of Richard R. Riddle, who is a citizen, by blood of the Choctaw Nation; that a female child was born to me on 11th day of September, 1903; that said child has been named Lee Ray Riddle, and was living March 4, 1905.

Florence Riddle

Witnesses To Mark:

Subscribed and sworn to before me this 23rd day of March, 1905

Wirt Franklin
Notary Public.

AFFIDAVIT OF ATTENDING PHYSICIAN OR MID-WIFE.

UNITED STATES OF AMERICA, Indian Territory, }
Central DISTRICT.

I, W.A. Cox, a physician, on oath state that I attended on Mrs. Florence Riddle, wife of Richard R. Riddle on the 11th day of September, 1903; that there was born to her on said date a female child; that said child was living March 4, 1905, and is said to have been named Lee Ray Riddle

W.A. Cox

Witnesses To Mark:

Applications for Enrollment of Choctaw Newborn
Act of 1905   Volume IV

Subscribed and sworn to before me this 23rd day of March, 1905

Wirt Franklin
Notary Public.

NB 212

Muskogee, Indian Territory, April 11, 1904.

Richard Riddle,
  Wilburton, Indian Territory.

Dear Sir:

Receipt is hereby acknowledged of the affidavits of Florence and Richard Riddle, relative to the birth of Lee Ray Riddle, infant daughter of Richard and Florence Riddle, September 11, 1903, which it is presumed have been forwarded to this office as an application for the enrollment of said child as a citizen by blood of the Choctaw Nation.

You are advised that under the provisions of the Act of Congress, approved July 1, 1902, the Commission is now without authority to receive or consider the original application of any person whomsoever for enrollment as a citizen of the Choctaw or Chickasaw Nation.

Respectfully,

Commissioner in Charge.

Choc New Born 213
  Henry G. Hampton
  (Born Nov. 2, 1902)
  Noel Hampton
  (Born Oct. 6, 1904)

BIRTH AFFIDAVIT.
DEPARTMENT OF THE INTERIOR,
COMMISSION TO THE FIVE CIVILIZED TRIBES.

IN RE Application for Enrollment, as a citizen of the Choctaw Nation, of Henry G. Hampton, born on the 2 day of November, 1902

Applications for Enrollment of Choctaw Newborn
Act of 1905   Volume IV

Name of Father: Sweeney Hampton a citizen of the Choctaw Nation.
Name of Mother: Elizabeth Hampton a citizen of the Choctaw Nation.

Post-Office: Wilburton

AFFIDAVIT OF MOTHER.

UNITED STATES OF AMERICA,
   INDIAN TERRITORY.
Central   District.

I, Elizabeth Hampton, on oath state that I am 25 years of age and a citizen by blood, of the Choctaw Nation; that I am the lawful wife of Sweeney Hampton, who is a citizen, by blood of the Choctaw Nation; that a female child was born to me on 2 day of Nov., 1902, that said child has been named Henry G. Hampton, and is now living.

                          her
             Elizabeth x Hampton
WITNESSES TO MARK: mark
  { R M Wilson
    Fred V Kinkade

Subscribed and sworn to before me this 23 *day of* Dec, 1902

            T. R. Humphrey
                NOTARY PUBLIC.

NEW-BORN AFFIDAVIT.

Number

...Choctaw Enrolling Commission...

IN THE MATTER OF THE APPLICATION FOR ENROLLMENT, as a citizen of the Choctaw Nation, of Henry Hampton

born on the 2 day of __November__ 1902

Name of father Sweeney Hampton   a citizen of   Choctaw
Nation final enrollment No. 9155
Name of mother Elizabeth Hampton   a citizen of   Choctaw
Nation final enrollment No. 9156

                Postoffice   Wilburton I.T.

Applications for Enrollment of Choctaw Newborn
Act of 1905 Volume IV

AFFIDAVIT OF MOTHER.

UNITED STATES OF AMERICA
INDIAN TERRITORY
Central   DISTRICT

I Elizabeth Hampton , on oath state that I am 30 years of age and a citizen by blood of the Choctaw Nation, and as such have been placed upon the final roll of the Choctaw Nation, by the Honorable Secretary of the Interior my final enrollment number being 9156 ; that I am the lawful wife of Sweeney Hampton , who is a citizen of the Choctaw Nation, and as such has been placed upon the final roll of said Nation by the Honorable Secretary of the Interior, his final enrollment number being 9155 and that a Male child was born to me on the 2nd day of November 1902 ; that said child has been named Henry Hampton , and is now living.

Witnesseth.   Elizabeth Hampton
Must be two
Witnesses who   Noel Anderson
are Citizens.   Silas Pusley

Subscribed and sworn to before me this 31st day of Jany 190 5

E.F. Lester
Notary Public.

My commission expires:
2/6/1906

AFFIDAVIT OF ATTENDING PHYSICIAN OR MIDWIFE

UNITED STATES OF AMERICA
INDIAN TERRITORY
Centra;   DISTRICT

I, Mrs Maggie Gore   a   midwife on oath state that I attended on Mrs. Sweeney Hampton wife of Sweeney Hampton on the 2nd day of November , 190 2 , that there was born to her on said date a male child, that said child is now living, and is said to have been named Henry Hampton

midwife
Mrs Maggie Gore

Subscribed and sworn to before me this, the 31st day of January 190 5

EF Lester Notary Public.

WITNESSETH:
Must be two witnesses   Noel Anderson
who are citizens   Silas Pusley

Applications for Enrollment of Choctaw Newborn
Act of 1905   Volume IV

We hereby certify that we are well acquainted with Mrs Maggie Gore a midwife and know her to be reputable and of good standing in the community.

Noel Anderson   Garvin I.T.

Silas Pusley   Damon IT

NEW-BORN AFFIDAVIT.

Number

...Choctaw Enrolling Commission...

IN THE MATTER OF THE APPLICATION FOR ENROLLMENT, as a citizen of the Choctaw Nation, of Noel Hampton

born on the 6 day of October 190 4

Name of father Sweeney Hampton   a citizen of Choctaw Nation final enrollment No. 9155
Name of mother Elizabeth Hampton   a citizen of Choctaw Nation final enrollment No. 9156

Postoffice Wilburton, I.T.

AFFIDAVIT OF MOTHER.

UNITED STATES OF AMERICA
INDIAN TERRITORY
Central   DISTRICT

I Elizabeth Hampton, on oath state that I am 30 years of age and a citizen by blood of the Choctaw Nation, and as such have been placed upon the final roll of the Choctaw Nation, by the Honorable Secretary of the Interior my final enrollment number being 9156 ; that I am the lawful wife of Sweeney Hampton, who is a citizen of the Choctaw Nation, and as such has been placed upon the final roll of said Nation by the Honorable Secretary of the Interior, his final enrollment number being 9155 and that a male child was born to me on the 6th day of October 190 4; that said child has been named Noel Hampton, and is now living.

Witnesseth.   Elizabeth Hampton
  Must be two ⎫ Noel Anderson
  Witnesses who ⎬
  are Citizens. ⎭ Silas Pusley

Applications for Enrollment of Choctaw Newborn
Act of 1905   Volume IV

Subscribed and sworn to before me this 22 day of February 190 5

EF Lester
Notary Public.

My commission expires: 2/6/1906

AFFIDAVIT OF ATTENDING PHYSICIAN OR MIDWIFE

UNITED STATES OF AMERICA
INDIAN TERRITORY
Central   DISTRICT

I, Mrs Maggie Gore a midwife on oath state that I attended on Mrs. Elizabeth Hampton wife of Sweeney Hampton on the 6th day of October, 190 4, that there was born to her on said date a male child, that said child is now living, and is said to have been named Noel Hampton

Mrs Maggie Gore ~~M.D.~~
midwife

WITNESSETH:
Must be two witnesses who are citizens and know the child.
{ Noel Anderson
  Silas Pusley

Subscribed and sworn to before me this, the 22 day of February 190 5

EF Lester   Notary Public.

We hereby certify that we are well acquainted with Mrs Maggie Gore a midwife and know her to be reputable and of good standing in the community.

{ Noel Anderson
  Silas Pusley

BIRTH AFFIDAVIT.

DEPARTMENT OF THE INTERIOR.
COMMISSION TO THE FIVE CIVILIZED TRIBES.

IN RE APPLICATION FOR ENROLLMENT, as a citizen of the Choctaw Nation, of Henry G. Hampton, born on the 2 day of November, 1902

Name of Father: Sweeney Hampton   a citizen of the Choctaw Nation.
Name of Mother: Elizabeth Hampton   a citizen of the Choctaw Nation.

Applications for Enrollment of Choctaw Newborn
Act of 1905   Volume IV

Postoffice   Wilburton, Indian Territory

AFFIDAVIT OF MOTHER.

UNITED STATES OF AMERICA, Indian Territory,
Central   DISTRICT.

I, Elizabeth Hampton, on oath state that I am 28 years of age and a citizen by blood, of the Choctaw Nation; that I am the lawful wife of Sweeney Hampton, who is a citizen, by blood of the Choctaw Nation; that a male child was born to me on 2 day of November, 1902; that said child has been named Henry G. Hampton, and was living March 4, 1905.

Elizabeth Hampton

Witnesses To Mark:

Subscribed and sworn to before me this 25 day of April, 1905

EF Lester
Notary Public.

AFFIDAVIT OF ATTENDING PHYSICIAN OR MID-WIFE.

UNITED STATES OF AMERICA, Indian Territory,
Central   DISTRICT.

I, Mrs Maggie Gore, a midwife, on oath state that I attended on Mrs. Elizabeth Hampton, wife of Sweeney Hampton on the 2 day of November, 1902; that there was born to her on said date a male child; that said child was living March 4, 1905, and is said to have been named Henry G. Hampton

Mrs Maggie Gore

Witnesses To Mark:

Subscribed and sworn to before me this 25 day of April, 1905

EF Lester
Notary Public.

Applications for Enrollment of Choctaw Newborn
Act of 1905 Volume IV

BIRTH AFFIDAVIT.

DEPARTMENT OF THE INTERIOR.
COMMISSION TO THE FIVE CIVILIZED TRIBES.

IN RE APPLICATION FOR ENROLLMENT, as a citizen of the Choctaw Nation, of Noel Hampton, born on the 6th day of October, 1904

Name of Father: Sweeney Hampton   a citizen of the Choctaw Nation.
Name of Mother: Elizabeth Hampton   a citizen of the Choctaw Nation.

Postoffice   Wilburton, I.T.

AFFIDAVIT OF MOTHER.

UNITED STATES OF AMERICA, Indian Territory,
Central   DISTRICT.

I, Elizabeth Hampton, on oath state that I am 28 years of age and a citizen by blood, of the Choctaw Nation; that I am the lawful wife of Sweeney Hampton, who is a citizen, by blood of the Choctaw Nation; that a male child was born to me on 6th day of October, 1904; that said child has been named, and was living March 4, 1905.

                               Elizabeth Hampton

Witnesses To Mark:

Subscribed and sworn to before me this 25 day of April, 1905

                               EF Lester
                                     Notary Public.

AFFIDAVIT OF ATTENDING PHYSICIAN OR MID-WIFE.

UNITED STATES OF AMERICA, Indian Territory,
Central   DISTRICT.

I, Mrs Maggie Gore, a midwife, on oath state that I attended on Mrs. Elizabeth Hampton, wife of Sweeney Hampton on the 6th day of October, 1904; that there was born to her on said date a male child; that said child was living March 4, 1905, and is said to have been named Noel Hampton

                               Mrs Maggie Gore

Witnesses To Mark:

Applications for Enrollment of Choctaw Newborn
Act of 1905   Volume IV

Subscribed and sworn to before me this 25th day of April, 1905

EF Lester
Notary Public.

COPY.   N.B. 213

Muskogee, Indian Territory, April 7, 1905.

Sweeney Hampton,
    Wilburton, Indian Territory.

Dear Sir:

There is inclosed you herewith for execution application for the enrollment of your infant child, Henry G. Hampton, born November 2, 1902.

The affidavit heretofore filed with the Commission shows the child was living on December 23, 1902. It is necessary, for the child to be enrolled, that he was living on March 5, 1905.

The above mentioned affidavit is of the mother only. You will notice from the inclosed application that the affidavit of the physician or midwife is also required. You will please insert the age of the mother in space provided for that purpose.

In having these affidavits executed care should be exercised to see that all the names are written in full as they appear in the body of the affidavit, and in the event that either of the persons signing the affidavit are unable to write, signatures by mark must be attested by two witnesses. Each affidavit must be executed before a Notary Public and the notarial seal and signature of the officer must be attached to each separate affidavit.

Respectfully,
SIGNED
T.B. Needles
LM 7-25   Commissioner in Charge.

Applications for Enrollment of Choctaw Newborn
Act of 1905   Volume IV

COPY.

Choctaw N.B. 213.
Choctaw 3164.

Muskogee, Indian Territory, May 1, 1905.

E. F. Lester,
 Attorney at Law,
  Wilburton, Indian Territory.

Dear Sir:

Receipt is hereby acknowledged of your letter of April 26, enclosing the affidavits of Elizabeth Hampton and Mrs. Maggie Gore to the birth of Henry G. Hampton and Noe. Hampton, children of Sweeney and Elizabeth Hampton, November 2, 1902 and October 6, 1904, respectively, and the same have been filed with our records in the matter of the enrollment of said children.

Respectfully,
SIGNED
Tams Bixby
Chairman.

7-NB-213

Muskogee, Indian Territory, September 8, 1905.

Arnote & Lester,
 Attorneys at Law,
  Wilburton, Indian Territory.

Gentlemen:

Replying to your letter of September 5th, you are advised that on June 30, 1905, the Secretary of the Interior approved the enrollment of Henry G. and Noel Hampton as New-born citizens by blood of the Choctaw Nation, and the names of the children appear upon the roll of such citizens, opposite numbers 214 and 215, respectively.

The children now being entitled to allotments, selection thereof should be made without delay at the land office for the nation in which the prospective allotments are located.

Respectfully,

Acting Commissioner.

Applications for Enrollment of Choctaw Newborn
Act of 1905   Volume IV

Choc New Born 214
    Capitolia Sparks
    (Born April 2, 1904)

BIRTH AFFIDAVIT.

DEPARTMENT OF THE INTERIOR.
COMMISSION TO THE FIVE CIVILIZED TRIBES.

IN RE APPLICATION FOR ENROLLMENT, as a citizen of the Choctaw Nation, of Capitolia Sparks, born on the 2nd day of April, 1904

Name of Father: John F. Sparks   a citizen of the United States ~~Nation~~.
Name of Mother: Cornelia Maye Sparks   a citizen of the Choctaw Nation.

                Postoffice   Newburg, I.T.

AFFIDAVIT OF MOTHER.

UNITED STATES OF AMERICA, Indian Territory, }
    Central   DISTRICT.

    I, Cornelia Maye Sparks, on oath state that I am 26 years of age and a citizen by blood, of the Choctaw Nation; that I am the lawful wife of John F. Sparks, who is a citizen, ~~by~~ .... of the United States ~~Nation~~; that a female child was born to me on 2nd day of April, 1904; that said child has been named Capitolia Sparks, and was living March 4, 1905.

                            Cornelia Maye Sparks

Witnesses To Mark:
{

    Subscribed and sworn to before me this 17th day of March, 1905

                            Wirt Franklin
                            Notary Public.

AFFIDAVIT OF ATTENDING PHYSICIAN OR MID-WIFE.

UNITED STATES OF AMERICA, Indian Territory, }
    Central   DISTRICT.

    I, Rebecca Burris, a mid-wife, on oath state that I attended on Mrs. Cornelia Maye Sparks, wife of John F. Sparks on the 2nd day of

Applications for Enrollment of Choctaw Newborn
Act of 1905   Volume IV

April   , 1904; that there was born to her on said date a   female   child; that said child was living March 4, 1905, and is said to have been named Capitolia Sparks

                                                Mrs. Rebeca Burris

Witnesses To Mark:
{

    Subscribed and sworn to before me this   17th day of   March   , 1905

                                               Wirt Franklin
                                                  Notary Public.

                                            7-NB-214

                            Muskogee, Indian Territory, July 15, 1905.

Cornelia Maye Sparks,
    Newburg, Indian Territory.

Dear Madam:

    Receipt is hereby acknowledged of your letter of July 10, 1905, asking if the enrollment of your child Capitolia Sparks has been approved.

    In reply to your letter you are advised that on June 30, 1905, the Secretary of the Interior approved the enrollment of your child Capitolia Sparks as a citizen by blood of the Choctaw Nation.

                                              Respectfully,

                                                       Commissioner.

Applications for Enrollment of Choctaw Newborn
Act of 1905   Volume IV

Choc New Born 215
    Robert Nail
    (Born June 8, 1903)
    Lillie Nail
    (Born Feb. 11, 1905)

NEW BORN AFFIDAVIT

No _____

CHOCTAW ENROLLING COMMISSION

IN THE MATTER OF THE APPLICATION FOR ENROLLMENT as a citizen of the Choctaw Nation, of   Robert Nail   born on the   8   day of   June   190 3

Name of father   Silas W. Nail   a citizen of   Chickasaw   Nation, final enrollment No.   2052

Name of mother   Rosa Nail (nee Carter)   a citizen of   Choctaw   Nation, final enrollment No.   9335

                    Alderson I.T.   Postoffice.

AFFIDAVIT OF MOTHER

UNITED STATES OF AMERICA
   INDIAN TERRITORY
DISTRICT   Central

I Rosa Nail (nee Carter)   , on oath state that I am   23   years of age and a citizen by   blood   of the   Choctaw   Nation, and as such have been placed upon the final roll of the   Choctaw   Nation, by the Honorable Secretary of the Interior my final enrollment number being   9335   ; that I am the lawful wife of   Silas W. Nail   , who is a citizen of the   Chickasaw   Nation, and as such has been placed upon the final roll of said Nation by the Honorable Secretary of the Interior, his final enrollment number being   2052   and that a   Male   child was born to me on the   8   day of   June   190 3; that said child has been named   Robert Nail   , and is now living.

WITNESSETH: Rosa Nail

Must be two witnesses { Frank Pope
who are citizens   { Columbus Campelube

Applications for Enrollment of Choctaw Newborn
Act of 1905 Volume IV

Subscribed and sworn to before me this, the 15 day of March , 190 5

                                          James Bower
                                               Notary Public.

My Commission Expires:
Sept. 23 1907.

Affidavit of Attending Physician or Midwife

UNITED STATES OF AMERICA,
    INDIAN TERRITORY,
Central   DISTRICT

I, Nellie Carney[sic] a Midwife on oath state that I attended on Mrs. Rosa Nail (nee Carney[sic]) wife of Silas W. Nail on the 8 day of June , 190 3, that there was born to her on said date a male child, that said child is now living, and is said to have been named Robert Nail

                                            her
                                      Nellie x Comey   M. D.
                                        mark

Subscribed and sworn to before me this the 15 day of March 1905

                                          James Bower
                                            Notary Public.

WITNESSETH:
    Must be two witnesses who are citizens and know the child.   { Columbus Campelube
                                                  Frank Pope

We hereby certify that we are well acquainted with Nellie Comey a midwife and know her to be reputable and of good standing in the community.

                              Must be two citizen witnesses.   { Frank Pope
                                                                     Columbus Campelube

Applications for Enrollment of Choctaw Newborn
Act of 1905   Volume IV

Affidavit of Attending Physician or Midwife

UNITED STATES OF AMERICA,
    INDIAN TERRITORY,
Central   DISTRICT

I, Nellie Carney[sic] a Midwife on oath state that I attended on Mrs. Rosa Nail (nee Carter) wife of Silas W. Nail on the 11 day of February, 190 5, that there was born to her on said date a Female child, that said child is now living, and is said to have been named LIllie Nail

    her
Nellie x Comey   M. D.
    mark

Subscribed and sworn to before me this the 15 day of March 1905

James Bower
Notary Public.

WITNESSETH:
Must be two witnesses who are citizens and know the child.
- Frank Pope
- Columbus Campelube

We hereby certify that we are well acquainted with Nellie Comey a midwife and know her to be reputable and of good standing in the community.

Must be two citizen witnesses.
- Frank Pope
- Columbus Campelube

NEW BORN AFFIDAVIT

No

CHOCTAW ENROLLING COMMISSION

IN THE MATTER OF THE APPLICATION FOR ENROLLMENT as a citizen of the Choctaw Nation, of Lillie Nail born on the 11 day of February 190 5

Name of father Silas W. Nail   a citizen of Chickasaw Nation, final enrollment No. 2052

Name of mother Rosa Nail (nee Carter)   a citizen of Choctaw Nation, final enrollment No. 9335

Alderson I.T.   Postoffice.

Applications for Enrollment of Choctaw Newborn
Act of 1905 Volume IV

AFFIDAVIT OF MOTHER

UNITED STATES OF AMERICA
INDIAN TERRITORY
DISTRICT Central

I Rosa Nail (nee Carter), on oath state that I am 23 years of age and a citizen by blood of the Choctaw Nation, and as such have been placed upon the final roll of the Choctaw Nation, by the Honorable Secretary of the Interior my final enrollment number being 9335 ; that I am the lawful wife of Silas W. Nail, who is a citizen of the Chickasaw Nation, and as such has been placed upon the final roll of said Nation by the Honorable Secretary of the Interior, his final enrollment number being 2052 and that a Female child was born to me on the 11 day of February 190 5; that said child has been named Lillie Nail, and is now living.

WITNESSETH: Rosa Nail

Must be two witnesses Frank Pope
who are citizens Columbus Campelube

Subscribed and sworn to before me this, the 15 day of March , 190 5

James Bower
Notary Public.

My Commission Expires:
Sept. 23 1907.

BIRTH AFFIDAVIT.

DEPARTMENT OF THE INTERIOR.
COMMISSION TO THE FIVE CIVILIZED TRIBES.

IN RE APPLICATION FOR ENROLLMENT, as a citizen of the Choctaw Nation, of Robert Nail , born on the 8th day of June , 1903

Name of Father: Silas Nail a citizen of the Chickasaw Nation.
Name of Mother: Rosa Nail a citizen of the Choctaw Nation.

Postoffice Alderson, I.T.

Applications for Enrollment of Choctaw Newborn
Act of 1905   Volume IV

AFFIDAVIT OF MOTHER.

UNITED STATES OF AMERICA, Indian Territory, }
Central   DISTRICT.

    I, Rosa Nail, on oath state that I am 23 years of age and a citizen by blood, of the Choctaw Nation; that I am the lawful wife of Silas Nail, who is a citizen, by blood of the Chickasaw Nation; that a male child was born to me on the 8th day of June, 1903; that said child has been named Robert Nail, and was living March 4, 1905; and I elect for said child to be finally enrolled as a Choctaw.

                                    Rosa Nail

Witnesses To Mark:

    Subscribed and sworn to before me this 17th day of March, 1905

                            Wirt Franklin
                            Notary Public.

AFFIDAVIT OF ATTENDING PHYSICIAN OR MID-WIFE.

UNITED STATES OF AMERICA, Indian Territory, }
Central   DISTRICT.

    I, Nellie Carter, a mid-wife, on oath state that I attended on Mrs. Rosa Nail, wife of Silas Nail on the 8th day of June, 1903; that there was born to her on said date a male child; that said child was living March 4, 1905, and is said to have been named Robert Nail

                                  her
                            Nellie x Carter
Witnesses To Mark: mark
    [Illegible] Collins
    Charlee Ward

    Subscribed and sworn to before me this 17th day of March, 1905

                            Wirt Franklin
                            Notary Public.

Applications for Enrollment of Choctaw Newborn
Act of 1905 Volume IV

BIRTH AFFIDAVIT.

DEPARTMENT OF THE INTERIOR.
COMMISSION TO THE FIVE CIVILIZED TRIBES.

IN RE APPLICATION FOR ENROLLMENT, as a citizen of the Choctaw Nation, of Lillie Nail, born on the 11th day of February, 1905

Name of Father: Silas Nail   a citizen of the Chickasaw Nation.
Name of Mother: Rosa Nail   a citizen of the Choctaw Nation.

Postoffice   Alderson, I.T.

AFFIDAVIT OF MOTHER.

UNITED STATES OF AMERICA, Indian Territory,
Central   DISTRICT.

I, Rosa Nail, on oath state that I am 23 years of age and a citizen by blood, of the Choctaw Nation; that I am the lawful wife of Silas Nail, who is a citizen, by blood of the Chickasaw Nation; that a female child was born to me on the 11th day of February, 1905; that said child has been named Lillie Nail, and was living March 4, 1905; and I elect for said child to be finally enrolled as a Choctaw.

Rosa Nail

Witnesses To Mark:

Subscribed and sworn to before me this 17th day of March, 1905

Wirt Franklin
Notary Public.

AFFIDAVIT OF ATTENDING PHYSICIAN OR MID-WIFE.

UNITED STATES OF AMERICA, Indian Territory,
Central   DISTRICT.

I, Nellie Carter, a mid wife, on oath state that I attended on Mrs. Rosa Nail, wife of Silas Nail on the 11th day of February, 1905; that there was born to her on said date a female child; that said child was living March 4, 1905, and is said to have been named Lillie Nail

her
Nellie x Carter
mark

Applications for Enrollment of Choctaw Newborn
Act of 1905 Volume IV

Witnesses To Mark:
{ Robt. R. Barnett
{ Geo. W. Nachtel

    Subscribed and sworn to before me this 17th day of March, 1905

                            Wirt Franklin
                            Notary Public.

United States of America, }
Indian Territory, }
Central District. }

    I, Silas Nail, on oath state that I am about 30 years of age and a citizen by blood of Chickasaw Nation; that I am the lawful husband of Rosa Nail (nee Carter); that I am father of Lillie Nail and Robert Nail; that I hereby elect to have said children enrolled as citizens by blood of the Choctaw Nation, provided the Commission should determine that said children are entitled to enrollment and allotment in the Choctaw and Chickasaw Nations. enrollment in either the Choctaw or Chickasaw Nation; and that, if said children are finally enrolled as citizens by blood of the Choctaw Nation, I hereby relinquish whatever right, title and interest said children may have in and to the tribal property of the Chickasaw Nation.

                            Silas Nail

    Subscribed and sworn to before me this 17th day of March, 1905.

                            Wirt Franklin
                            Notary Public

Applications for Enrollment of Choctaw Newborn
Act of 1905   Volume IV

Choc New Born 216
    Joseph Kemp
    (Born April 22, 1904)

NB-216.
DEPARTMENT OF THE INTERIOR,
COMMISSION TO THE FIVE CIVILIZED TRIBES.
SOUTH McAlester, I. T.   APRIL 24, 1905.

In the matter of the application for the enrollment of Joseph Kemp as a citizen by blood of the Choctaw Nation.

Frances Kemp being first duly sworn testifies as follows:

EXAMINATION BY THE COMMISSION:

Q What is your name?   A Frances Kemp.
Q What is your age?   A Twenty-four.
Q What kis your post office address?   A McAlester.
Q Are you a citizen by blood of the Choctaw Nation?   A Yes, sir.
Q You present here a letter from the Commission to the Five Civilized Tribes dated April 8, 1905 wherein they acknowledge receipt of the application for the enrollment of your infant child Joseph Kemp as a citizen of the Choctaw Nation; when was this child born: A April 22, 1904.
Q How long have you been married to Mr. Kemp?   A Married October 3, 1903.
Q What was your name prior to your marriage to Mr. Kemp?   A Frances Carter.
Q Is that the way your allotment certificate reads - Frances Carter   A Yes, sir.
Q Your roll number is 13324?   A Yes, sir.
Q Your child is living today?   A Yes, sir.

                Witness excused.

Chas. T. Difendafer be first duly sworn states that the above and foregoing is a full, true and correct transcript of his stenographic notes taken in said cause on said date.

                Chas. T. Difendafer

Subscribed and sworn to before me this 24th day of April 1905.

                OL Johnson
                Notary Public.

Applications for Enrollment of Choctaw Newborn
Act of 1905   Volume IV

United States of America,
Indian Territory,
Central District.

  I, Daniel E. Johnson, on oath state that I am 35 years old and am a citizen by blood of the Choctaw Nation; that I am personally acquainted with Frances Kemp and her husband, Warren Kemp; that there was born to them on the 22nd day of April, 1904, a male child; that said child is said to have been named Joseph Kemp and is now living; that my mother, Eliza A. Johnson, attended the said Frances Kemp at the birth of said child, acting in the capacity of mid-wife; that I learned the facts surrounding the birth of said child from my mother and that my mother died September 24, 1904.

            Daniel E Johnson

Subscribed and sworn to before me this 21st day of March, 1905.

            Wirt Franklin
             Notary Public.

BIRTH AFFIDAVIT.

DEPARTMENT OF THE INTERIOR.
COMMISSION TO THE FIVE CIVILIZED TRIBES.

  IN RE APPLICATION FOR ENROLLMENT, as a citizen of the Choctaw Nation, of Joseph Kemp, born on the 22nd day of April, 1904

Name of Father: Warren Kemp   a citizen of the Choctaw Nation.
Name of Mother: Frances Kemp   a citizen of the Choctaw Nation.

        Postoffice   McAlester, I.T.

AFFIDAVIT OF MOTHER.

UNITED STATES OF AMERICA, Indian Territory,
  Central   DISTRICT.

  I, Frances Kemp, on oath state that I am 24 years of age and a citizen by blood, of the Choctaw Nation; that I am the lawful wife of Warren Kemp, who is a citizen, by blood of the Choctaw Nation; that a male child was born to me on 22nd day of April, 1904; that said child has been named Joseph Kemp, and was living March 4, 1905.

            Frances Kemp

Witnesses To Mark:

Applications for Enrollment of Choctaw Newborn
Act of 1905   Volume IV

Subscribed and sworn to before me this 21st day of March, 1905

Wirt Franklin
Notary Public.

COMMISSIONERS:
TAMS BIXBY,
THOMAS B. NEEDLES,
C.R. BRECKINBRIDGE.

WM. O. BEALL
Secretary

**DEPARTMENT OF THE INTERIOR,
COMMISSIONER TO THE FIVE CIVILIZED TRIBES.**

$W^m O.B.$

REFER IN REPLY TO THE FOLLOWING:

N. B. 216

ADDRESS ONLY THE
COMMISSION TO THE FIVE CIVILIZED TRIBES.

Muskogee, Indian Territory, April 8, 1905.

Warren Kemp,
McAlester, Indian Territory.

Dear Sir:

Referring to the affidavits heretofore forwarded, relative to the birth of your infant child, Joseph Kemp, born April 22, 1904, it is stated in the affidavit of the mother, Frances Kemp, that she is a citizen by blood of the Choctaw Nation.

If this is correct you are requested to state when, where and under what name she was listed for enrollment, the names of her parents and other members of her family for whom application was made at the same time, and if she has selected an allotment to give her roll number as the same appears upon her allotment certificate.

Respectfully,

T.B. Needles
Commissioner in Charge.

Roll No. 13324 - Frances Carter.

Applications for Enrollment of Choctaw Newborn
Act of 1905   Volume IV

7-NB-216

Muskogee, Indian Territory, February 27, 1906.

Warren Kemp,
    Vireton, Indian Territory.

Dear Sir:

    Receipt is hereby acknowledged of your letter of February 23, 1906, asking the roll number of your son Joseph Kemp.

    In reply to your letter you are advised that the name of your son Joseph Kemp appears upon the approved roll of new born citizens of the Choctaw Nation opposite No. 219 and his enrollment was approved by the Secretary of the Interior, June 30, 1905.

                  Respectfully,

                                Acting Commissioner.

Choc New Born 217
    Willie Lee Pusley
    (Born Feb. 18, 1903)

NEW-BORN AFFIDAVIT.

        Number..............

...Choctaw Enrolling Commission...

IN THE MATTER OF THE APPLICATION FOR ENROLLMENT, as a citizen of the Choctaw Nation, of Willie Lee Pusley

born on the 18 day of _____Feb_____ 190 3

Name of father John Pusley	a citizen of Choctaw
Nation final enrollment No. 9652	
Name of mother Nannie B. Pusley	a citizen of Choctaw
Nation final enrollment No. 314	
	Postoffice Guertie, I.T.

Applications for Enrollment of Choctaw Newborn
Act of 1905   Volume IV

AFFIDAVIT OF MOTHER.

UNITED STATES OF AMERICA
INDIAN TERRITORY
Central   DISTRICT

I   Nannie B. Pusley   , on oath state that I am 33 years of age and a citizen by   Int. Mar.   of the   Choctaw   Nation, and as such have been placed upon the final roll of the   Choctaw   Nation, by the Honorable Secretary of the Interior my final enrollment number being   314 ; that I am the lawful wife of   John Pusley   , who is a citizen of the   Choctaw   Nation, and as such has been placed upon the final roll of said Nation by the Honorable Secretary of the Interior, his final enrollment number being   9562   and that a   Female   child was born to me on the   18   day of   Feb   190 3; that said child has been named   Willie Lee Pusley   , and is now living.

Witnesseth.   Nannie B. Pusley

Must be two Witnesses who are Citizens.
Lizzie Pusley
Mrs. Cora A. Gulley

Subscribed and sworn to before me this   2   day of   Feb   190 5

J. I. Givens
Notary Public.

My commission expires: Feb. 1st 1908

AFFIDAVIT OF ATTENDING PHYSICIAN OR MIDWIFE

UNITED STATES OF AMERICA
INDIAN TERRITORY
Central   DISTRICT

I,   C. C. Martin   a   Physician   on oath state that I attended on Mrs.   Pusley   wife of   John Pusley   on the   18   day of   Feb   , 190 3 , that there was born to her on said date a   Female   child, that said child is now living, and is said to have been named   Willie Lee Pusley

C. C. Martin M.D.

Subscribed and sworn to before me this, the   2nd   day of   Feb   190 5

WITNESSETH: J.I. Givens   Notary Public.

Must be two witnesses who are citizens
Lizzie Pusley
Mrs Cora A Gulley

Applications for Enrollment of Choctaw Newborn
Act of 1905 Volume IV

We hereby certify that we are well acquainted with Dr. C. C. Martin a Physician and know him to be reputable and of good standing in the community.

Lizzie Pusley _____

Mrs. Cora R. Gulley _____

BIRTH AFFIDAVIT.

DEPARTMENT OF THE INTERIOR.
COMMISSION TO THE FIVE CIVILIZED TRIBES.

IN RE APPLICATION FOR ENROLLMENT, as a citizen of the Choctaw Nation, of Willie Lee Pusley, born on the 18 day of Feb, 1903

Name of Father: John Pusley a citizen of the Choctaw Nation.
Name of Mother: Nannie B. Pusley a citizen of the Choctaw Nation.

Postoffice Guertie, I.T.

AFFIDAVIT OF MOTHER.

UNITED STATES OF AMERICA, Indian Territory,
Central DISTRICT.

I, Nannie B. Pusley, on oath state that I am 33 years of age and a citizen by Int. Marriage, of the Choctaw Nation; that I am the lawful wife of John Pusley, who is a citizen, by blood of the Choctaw Nation; that a Female child was born to me on 18 day of Feb, 1903; that said child has been named Willie Lee Pusley, and was living March 4, 1905.

Nannie B. Pusley

Witnesses To Mark:

Subscribed and sworn to before me this 23 day of March, 1905

J.I. Givens
Notary Public.

Applications for Enrollment of Choctaw Newborn
Act of 1905   Volume IV

AFFIDAVIT OF ATTENDING PHYSICIAN OR MID-WIFE.

UNITED STATES OF AMERICA, Indian Territory, }
Central   DISTRICT.

I, C. C. Martin, a Physician, on oath state that I attended on Mrs. Nannie B. Pusley, wife of John Pusley on the 18 day of Feb, 1903; that there was born to her on said date a Female child; that said child was living March 4, 1905, and is said to have been named Willie Lee Pusley

C. C. Martin M.D.

Witnesses To Mark:
{

Subscribed and sworn to before me this 23 day of March, 1905

J.I. Givens
Notary Public.

7-3332

Muskogee, Indian Territory, March 28, 1905.

John Pusley,
    Guertie, Indian Territory.

Dear Sir:

Receipt is hereby acknowledged of the affidavits of Nancy[sic] B. Pusley and C. C. Martin to the birth of Willie Lee Pusley daughter of John and Nancy B. Pusley, February 18, 1903, and the same have been filed with our records as an application for the enrollment of said child.

Respectfully,

Chairman.

Applications for Enrollment of Choctaw Newborn
Act of 1905   Volume IV

Choc New Born 218
    Alfred Henry Estes
    (Born Sep. 14, 1903)

BIRTH AFFIDAVIT.

DEPARTMENT OF THE INTERIOR.
COMMISSION TO THE FIVE CIVILIZED TRIBES.

IN RE APPLICATION FOR ENROLLMENT, as a citizen of the Choctaw Nation, of Alfred Henry Estes, born on the 14th day of September, 1903

Name of Father: Joe S. Estes   a citizen of the United States ~~Nation~~.
Name of Mother: Lorena Estes   a citizen of the Choctaw Nation.

Postoffice   Calvin, I.T.

AFFIDAVIT OF MOTHER.

UNITED STATES OF AMERICA, Indian Territory, }
    Central   DISTRICT.

I, Lorena Estes, on oath state that I am 21 years of age and a citizen by blood, of the Choctaw Nation; that I am the lawful wife of Joe S. Estes, who is a citizen, ~~by~~ of the United States ~~Nation~~; that a male child was born to me on 14th day of September, 1903; that said child has been named Alfred Henry Estes, and was living March 4, 1905.

                         Lorena Estes

Witnesses To Mark:
{

Subscribed and sworn to before me this 17th day of March, 1905

                         Wirt Franklin
                         Notary Public.

AFFIDAVIT OF ATTENDING PHYSICIAN OR MID-WIFE.

UNITED STATES OF AMERICA, Indian Territory, }
    Central   DISTRICT.

I, Jennetta Paxson, a midwife, on oath state that I attended on Mrs. Lorena Estes, wife of Joe S. Estes on the 14th day of September,

Applications for Enrollment of Choctaw Newborn
Act of 1905   Volume IV

1903; that there was born to her on said date a male child; that said child was living March 4, 1905, and is said to have been named Alfred Henry Estes

Mrs. Janetta[sic] Parson

Witnesses To Mark:
{

Subscribed and sworn to before me this 18th day of March , 1905

Wirt Franklin
Notary Public.

Choc New Born 219
    Corinne Moore
    (Born April 25, 1904)

NEW-BORN AFFIDAVIT.

Number..............

...Choctaw Enrolling Commission...

IN THE MATTER OF THE APPLICATION FOR ENROLLMENT, as a citizen of the Choctaw Nation, of Corinne Moore

born on the 25 day of ~~May~~ April 190 4

Name of father Herbert M Moore   a citizen of Choctaw Nation final enrollment No. 7845
    Known as McCurtain
Name of mother Lena Moore   a citizen of Choctaw Nation final enrollment No.

Postoffice   Kinta I.T.

Applications for Enrollment of Choctaw Newborn
Act of 1905 Volume IV

AFFIDAVIT OF MOTHER.

UNITED STATES OF AMERICA
INDIAN TERRITORY
Western   DISTRICT

I   Lena Moore   , on oath state that I am 24 years of age and a citizen by blood of the Choctaw Nation, and as such have been placed upon the final roll of the Choctaw Nation, by the Honorable Secretary of the Interior my final enrollment number being ....; that I am the lawful wife of Herbert M Moore , who is a citizen of the Choctaw Nation, and as such has been placed upon the final roll of said Nation by the Honorable Secretary of the Interior, his final enrollment number being 7845 and that a female child was born to me on the 25 day of ~~May~~ April 190 4 ; that said child has been named Corinne Moore , and is now living.

                                                                    Lena Moore

Witnesseth.
Must be two Witnesses who are Citizens.   } Rufus Rabon
                                            J W. Rabon

Subscribed and sworn to before me this 12" day of Jan 190 5

                                                    L.C. Tiney
                                                        Notary Public.

My commission expires: Jan 17-1907

AFFIDAVIT OF ATTENDING PHYSICIAN OR MIDWIFE

UNITED STATES OF AMERICA
INDIAN TERRITORY
Western   DISTRICT

I, E. Johnson a practicing physician on oath state that I attended on Mrs. Lena Moore wife of Herbert M Moore on the 25 day of ~~May~~ April , 190 4 , that there was born to her on said date a female child, that said child is now living, and is said to have been named Corinne Moore

                                        E. Johnson M.D.

Subscribed and sworn to before me this, the 6" day of Jan 190 5

WITNESSETH: L.C. Tiney   Notary Public.
Must be two witnesses who are citizens { Rufus Rabon
                                          J.W. Rabon

Applications for Enrollment of Choctaw Newborn
Act of 1905   Volume IV

We hereby certify that we are well acquainted with   E. Johnson a practicing physician   and know   him   to be reputable and of good standing in the community.

Rufus Rabon   _____

J.W. Rabon   _____

BIRTH AFFIDAVIT.

DEPARTMENT OF THE INTERIOR.
COMMISSION TO THE FIVE CIVILIZED TRIBES.

IN RE APPLICATION FOR ENROLLMENT, as a citizen of the   Choctaw   Nation, of   Corinne Moore   , born on the 25th day of   April   , 1904

Name of Father: Herbert M Moore   a citizen of the   Choctaw   Nation.
Name of Mother: Lena McCurtain   a citizen of the   Choctaw   Nation.

Postoffice   Kinta Ind Ter

AFFIDAVIT OF MOTHER.

UNITED STATES OF AMERICA, Indian Territory, }
   Western   DISTRICT.

I, Lena Moore   , on oath state that I am   24   years of age and a citizen by blood   , of the   Choctaw   Nation; that I am the lawful wife of   Herbert M Moore, who is a citizen, by blood   of the   Choctaw   Nation; that a   female   child was born to me on   25th day of   April   , 1904; that said child has been named Corinne Moore   , and was living March 4, 1905.

    Lena Moore

Witnesses To Mark:
{

Subscribed and sworn to before me this   20th day of   March   , 1904

    [Name Illegible]
    Notary Public.

My Commission expires March 4th 1907

Applications for Enrollment of Choctaw Newborn
Act of 1905   Volume IV

AFFIDAVIT OF ATTENDING PHYSICIAN OR MID-WIFE.

UNITED STATES OF AMERICA, Indian Territory,
Western   DISTRICT.

I, E Johnson , a physician , on oath state that I attended on Mrs. Lena Moore , wife of Herbert M Moore on the 25th day of April , 1904; that there was born to her on said date a female child; that said child was living March 4, 1905, and is said to have been named Corinne Moore

E Johnson MD

Witnesses To Mark:

{

Subscribed and sworn to before me this 20th day of March , 1904

[Name Illegible]
Notary Public.

My Commission expires March 4th 1907

7-1931

Muskogee, Indian Territory, March 25, 1905.

Herbert M. Moore,
    Kinta, Indian Territory.

Dear Sir:

Receipt is hereby acknowledged of your letter without date enclosing affidavits of Lena Moore and E. Johnson to the birth of Corine[sic] Moore, daughter of Herbert M. and Lena Moore, April 25, 1904, and the same have been filed with our records as an application for the enrollment of said child.

Respectfully,

Chairman.

Applications for Enrollment of Choctaw Newborn
Act of 1905   Volume IV

7-NB-219

Muskogee, Indian Territory, July 18, 1905.

H. M. Moore,
    Kinta, Indian Territory.

Dear Sir:

    Receipt is hereby acknowledged of your letter of July 7, 1905, stating that you have a child who will come in under the new roll and you which to be advised when selection of allotment can be made; you also ask whether it will be necessary for the mother of the child to appear at the land office or if you will be permitted to file for said child.

    In reply to your letter you are advised that the enrollment of your child Corinne Moore was on June 30, 1905 approved by the Secretary of the Interior and selection of allotment may now be made in her behalf.

    You are advised that being a citizen you will be permitted to select an allotment for said child and it will not be necessary for the mother to appear at the land office for that purpose.

                  Respectfully,

                  Commissioner.

Choc New Born 220
    Houston Leflore
    (Born Nov. 24, 1902)

BIRTH AFFIDAVIT.

Department of the Interior,
COMMISSION TO THE FIVE CIVILIZED TRIBES.

    IN RE APPLICATION FOR ENROLLMENT, as a citizen of the Choctaw Nation, of Houston Leflore, born on the 24 day of November, 1902

Name of Father: Joseph Leflore   a citizen of the Choctaw Nation.
Name of Mother: Selina Leflore   a citizen of the Choctaw Nation.

                Post-Office: Leflore I.T.

Applications for Enrollment of Choctaw Newborn
Act of 1905   Volume IV

AFFIDAVIT OF MOTHER.

UNITED STATES OF AMERICA,
INDIAN TERRITORY,
Central District.

I, Selina Leflore, on oath state that I am 36 years of age and a citizen by Blood, of the Choctaw Nation; that I am the lawful wife of Joseph Leflore, who is a citizen, by Blood of the Choctaw Nation; that a male child was born to me on 24 day of November, 190 2, that said child has been named Houston Leflore, and is now living.

                                          her
                                  Selina x Leflore

WITNESSES TO MARK: mark
    { James Adames[sic]
      Jeff Goin

Subscribed and sworn to before me this 19 day of December, 190 2.

My Com Expires   James Culberson
Feb-26-1906   *Notary Public.*

AFFIDAVIT OF ATTENDING PHYSICIAN OR MID-WIFE.

UNITED STATES OF AMERICA,
INDIAN TERRITORY,
Central District.

I, Sillis Yotah, a nurse, on oath state that I attended on Mrs. Selina Leflore, wife of Joseph Leflore on the 24 day of November, 190 2 ; that there was born to her on said date a male child; that said child is now living and is said to have been named Houston Leflore

                                          her
                                  Sillis x Yotah

WITNESSES TO MARK: mark
    { James Adames[sic]
      Jeff Goin

Subscribed and sworn to before me this 19 day of December, 190 2.

My Com Expires   James Culberson
Feb-26-1906   *Notary Public.*

Applications for Enrollment of Choctaw Newborn
Act of 1905   Volume IV

NEW BORN AFFIDAVIT

No _____

CHOCTAW ENROLLING COMMISSION

IN THE MATTER OF THE APPLICATION FOR ENROLLMENT as a citizen of the Choctaw Nation, of   Houston Leflore   born on the   14[sic] day of   November   190 2

Name of father   Joseph Leflore   a citizen of   Choctaw   Nation, final enrollment No.   13951
Name of mother   Selina Leflore   a citizen of   Choctaw   Nation, final enrollment No.   8563

Leflore I.T.   Postoffice.

AFFIDAVIT OF MOTHER

UNITED STATES OF AMERICA
INDIAN TERRITORY
DISTRICT   Central

I   Selina Leflore   , on oath state that I am   38   years of age and a citizen by   blood   of the   Choctaw   Nation, and as such have been placed upon the final roll of the   Choctaw   Nation, by the Honorable Secretary of the Interior my final enrollment number being   8563   ; that I am the lawful wife of   Joseph Leflore   , who is a citizen of the   Choctaw   Nation, and as such has been placed upon the final roll of said Nation by the Honorable Secretary of the Interior, his final enrollment number being   13951   and that a   Male   child was born to me on the   14[sic] day of   November   190 2; that said child has been named   Houston Leflore   , and is now living.

WITNESSETH:
Must be two witnesses who are citizens { Willy Blue
Thomas Adams

her
Selina x Leflore
mark

Subscribed and sworn to before me this, the   17   day of   February   , 190 5

James Bower
Notary Public.

My Commission Expires:
Sept 23, 1907

Applications for Enrollment of Choctaw Newborn
Act of 1905   Volume IV

Affidavit of Attending Physician or Midwife

UNITED STATES OF AMERICA,
INDIAN TERRITORY,
Central   DISTRICT

I, Joseph Leflore   a n   Attendant on oath state that I attended on Mrs. Selina Leflore wife of Joseph Leflore on the 14[sic] day of November, 190 2, that there was born to her on said date a male child, that said child is now living, and is said to have been named Houston Leflore

Joseph Leflore   M. D.

Subscribed and sworn to before me this the   17   day of   February   1905

James Bower
Notary Public.

WITNESSETH:
Must be two witnesses who are citizens and know the child.
{ Willy Blue
  Thomas Adams

We hereby certify that we are well acquainted with   Joseph Leflore   a n   Attendant   and know   him   to be reputable and of good standing in the community.

Must be two citizen witnesses.
{ Willy Blue
  Thomas Adams

BIRTH AFFIDAVIT.

DEPARTMENT OF THE INTERIOR.
COMMISSION TO THE FIVE CIVILIZED TRIBES.

IN RE APPLICATION FOR ENROLLMENT, as a citizen of the   Choctaw   Nation, of   Houston LeFlore   , born on the 14[sic] day of November   , 1902

Name of Father: Joseph LeFlore   a citizen of the   Choctaw   Nation.
Name of Mother: Selina LeFlore   a citizen of the   Choctaw   Nation.

Postoffice   LeFlore I.T.

Applications for Enrollment of Choctaw Newborn
Act of 1905   Volume IV

AFFIDAVIT OF MOTHER.

UNITED STATES OF AMERICA, Indian Territory,
Central   DISTRICT.

 I, Selina LeFlore, on oath state that I am 38 years of age and a citizen by blood, of the Choctaw Nation; that I am the lawful wife of Joseph LeFlore, who is a citizen, by blood of the Choctaw Nation; that a male child was born to me on 14[sic] day of November, 1902; that said child has been named Houston LeFlore, and was living March 4, 1905.

           her
         Selina x LeFlore
Witnesses To Mark: mark
 { R.B. Green
   S.G. Tiffer

 Subscribed and sworn to before me this 8 day of April, 1905

         Robert E. Lee
          Notary Public.
My com. expires Jan. 11-1906

AFFIDAVIT OF ATTENDING PHYSICIAN OR MID-WIFE.

UNITED STATES OF AMERICA, Indian Territory,
Central   DISTRICT.

 I, Cillis Yota, a midwife, on oath state that I attended on Mrs. , wife of on the 14[sic] day of November, 1902; that there was born to her on said date a male child; that said child was living March 4, 1905, and is said to have been named Houston LeFlore

         her
        Cillis x Yota
Witnesses To Mark: mark
 { R.B. Green
   S.G. Tiffer

 Subscribed and sworn to before me this 8 day of April, 1905

         Robert E. Lee
          Notary Public.
My com. expires Jan. 11-1906

Final enrollment of Joseph LeFlore being No. 13951
Final enrollment of Selina LeFlore being No. 8563

Applications for Enrollment of Choctaw Newborn
Act of 1905   Volume IV

7-2908.

Muskogee, Indian Territory, December 30, 1902.

Selina LeFlore,
    LeFlore, Indian Territory.

Dear Madam:

    Receipt is hereby acknowledged of the application for enrollment as a citizen of the Choctaw Nation of Houston Leflore, infant son of Joseph and Selina LeFlore, born November 24, 1902.

    You are advised that the Commission is without authority to enroll this child, it appearing that it was born November 24, 1902, subsequent to the date of the ratification on September 25, 1902, of the act of Congress approved July 1, 1902.

    Section twenty-eight thereof is as follows:

    "The names of all persons living on the date of the final ratification of this agreement entitled to be enrolled as provided in section 27 hereof shall be placed upon the rolls made by said Commission; and no child born thereafter to a citizen or freedman and no person intermarried thereafter to a citizen shall be entitled to enrollment or to participate in the distribution of the tribal property of the Choctaws and Chickasaws."

    Respectfully,

    Acting Chairman.

COPY.   N. B. 220

Muskogee, Indian Territory, April 7, 1905.

Joseph LeFlore,
    LeFlore, Indian Territory.

Dear Sir:

    There is inclosed you herewith for execution application for the enrollment of your infant child, Houston LeFlore, born November 24, 1902.

    The affidavits heretofore filed with the Commission show the child was living on December 19, 1902. It is necessary, for the child to be enrolled, that he was living on March 4, 1905.

    In having these affidavits executed care should be exercised to see that all the names are written in full as they appear in the body of the affidavit, and in the event that either of the persons signing the affidavit are unable to write, signatures by mark must be

Applications for Enrollment of Choctaw Newborn
Act of 1905   Volume IV

attested by two witnesses. Each affidavit must be executed before a Notary Public and the notarial seal and signature of the officer must be attached to each separate affidavit.

Respectfully,
SIGNED

T.B. Needles

LM 7-20   Commissioner in Charge.

Choctaw 2908.

Muskogee, Indian Territory, April 12, 1905.

Joseph Le Flore,
      Le Flore, Indian Territory.

Dear Sir:

   Receipt is hereby acknowledged of the affidavits of Selina Le Flore and Cillis Yota to the birth of Houston Le Flore, son of Joseph and Selina Le Flore, November 14th[sic], 1902, and the same have been filed with our records as an application for the enrollment of said child.

Respectfully,

Commissioner in Charge.

[The letter below does not belong with the current applicant.]

9-NB-220

Muskogee, Indian Territory, July 24, 1905.

Lankford Anatubby,
      Isom Springs, Indian Territory.

Dear Sir:

   Receipt is hereby acknowledged of your letter of July 18, 1905, in which you state that your wife is a Chickasaw by blood and is named Jane Anatubby and that you know nothing whatever about the child of Letice Arpela who claims to be your wife.

   This information has been made a matter of record.

Respectfully,

Commissioner.

Applications for Enrollment of Choctaw Newborn
Act of 1905   Volume IV

Choc New Born 221
    Mutien Pope
    (Born June 15, 1914)

- D E P A R T M E N T OF THE I N T E R I O R -
Commission to the Five Civilized Tribes.

APPLICATION FOR ENROLLMENT, as a citizen of the Choctaw Natoin[sic], of Mutien Pope born on the 15 Dau of June 1904. Name of Father, Gilbert Pope a citizen of the Choctaw Nation. Name of Mother: Lucy Pope a citizen of the Choctaw Nation.

POST OFFICE: Krebs I.T.

Affidavit of Mother.

UNITED STATES OF AMERICA|
    Indian Territory. |
  Central   District |

I Lucy Pope on oath state that I am 26 Years of age and a Citizen by Blood of the Choctaw Nation, that I am the lawful wife of Gilbert Pope who is a citizen by Blood of the Choctaw Nation, that a Male child was born to me on the 15 day of June 1904, that said child has been Names Mutien Pope and is now living[sic] ….

                                          her
                               Lucy x Pope
                                 mark

Must be to[sic] | Lee Silmon
witnesses. | John Emos

Subscribed and sworn to before me this 9 day of Jan 1905.

                            W.J. Oglesby
                            Notary Public.

                Affidavid[sic] of attending Physician or Midwife.
Central District.
Indian Territory.
          I Fannie Sam a Midwife on oath state that I attended on Mrs Lucy Pope wife of Gilbert Pope on the 15 day of June 1904 that there was born to her on said date a male child; that said child is now living and is said to have been named Mutien Pope

                                 Fannie x Sam

Applications for Enrollment of Choctaw Newborn
Act of 1905   Volume IV

Lee Silmon
John Emos

Subscribed and sworn to before me this 9 day of Jan 1905.

         W.J. Oglesby   Notary Public.

BIRTH AFFIDAVIT.

DEPARTMENT OF THE INTERIOR.
COMMISSION TO THE FIVE CIVILIZED TRIBES.

  IN RE APPLICATION FOR ENROLLMENT, as a citizen of the   Choctaw   Nation, of   Mutien Pope   , born on the   15   day of   June   , 1904

Name of Father: Gilbert Pope   a citizen of the   Choctaw   Nation.
Name of Mother: Lucy Pope   a citizen of the   Choctaw   Nation.

      Postoffice   Krebs   I.T.

AFFIDAVIT OF MOTHER.

UNITED STATES OF AMERICA, Indian Territory, }
 Central   DISTRICT. }

  I,   Lucy Pope   , on oath state that I am   26   years of age and a citizen by blood   , of the   Choctaw   Nation; that I am the lawful wife of   Gilbert   , who is a citizen, by blood   of the   Choctaw   Nation; that a   Male   child was born to me on   15   day of   June   , 1904; that said child has been named   Mutien Pope   , and was living March 4, 1905.

           her
         Lucy x Pope
Witnesses To Mark: mark
 { Jno [Illegible]
 { Minnie Oglesby

  Subscribed and sworn to before me this   22   day of   March   , 1905

         W J Oglesby
          Notary Public.

Applications for Enrollment of Choctaw Newborn
Act of 1905   Volume IV

AFFIDAVIT OF ATTENDING PHYSICIAN OR MID-WIFE.

UNITED STATES OF AMERICA, Indian Territory, }
Central   DISTRICT. }

I, Sallie Riply   , a   Mid Wife   , on oath state that I attended on Mrs. Lucy Pope   , wife of Gilbert Pope   on the 15 day of June   , 1904; that there was born to her on said date a   male   child; that said child was living March 4, 1905, and is said to have been named   Mutien Pope

                                her
                            Sallie x Riply
Witnesses To Mark: mark
 { Jno [Illegible]
 { Minnie Oglesby

Subscribed and sworn to before me this 22 day of   March   , 1905

                            W J Oglesby
                                Notary Public.

7-2933

Muskogee, Indian Territory, January 19, 1905.

Gilbert Pope,
        Krebs, Indian Territory.

Dear Sir:

Receipt is hereby acknowledged of the affidavits of Lucy Pope and Fannie Sam to the birth of Mutien Pope, minor son of Gilbert and Lucy Pope June 15, 1904, which it is presumed have been forwarded as an application for the enrollment of said child.

You are advised that under the provisions of the act of Congress approved July 1, 1902, no children born to recognized and enrolled citizens of the Choctaw and Chickasaw Nations subsequent to September 25, 1902, the date of the ratification of said act, are entitled to enrollment and allotment in the Choctaw and Chickasaw Nations.

            Respectfully,

                    Chairman.

Applications for Enrollment of Choctaw Newborn
Act of 1905 Volume IV

7-2933

Muskogee, Indian Territory, March 25, 1905.

Gilbert Pope,
    Krebs, Indian Territory.

Dear Sir:

    Receipt is hereby acknowledged of the affidavits of Lucy Pope and Sallie Ripley[sic] to the birth of Mutien Pope, son of Gilbert and Lucy Pope, June 15, 1904, and the same have been filed with our records as an application for the enrollment of said child.

    Respectfully,

    Chairman.

Choc New Born 222
    Amanda May Fetter
    (Born May 25, 1903)
    Nina Belle Fetter
    (Born Feb. 3, 1905)

BIRTH AFFIDAVIT.

DEPARTMENT OF THE INTERIOR,
COMMISSION TO THE FIVE CIVILIZED TRIBES.

In Re Application for Enrollment, as a citizen of the Choctaw Nation, of Manda May Fetter , born on the 25 day of May 1903 , 1......

Name of Father: O.B. Fetter   a citizen of the Choctaw Nation.
Name of Mother: Abbie Fetter   a citizen of the Choctaw Nation.

    Post-office   Lutie I.T.

Applications for Enrollment of Choctaw Newborn
Act of 1905   Volume IV

AFFIDAVIT OF MOTHER.

UNITED STATES OF AMERICA, }
 INDIAN TERRITORY,
................................District. }

I, Abbie Fetter , on oath state that I am 26 years of age and a citizen by Blood , of the Choctaw Nation; that I am the lawful wife of O.B. Fetter , who is a citizen, by Marriage of the Choctaw Nation; that a Female child was born to me on 25 day of May 1903 , 1......., that said child has been named Mandy[sic] May Fetter , and is now living.

her
Abbie Fetter x
mark

WITNESSES TO MARK:
{ Bell Reynolds
{ Mrs M H Bain

Subscribed and sworn to before me this 15 day of March , 1904

R.J. Charles
NOTARY PUBLIC.

AFFIDAVIT OF ATTENDING PHYSICIAN OR MID-WIFE.

UNITED STATES OF AMERICA, }
 INDIAN TERRITORY,
 Central   District. }

I, Bell Reynolds , a Midwife , on oath state that I attended on Mrs. Abbie Fetter , wife of O.B. Fetter on the 25 day of May , 1903 ; that there was born to her on said date a Female child; that said child is now living and is said to have been named Mandy May Fetter

Bell Reynolds

WITNESSES TO MARK:
{
{

Subscribed and sworn to before me this 15 day of March , 1904

R.J. Charles
NOTARY PUBLIC.

Applications for Enrollment of Choctaw Newborn
Act of 1905 Volume IV

BIRTH AFFIDAVIT.

DEPARTMENT OF THE INTERIOR,
COMMISSION TO THE FIVE CIVILIZED TRIBES.

In Re Application for Enrollment, as a citizen of the Choctaw Nation, of Nina Belle Fetter, born on the 3 day of February, 1905

Name of Father: Olliver B. Fetter   a citizen of the Choctaw Nation.
Name of Mother: Abigail Fetter   a citizen of the Choctaw Nation.

Post-office   Lutie Ind Ter

AFFIDAVIT OF MOTHER.

UNITED STATES OF AMERICA,
INDIAN TERRITORY,
.... District.

I, Abigail Fetter, on oath state that I am 27 years of age and a citizen by Blood, of the Choctaw Nation; that I am the lawful wife of Olliver B. Fetter, who is a citizen, by Marriage of the Choctaw Nation; that a Female child was born to me on 3rd day of February, 1905, that said child has been named Nina Belle Fetter, and is now living.

                       her
                Abbie Fetter x
WITNESSES TO MARK: mark
   { Harry Fetters[sic]
     A J Charles

Subscribed and sworn to before me this 15 day of February, 1905

                    R.J. Charles
                       NOTARY PUBLIC.

AFFIDAVIT OF ATTENDING PHYSICIAN OR MID-WIFE.

UNITED STATES OF AMERICA,
INDIAN TERRITORY,
.... District.

I, James C. Johnston, a regular physician, on oath state that I attended on Mrs. Abigail Fetter, wife of Olliver B. Fetter on the 3 day of February, 1905 ; that there was born to her on said date a Female child; that said child is now living and is said to have been named Nina Belle Fetter

                Dr James C Johnston

Applications for Enrollment of Choctaw Newborn
Act of 1905 Volume IV

WITNESSES TO MARK:

Subscribed and sworn to before me this 16 day of February , 1905

R.J. Charles
NOTARY PUBLIC.

BIRTH AFFIDAVIT.

DEPARTMENT OF THE INTERIOR.
COMMISSION TO THE FIVE CIVILIZED TRIBES.

IN RE APPLICATION FOR ENROLLMENT, as a citizen of the Choctaw Nation, of Amanda May Fetter , born on the 25th day of May , 1903

Name of Father: Oliver B. Better   a citizen of the United States ~~Nation~~.
Name of Mother: Abigail Fetter   a citizen of the Choctaw Nation.

Postoffice Lutie, I.T.

AFFIDAVIT OF MOTHER.

UNITED STATES OF AMERICA, Indian Territory,
Central   **DISTRICT.**

I, Abigail Fetter , on oath state that I am 28 years of age and a citizen by blood , of the Choctaw Nation; that I am the lawful wife of Oliver B. Fetter , who is a citizen, ~~by~~ .... of the United States ~~Nation~~; that a female child was born to me on 25th day of May , 1903; that said child has been named Amanda May Fetter , and was living March 4, 1905.

                             her
                      Abigail x Fetter
Witnesses To Mark: mark
   Richard R. Riddle
   Thomas Riddle

Subscribed and sworn to before me this 23rd day of March , 1905

Wirt Franklin
Notary Public.

Applications for Enrollment of Choctaw Newborn
Act of 1905   Volume IV

AFFIDAVIT OF ATTENDING PHYSICIAN OR MID-WIFE.

UNITED STATES OF AMERICA, Indian Territory, }
Central   DISTRICT. }

I, Cecelia Hunter , a -------------- , on oath state that I attended on Mrs. Abigail Fetter , wife of Oliver B. Fetter on the 25th day of May , 1903; that there was born to her on said date a female child; that said child was living March 4, 1905, and is said to have been named Amanda May Fetter

                                            her
                                  Cecelia x Hunter

Witnesses To Mark: mark
   { Peter Maytubby, Jr
   { Victor M Locke Jr

Subscribed and sworn to before me this 23rd day of March , 1905

                                      Wirt Franklin
                                            Notary Public.

BIRTH AFFIDAVIT.

DEPARTMENT OF THE INTERIOR.
COMMISSION TO THE FIVE CIVILIZED TRIBES.

IN RE APPLICATION FOR ENROLLMENT, as a citizen of the Choctaw Nation, of Nina Belle Fetter[sic] , born on the 3rd day of February , 1905

Name of Father: Oliver B. Better   a citizen of the United States ~~Nation~~.
Name of Mother: Abigail Fetter   a citizen of the Choctaw Nation.

                          Postoffice   Lutie, I.T.

AFFIDAVIT OF MOTHER.

UNITED STATES OF AMERICA, Indian Territory, }
Central   DISTRICT. }

I, Abigail Fetter , on oath state that I am 28 years of age and a citizen by blood , of the Choctaw Nation; that I am the lawful wife of Oliver B. Fetter , who is a citizen, ~~by~~ ....of the United States ~~Nation~~; that a female child was born to me on 25th day of May , 1903; that said child has been named Amanda May Fetter , and was living March 4, 1905.   her
                                        Abigail x Fetter
                                          mark

Applications for Enrollment of Choctaw Newborn
Act of 1905   Volume IV

Witnesses To Mark:
  { Richard R. Riddle
  { Thomas Riddle

    Subscribed and sworn to before me this   23rd day of   March   , 1905

                                    Wirt Franklin
                                      Notary Public.

AFFIDAVIT OF ATTENDING PHYSICIAN OR MID-WIFE.

UNITED STATES OF AMERICA, Indian Territory, }
  Central   DISTRICT. }

    I,   Cecelia Hunter   , a -------------- , on oath state that I attended on Mrs. Abigail Fetter   , wife of   Oliver B. Fetter   on the 25th day of   May , 1903; that there was born to her on said date a   female   child; that said child was living March 4, 1905, and is said to have been named   Amanda May Fetter
                                        her
                               Cecelia   x   Hunter
Witnesses To Mark: mark
  { Peter Maybubby Jr
  { Victor M Locke Jr.

    Subscribed and sworn to before me this 23rd   day of   March   , 1905

                                      Wirt Franklin
                                      Notary Public.

BIRTH AFFIDAVIT.
                          DEPARTMENT OF THE INTERIOR.
                 COMMISSION TO THE FIVE CIVILIZED TRIBES.

    IN RE APPLICATION FOR ENROLLMENT, as a citizen of the   Choctaw   Nation, of Nina Belle Fetter   , born on the 3rd   day of February , 1905

Name of Father: Oliver B. Better   a citizen of the United States Nation.
Name of Mother: Abigail Fetter   a citizen of the   Choctaw   Nation.

                        Postoffice   Lutie, I.T.

Applications for Enrollment of Choctaw Newborn
Act of 1905   Volume IV

AFFIDAVIT OF MOTHER.

UNITED STATES OF AMERICA, Indian Territory, }
Central   DISTRICT.

I, Abigail Fetter, on oath state that I am 28 years of age and a citizen by blood, of the Choctaw Nation; that I am the lawful wife of Oliver B. Fetter, who is a citizen, by ....of the United States Nation; that a female child was born to me on 3rd day of February, 1905; that said child has been named Nina Belle Fetter, and was living March 4, 1905.

             her
            Abigail x Fetter
             mark

Witnesses To Mark:
{ Wm Fetter
{ Thomas Riddle

Subscribed and sworn to before me this 23rd day of March, 1905

            Wirt Franklin
             Notary Public.

AFFIDAVIT OF ATTENDING PHYSICIAN OR MID-WIFE.

UNITED STATES OF AMERICA, Indian Territory, }
Central   DISTRICT.

I, Cecelia Hunter, a --------------, on oath state that I attended on Mrs. Abigail Fetter, wife of Oliver B. Fetter on the 3rd day of February, 1905; that there was born to her on said date a female child; that said child was living March 4, 1905, and is said to have been named Nina Belle Fetter

             her
           Cecelia x Hunter
Witnesses To Mark: mark
{ Robt. R. Bennett
{ George W. Wachtel

Subscribed and sworn to before me this 23rd day of March, 1905

            Wirt Franklin
             Notary Public.

Applications for Enrollment of Choctaw Newborn
Act of 1905 Volume IV

7-NB-222.

Muskogee, Indian Territory, June 10, 1905.

O. B. Fetter,
    Lutie, Indian Territory.

Dear Sir:

    Receipt is hereby acknowledged of your letter of June 1, asking if the enrollment of your children, Amanda May and Nina Belle Fetter, has been approved.

    In reply to your letter you are advised that the names of your children, Amanda May Fetter and Nina Belle Fetter, have been placed upon a schedule of citizens by blood of the Choctaw Nation, which has been forwarded to the Secretary of the Interior, and you will be informed when their enrollment is approved by him.

Respectfully,

Chairman.

Choc New Born 223
    Rebecca Jency Hembree
    (Born Dec. 4, 1903)

BIRTH AFFIDAVIT.

DEPARTMENT OF THE INTERIOR,
COMMISSION TO THE FIVE CIVILIZED TRIBES.

In Re Application for Enrollment, as a citizen of the Choctaw Nation, of Ind Ter , born on the 4 day of December , 1903

Name of Father: William Hembree   a citizen of the Choctaw Nation.
Name of Mother: Amy Hembree   a citizen of the Choctaw Nation.

Post-office   Farris, Ind Ter

Applications for Enrollment of Choctaw Newborn
Act of 1905 Volume IV

AFFIDAVIT OF MOTHER.

UNITED STATES OF AMERICA,
   INDIAN TERRITORY,
Central   District.

I, Amy Hembree, on oath state that I am 22 years of age and a citizen by blood, of the Choctaw Nation; that I am the lawful wife of William Hembree, who is a citizen, by marriage of the Choctaw Nation; that a female child was born to me on 4 day of December, 1903, that said child has been named Rebecca Jency Hembree, and is now living.

                                      Amy Hembree

WITNESSES TO MARK:
- A.J. Stewart
- J F Allen

Subscribed and sworn to before me this 25 day of January, 1904

                                       A F Keener
                                       NOTARY PUBLIC.

AFFIDAVIT OF ATTENDING PHYSICIAN OR MID-WIFE.

UNITED STATES OF AMERICA,
   INDIAN TERRITORY,
Central   District.

I, Dr Wm Davis, a Physician, on oath state that I attended on Mrs. Amy Hembree, wife of William Hembree on the 4 day of December, 1903; that there was born to her on said date a female child; that said child is now living and is said to have been named Rebecca Jency Hembree

                                       William Davis

WITNESSES TO MARK:
- J.R. McDonald
- C W Gould

Subscribed and sworn to before me this 25 day of ...., 190....

                                     A F Keener N.P.
                                       NOTARY PUBLIC.

Applications for Enrollment of Choctaw Newborn
Act of 1905   Volume IV

NEW-BORN AFFIDAVIT.

Number..........

...Choctaw Enrolling Commission...

IN THE MATTER OF THE APPLICATION FOR ENROLLMENT, as a citizen of the Choctaw Nation, of Rebecca Jincy[sic] Hembree

born on the 4th day of December 190 4[sic]

Name of father William Hembree   a citizen of Choctaw
Nation final enrollment No. 310
Name of mother Amy Hembree   a citizen of Choctaw
Nation final enrollment No. 9467

Postoffice   Farris I.T.

AFFIDAVIT OF MOTHER.

UNITED STATES OF AMERICA
INDIAN TERRITORY
   Central   DISTRICT

I Amy Hembree, on oath state that I am 23 years of age and a citizen by blood of the Choctaw Nation, and as such have been placed upon the final roll of the Choctaw Nation, by the Honorable Secretary of the Interior my final enrollment number being 9467 ; that I am the lawful wife of William Hembree, who is a citizen of the Choctaw Nation, and as such has been placed upon the final roll of said Nation by the Honorable Secretary of the Interior, his final enrollment number being 310 and that a Female child was born to me on the 4th day of December 190 4; that said child has been named Rebecca Jincey Hembree, and is now living.

                                                Amy Hembree

Witnesseth.
   Must be two ⎫ William P Anderson
   Witnesses who ⎬
   are Citizens. ⎭ Jackson Corn

Subscribed and sworn to before me this 4th day of March 190 5

                                    A.E. Folsom
                                        Notary Public.

My commission expires:
   Jan 9-1909

Applications for Enrollment of Choctaw Newborn
Act of 1905 Volume IV

AFFIDAVIT OF ATTENDING PHYSICIAN OR MIDWIFE

UNITED STATES OF AMERICA
INDIAN TERRITORY
Central   DISTRICT

I, William Davis   a   Practicing Physician on oath state that I attended on Mrs. Amy Hembree   wife of William Hembree on the 4th day of December , 190 4, that there was born to her on said date a   Female child, that said child is now living, and is said to have been named   Rebecca Jincey Hembree

William Davis   M.D.

WITNESSETH:
Must be two witnesses who are citizens and know the child.
{ William P Anderson
  Jackson Corn

Subscribed and sworn to before me this, the   4   day of March   190 5

Calvin W Meek   Notary Public.

We hereby certify that we are well acquainted with   Dr William Davis   a Practicing Physician   and know   him   to be reputable and of good standing in the community.

{ William P Anderson
  Jackson Corn

BIRTH AFFIDAVIT.

DEPARTMENT OF THE INTERIOR.
COMMISSION TO THE FIVE CIVILIZED TRIBES.

IN RE APPLICATION FOR ENROLLMENT, as a citizen of the   Choctaw   Nation, of   Rebeca Jencey Hembree[sic] , born on the 4th day of December , 1904

Name of Father: William Hembree   a citizen of the Choctaw   Nation.
Name of Mother: Amy Hembree   a citizen of the Choctaw   Nation.

Postoffice   Farris Indian Territory

Applications for Enrollment of Choctaw Newborn
Act of 1905   Volume IV

AFFIDAVIT OF MOTHER.

UNITED STATES OF AMERICA, Indian Territory, }
Central   DISTRICT.

I, Amy Hembree, on oath state that I am 23 years of age and a citizen by Blood, of the Choctaw Nation; that I am the lawful wife of William Hembree, who is a citizen, by Marriage of the Choctaw Nation; that a Female child was born to me on 4th day of December, 1904; that said child has been named Rebecca Jencey Hembree, and was living March 4, 1905.

                                      Amy Hembree

Witnesses To Mark:
  { George Burney
    Willie Kenup

Subscribed and sworn to before me this 15th day of March, 1905

                                      C B Prather
                                      Notary Public.

AFFIDAVIT OF ATTENDING PHYSICIAN OR MID-WIFE.

UNITED STATES OF AMERICA, Indian Territory, }
Central   DISTRICT.

I, William Davis, a midwife[sic], on oath state that I attended on Mrs. Amy Hembree, wife of William Hembree on the 4th day of December, 1904; that there was born to her on said date a Female child; that said child was living March 4, 1905, and is said to have been named Rebecca Jencey Hembree

                                      William Davis

Witnesses To Mark:
  { George Burney
    Willie Kenup

Subscribed and sworn to before me this 15th day of March, 1905

                                      C B Prather
                                      Notary Public.

Applications for Enrollment of Choctaw Newborn
Act of 1905   Volume IV

BIRTH AFFIDAVIT.

DEPARTMENT OF THE INTERIOR.
COMMISSION TO THE FIVE CIVILIZED TRIBES.

IN RE APPLICATION FOR ENROLLMENT, as a citizen of the Choctaw Nation, of Rebecca Jincy[sic] Hembree, born on the 4" day of December, 1904

Name of Father: William Hembree   a citizen of the Choctaw Nation.
Name of Mother: Amy Hembree   a citizen of the Choctaw Nation.

Postoffice   Farris Indian Territory

AFFIDAVIT OF MOTHER.

UNITED STATES OF AMERICA, Indian Territory,
Central   DISTRICT.

I, Amy Hembree, on oath state that I am 23 years of age and a citizen by blood, of the Choctaw Nation; that I am the lawful wife of William Hembree, who is a citizen, by intermarriage of the Choctaw Nation; that a Female child was born to me on 4" day of December, 1903; that said child has been named Rebecca Jincy Hembree, and was living March 4, 1905.

Amy Hembree

Witnesses To Mark:
 { Vinson Camp
   Tilson Jones

Subscribed and sworn to before me this 15th day of May, 1905

C B Prather
Notary Public.

AFFIDAVIT OF ATTENDING PHYSICIAN OR MID-WIFE.

UNITED STATES OF AMERICA, Indian Territory,
Central   DISTRICT.

I, William Davis, a midwife[sic], on oath state that I attended on Mrs. Amy Hembree, wife of William Hembree on the 4" day of December, 1903; that there was born to her on said date a female child; that said child was living March 4, 1905, and is said to have been named Rebecca Jincy Hembree

William Davis

Applications for Enrollment of Choctaw Newborn
Act of 1905   Volume IV

Witnesses To Mark:
- Vinson Camp
- Tilson Jones

Subscribed and sworn to before me this 15th day of May, 1905

C B Prather
Notary Public.

COMMISSIONERS:
TAMS BIXBY,
THOMAS B. NEEDLES,
C.R. BRECKINBRIDGE.

WM. O. BEALL
Secretary

DEPARTMENT OF THE INTERIOR,
COMMISSIONER TO THE FIVE CIVILIZED TRIBES.

$W^m O.B.$

REFER IN REPLY TO THE FOLLOWING:

7-3282

ADDRESS ONLY THE
COMMISSION TO THE FIVE CIVILIZED TRIBES.

Muskogee, Indian Territory, March 21, 1905.

William Hembree,
   Paris, Indian Territory.

Dear Sir:

   Receipt is hereby acknowledged of the affidavits of Amy Hembree and William Davis to the birth of Rebecca Jencey Hembree, daughter of William and Amy Hembree, December 4, 1904, and the same have been filed with our records as an application for the enrollment of said child.

   Respectfully,

   Tams Bixby
   Chairman.

COPY.   7-N.B.223.

Muskogee, Indian Territory, May 11. 1905.

William Hembree,
   Farris, Indian Territory.

Dear Sir:

   There is enclosed you herewith for execution application for the enrollment of your infant child, Rebecca Jincy Hembree, born December 4, 1903.

Applications for Enrollment of Choctaw Newborn
Act of 1905   Volume IV

In the affidavit of January 25, 1904, heretofore filed with the Commission, the date of the birth of the applicant is given as December 4, 1903, while in those of March 15, 1905, it is given a December 4, 1904. In the enclosed application, which you will please have executed and return, it is inserted as December 4, 1903, which is evidently correct.

In having these affidavits executed care should be exercised to see that all the names are written in full as they appear in the body of the affidavit, and in the event that either of the persons signing the affidavit are unable to write, signatures by mark must be attested by two witnesses. Each affidavit must be executed before a Notary Public and the notarial seal and signature of the officer must be attached to each separate affidavit.

Respectfully,
SIGNED

Tams Bixby

V. 11/8

Chairman.

7--N.B.223.

Muskogee, Indian Territory, May 25, 1905.

William Hembree,
    Farris, Indian Territory.

Dear Sir:

Receipt is hereby acknowledged of the affidavits of Amy Hembree and William Davis, to the birth of Rebecca Jincy Hembree, daughter of William and Amy Hembree, December 4, 1903, and the same have been filed with our records in the matter of the application for the enrollment of said child.

Respectfully,

Chairman

Applications for Enrollment of Choctaw Newborn
Act of 1905   Volume IV

Choc New Born 224
    Addie F. Case
    (Born March 9, 1905)

BIRTH AFFIDAVIT.

DEPARTMENT OF THE INTERIOR.
COMMISSION TO THE FIVE CIVILIZED TRIBES.

IN RE APPLICATION FOR ENROLLMENT, as a citizen of the   Choctaw   Nation, of   Addie F. Case   , born on the 9th   day of   March , 1903

                                                                        By intermarriage
Name of Father: Lee Case   a citizen of the   Choctaw   Nation.
Name of Mother: Lucy Case   a citizen of the   Choctaw   Nation.

                          Postoffice   Pauls Valley I.T.

AFFIDAVIT OF MOTHER.

UNITED STATES OF AMERICA, Indian Territory, }
   Southern   DISTRICT.

       I,   Lucy Case   , on oath state that I am   32   years of age and a citizen by Blood , of the   Choctaw   Nation; that I am the lawful wife of Lee Case   , who is a citizen, by intermarriage   of the   Choctaw   Nation; that a   Female child was born to me on   9th   day of   March   , 1903, that said child has been named   Addie F. Case   , and is now living.

                                                                    Lucy Case
Witnesses To Mark:
{

       Subscribed and sworn to before me this   11th   day of   March   , 1905.

                                                 Marion Henderson
                                                    Notary Public.

AFFIDAVIT OF ATTENDING PHYSICIAN OR MID-WIFE.

UNITED STATES OF AMERICA, Indian Territory, }
   Central   DISTRICT.

       I,   Lizzie F Bell   , a   midwife   , on oath state that I attended on Mrs.   Lucy Case   , wife of   Lee Case   on the   9" day of   March , 1903; that there was born to her on said date a   male   child; that said child is now living and is said to have been named   Addie F. Case

Applications for Enrollment of Choctaw Newborn
Act of 1905   Volume IV

Lizzie F Bell

Witnesses To Mark:
{ W Y Wooley
{ William Elliott

Subscribed and sworn to before me this 18 day of March , 1905.

Jas H Elliott
Notary Public.

7-3283

Muskogee, Indian Territory, March 22, 1905.

Lee Case,
    Pauls Valley, Indian Territory.

Dear Sir:

    Receipt is hereby acknowledged of the affidavits of Lucy Case and Lizzie F. Bell to the birth of Addie F. Case, daughter of Lee and Lucy Case, March 9, 1903, and the same have been filed with our records as an application for the enrollment of said child.

Respectfully,

Chairman.

Applications for Enrollment of Choctaw Newborn
Act of 1905   Volume IV

Choc New Born 225
    Martha Iler Dilbeck
    (Born March 2, 1904)

BIRTH AFFIDAVIT.

DEPARTMENT OF THE INTERIOR.
COMMISSION TO THE FIVE CIVILIZED TRIBES.

IN RE APPLICATION FOR ENROLLMENT, as a citizen of the Choctaw Nation, of Martha Iler Dilbeck, born on the 2 day of March, 1904.

Name of Father: S M Dilbeck   a citizen of the Choctaw Nation.
Name of Mother: Emeline Dilbeck   a citizen of the Choctaw Nation.

Postoffice   Non I.T.

AFFIDAVIT OF MOTHER.

UNITED STATES OF AMERICA, Indian Territory, }
    Central Dist.   DISTRICT. }

I, Emeline Dilbeck, on oath state that I am twenty five years of age and a citizen by Blood, of the Choctaw Nation; that I am the lawful wife of S. M. Dilbeck, who is a citizen, by Blood of the Choctaw Nation; that a female child was born to me on 2 day of March, 1904, that said child has been named Martha Iler Dilbeck, and is now living.

                                           Emeline Dilbeck

Witnesses To Mark:
{

Subscribed and sworn to before me this 19 day of Nov, 1904.

                                      C E McCain
                                         Notary Public.

AFFIDAVIT OF ATTENDING PHYSICIAN OR MID-WIFE.

UNITED STATES OF AMERICA, Indian Territory, }
    Central   DISTRICT. }

I, Phema Prince, a mid wife, on oath state that I attended on Mrs. Emeline Dilbeck, wife of S. M. Dilbeck on the 2 day of March,

Applications for Enrollment of Choctaw Newborn
Act of 1905   Volume IV

1904; that there was born to her on said date a   female   child; that said child is now living and is said to have been named   Martha Iler Dilbeck

                                              her
Witnesses To Mark: Phema x Prince
{ P.M. Parker   mark
{ S. M. Dilbeck

        Subscribed and sworn to before me this   19 day of   Nov   , 1904.

                                    C E McCain
                                    Notary Public.

NEW BORN AFFIDAVIT

No

CHOCTAW ENROLLING COMMISSION

    IN THE MATTER OF THE APPLICATION FOR ENROLLMENT as a citizen of the Choctaw Nation, of   Martha Iler Irine[sic] Dilbeck   born on the 2 day of   March   190 4

    Name of father   Stephen M Dilbeck   a citizen of   Choctaw   Nation, final enrollment No.   not enroled[sic]
    Name of mother   Emiline Delbek[sic]   a citizen of   Choctaw   Nation, final enrollment No.   9510

                                        Non   Postoffice.

AFFIDAVIT OF MOTHER

UNITED STATES OF AMERICA }
    INDIAN TERRITORY }
District   Central

    I Emiline Delbeck   , on oath state that I am   25   years of age and a citizen by   Blood   of the   Choctaw   Nation, and as such have been placed upon the final roll of the   Choctaw   Nation, by the Honorable Secretary of the Interior my final enrollment number being   9510   ; that I am the lawful wife of   Stephen M Dilbeck   , who is a citizen of the   Choctaw   Nation, and as such has been placed upon the final roll of said Nation by the Honorable Secretary of the Interior, his final enrollment number being

Applications for Enrollment of Choctaw Newborn
Act of 1905   Volume IV

0   and that a   female   child was born to me on the   2   day of   March   190 4; that said child has been named   Martha Iler Irine Dilbeck   , and is now living.

Emiline Dilbeck

WITNESSETH:
Must be two witnesses { S.W. Weaver
who are citizens   { E.A. Horner

Subscribed and sworn to before me this, the   17   day of   Feb   , 190 5

C. E. McCain
Notary Public.

My Commission Expires: May 17, 1908

Affidavit of Attending Physician or Midwife

UNITED STATES OF AMERICA,
    INDIAN TERRITORY,
Central   DISTRICT
Mrs.
    I,   Phema Prince   a   mid wife
on oath state that I attended on Mrs.   Emiline Dilbeck   wife of   Stephen M. Dilbeck
on the   2   day of   March   , 190 4, that there was born to her on said date a   female   child, that said child is now living, and is said to have been named   Martha Iler Irine Dilbeck

her
Mrs. Phema x Prince   M. W.
mark

Subscribed and sworn to before me this the   17   day of   Feb   1905

C.E. McCain
Notary Public.

WITNESSETH:
Must be two witnesses { S.W. Weaver
who are citizens and   {
know the child.   { E. A. Horner

We hereby certify that we are well acquainted with   Mrs. Phema Prince
a   mid wife   and know   her   to be reputable and of good standing in the community.

Must be two citizen { S.W. Weaver
witnesses.   { E.A. Horner

Applications for Enrollment of Choctaw Newborn
Act of 1905 Volume IV

BIRTH AFFIDAVIT.

DEPARTMENT OF THE INTERIOR.
COMMISSION TO THE FIVE CIVILIZED TRIBES.

IN RE APPLICATION FOR ENROLLMENT, as a citizen of the Choctaw Nation, of Martha Iler Dilbeck, born on the 2" day of March, 1904

Name of Father: S. M. Dilbeck   a citizen of the U.S. Nation.
Name of Mother: Emeline Dilbeck (Gillum)   a citizen of the Choctaw Nation.

Postoffice   Non, Ind. Ter.

AFFIDAVIT OF MOTHER.

UNITED STATES OF AMERICA, Indian Territory, DISTRICT.

enroled[sic] as
I, Emeline Dilbeck (Gillum), on oath state that I am 26 years of age and a citizen by Blood, of the Choctaw Nation; that I am the lawful wife of S.M. Dilbeck, who is a citizen, by -------------- of the United States Nation; that a Female child was born to me on 2" day of March, 1904; that said child has been named Martha Iler Dilbeck, and was living March 4, 1905.

                         Emeline Dilbeck

Witnesses To Mark:

Subscribed and sworn to before me this 15 day of Apr, 1905

                         C.E. McCain
                         Notary Public.

AFFIDAVIT OF ATTENDING PHYSICIAN OR MID-WIFE.

UNITED STATES OF AMERICA, Indian Territory, DISTRICT.

I, Phemey[sic] Prince, a Mid Wife, on oath state that I attended on Mrs. Emeline Dilbeck (Gillum), wife of S. M. Dilbeck on the 2" day of March, 1904; that there was born to her on said date a Female child; that said child was living March 4, 1905, and is said to have been named Martha Iler Dilbeck

                         her
                     Phemey x Prince
                        mark

Applications for Enrollment of Choctaw Newborn
Act of 1905 Volume IV

Witnesses To Mark:
{ John Prince
{ J.E. [Illegible]

Subscribed and sworn to before me this 15 day of Apr , 1905

C.E. McCain
Notary Public.

COPY.
Muskogee, Indian Territory, November 25, 1904.

Emeline Dilbeck,
Non, Indian Territory.

Dear Madam:

Receipt is hereby acknowledged of your affidavit and the affidavit of Phema Prince relative to the birth of Martha Iler Dilbeck, infant daughter of J.[sic] M. and Emma[sic] Dilbeck, March 2, 1904, which it is presumed have been forwarded as evidence of birth of the above named child.

You are advised from the information contained therein that the Commission is unable to identify you upon its records as an applicant for enrollment as a citizen of the Choctaw Nation and if application was made for your enrollment you are requested to state when, where, and under what name the same was made, the names of your parents, and the other members of the family who appeared at the same time, and any other information you may possess which will enable the Commission to identify you upon its records.

Respectfully,

SIGNED

Tams Bixby
Chairman.

Applications for Enrollment of Choctaw Newborn
Act of 1905   Volume IV

COPY.

N. B. 225

Muskogee, Indian Territory, April 11, 1905.

S. M. Dilbeck,
  Non, Indian Territory.

Dear Sir:

There is inclosed you herewith for execution application for the enrollment of your infant child, Martha Iler Dilbeck, born March 2, 1904.

The affidavits heretofore filed with the Commission show the child was living on November 19, 1904. It is necessary, for the child to be enrolled, that she was living on March 4, 1905. You will please insert the mother's age in the place left blank for that purpose.

In the affidavits heretofore forwarded it is stated that the mother, Emeline Dilbeck, is a citizen by blood of the Choctaw Nation.

If this is correct you are requested to state when, where and under what name she was listed for enrollment, the names of her parents and other members of her family for whom application was made at the same time, and if she has selected an allotment to give her roll number as the same appears upon her allotment certificate.

In having these affidavits executed care should be exercised to see that all the names are written in full as they appear in the body of the affidavit, and in the event that either of the persons signing the affidavit are unable to write, signatures by mark must be attested by two witnesses. Each affidavit must be executed before a Notary Public and the notarial seal and signature of the officer must be attached to each separate affidavit.

Respectfully,

SIGNED   T.B. Needles
Commissioner in Charge.

SEV 1-11

Applications for Enrollment of Choctaw Newborn
Act of 1905   Volume IV

                                      Choctaw N.B. 225,
COPY.   Choctaw 3307.

                Muskogee, Indian Territory, April 21, 1905.

Emeline Dilbeck,
      Non, Indian Territory.

Dear Madam:

      Receipt is hereby acknowledged of your letter of April 15, transmitting the affidavits of Emeline Dilbeck and Phemy Prince to the birth of Martha Iler Dilbeck, daughter of S. M. and Emeline Dilbeck (Gillum), March 2, 1904, and the same have been filed with our records in the matter of the enrollment of your child.

      Replying to that portion of your letter in which you state that since you were separated from your former husband, Gillum, you have married S. M. Dilbeck and you desire to have your name changed upon the rolls, you are advised that you have been enrolled by the Commission and your enrollment approved by the Secretary of the Interior under the name of Emeline Gillum and under that name you have selected an allotment of land in the Choctaw Nation.

      It is therefore impracticable to comply with your request that your name be changed upon the approved roll.

                                Respectfully,
                                SIGNED

                                Tams Bixby
                                Chairman.

Applications for Enrollment of Choctaw Newborn
Act of 1905   Volume IV

Choc New Born 226
    Ada Arlee Duer
    (Born Nov. 18, 1902)
    William Andrew Duer
    (Born Feb. 20, 1904)

After Sept. 25, 1902

BIRTH AFFIDAVIT.

DEPARTMENT OF THE INTERIOR,
COMMISSION TO THE FIVE CIVILIZED TRIBES.

    IN RE Application for Enrollment, as a citizen of the   Choctaw   Nation, of   Ada Arlee Duer   , born on the   18   day of   November   , 1902

Name of Father: Ephriam Duer   a citizen of the   Choctaw   Nation.
Name of Mother: Mary Duer   a citizen of the   Choctaw   Nation.

        Post-Office: Durant Ind. Terry

AFFIDAVIT OF MOTHER.

UNITED STATES OF AMERICA,
    INDIAN TERRITORY.
  Central   District.

    I,   Mary Duer   , on oath state that I am   22   years of age and a citizen by Marriage   , of the   Choctaw   Nation; that I am the lawful wife of   Ephriam Duer   , who is a citizen, by   Blood   of the   Choctaw   Nation; that a   Female   child was born to me on   18th day of   November   , 1902 , that said child has been named   Ada Arlee Duer   , and is now living.

                            Mary Duer

WITNESSES TO MARK:
    { Edna Terry
      Frances Duer

    Subscribed and sworn to before me this   20th *day of*   December   , 1902

                        B.S. Johnson
                            NOTARY PUBLIC.

Applications for Enrollment of Choctaw Newborn
Act of 1905   Volume IV

AFFIDAVIT OF ATTENDING PHYSICIAN OR MID-WIFE.

UNITED STATES OF AMERICA,
INDIAN TERRITORY.
Central District.

I, Mrs Jane Pate, a Non Citizen, on oath state that I attended on Mrs. Mary Duer, wife of Ephriam Duer on the 18th day of November, 190 2; that there was born to her on said date a Female child; that said child is now living and is said to have been named Ada Arlee Duer

Jane Pate

WITNESSES TO MARK:
Edna Terry
Frances Duer

Subscribed and sworn to before me this 20th day of December, 1902

B.S. Johnson
NOTARY PUBLIC.

BIRTH AFFIDAVIT.

DEPARTMENT OF THE INTERIOR.
COMMISSION TO THE FIVE CIVILIZED TRIBES.

IN RE APPLICATION FOR ENROLLMENT, as a citizen of the Choctaw Nation, of Ada Arlee Duer, born on the 18th day of November, 1902

Name of Father: Ephriham[sic] Duer   a citizen of the Choctaw Nation.
Name of Mother: Mary Duer   a citizen of the Choctaw Nation.

Postoffice   Durant, Ind. Terr.

AFFIDAVIT OF MOTHER.

UNITED STATES OF AMERICA, Indian Territory,
Central DISTRICT.

I, Mary Duer, on oath state that I am 25 years of age and a citizen by intermarriage, of the Choctaw Nation; that I am the lawful wife of Ephriham Duer, who is a citizen, by blood of the Choctaw Nation; that a female child was born to me on 18th day of November, 1902; that said child has been named Ada Arlee Duer, and was living March 4, 1905.

Mary Duer

Applications for Enrollment of Choctaw Newborn
Act of 1905   Volume IV

Witnesses To Mark:

{

Subscribed and sworn to before me this   26th   day of   April   , 1905

Com Ex Charles A. Phillips
Feb 8, 1908 Notary Public.

AFFIDAVIT OF ATTENDING PHYSICIAN OR MID-WIFE.

UNITED STATES OF AMERICA, Indian Territory, }
   Central   DISTRICT.

I,   Jane Pate   , a   Midwife   , on oath state that I attended on Mrs.   Mary Duer   , wife of   Ephriham Duer   on the   18th   day of   November , 1902; that there was born to her on said date a   female   child; that said child was living March 4, 1905, and is said to have been named   Ada Arlee Duer

Jane Pate

Witnesses To Mark:

{

Subscribed and sworn to before me this   26th   day of   April   , 1905

Com Ex Charles A. Phillips
Feb 8, 1908 Notary Public.

BIRTH AFFIDAVIT.

DEPARTMENT OF THE INTERIOR.
COMMISSION TO THE FIVE CIVILIZED TRIBES.

IN RE APPLICATION FOR ENROLLMENT, as a citizen of the   Choctaw   Nation, of   William Andrew Duer   , born on the   20th   day of   February   , 1904

Name of Father: Ephram Duer   a citizen of the   Choctaw   Nation.
Name of Mother: Mary Duer   a citizen of the   Choctaw   Nation.

Postoffice   Durant, Ind. Terr.

Applications for Enrollment of Choctaw Newborn
Act of 1905   Volume IV

AFFIDAVIT OF MOTHER.

UNITED STATES OF AMERICA, Indian Territory, }
Central   DISTRICT.

I, Mary Duer, on oath state that I am 25 years of age and a citizen by Intermarriage, of the Choctaw Nation; that I am the lawful wife of Ephram Duer, who is a citizen, by Blood of the Choctaw Nation; that a Male child was born to me on 20th day of February, 1904; that said child has been named William Andrew Duer, and was living March 4, 1905.

Com Ex
Feb 8, 1908   Mary Duer
Witnesses To Mark:
{

Subscribed and sworn to before me this 26th day of April, 1905

Charles A. Phillips
Notary Public.

AFFIDAVIT OF ATTENDING PHYSICIAN OR MID-WIFE.

UNITED STATES OF AMERICA, Indian Territory, }
Central   DISTRICT.

I, John J Stephens, a Physician, on oath state that I attended on Mrs. Mary Duer, wife of Ephram Duer on the 20th day of February, 1904; that there was born to her on said date a male child; that said child was living March 4, 1905, and is said to have been named William Andrew Duer

John J Stephens M.D.
Witnesses To Mark:
{

Subscribed and sworn to before me this 26th day of April, 1905

Com Ex   Charles A. Phillips
Feb 8, 1908   Notary Public.

Applications for Enrollment of Choctaw Newborn
Act of 1905 Volume IV

   THIS IS TO CERTIFY THAT Ephriam Duer of a Choctaw Indian ~~in the State~~ of Durant, I. T., and Miss Mary Pate of a U. S. citizen ~~in the state~~ of Durant, I. T. were by me Joined together in HOLY MATRIMONY on the 30th day of June in the Year of our Lord One Thousand ~~Eight~~ Nine Hundred and One (1901).

              J. H. Dickerson,
                Minister.

WITNESS.

   C. W. James,
   Florence James

INDIAN TERRITORY   )
BLUE COUNTY, CHOCTAW NATION.) SS

   I, F. E. Fulsom, Clerk of the County Court of said County do hereby certify that the foregoing instrument of writing, dated the 30" day of June ~~189~~ 1901 with its Certificate of Authentication was filed for record in my office the 17 day of Sept. ~~189~~ 1902 at ....o'clock......M., and duly recorded this 17 day of Sept. ~~189~~ 1902 at ......o'clock......M., in the records of said County in Volumn[sic] A on Pages 415 WITNESS my hand and seal of the county court of said county, at office in Caddo, the day and year last above mentioned.

            F. E. Folsom

          Clerk, County Court, Blue County.

Endorsed on back of Marriage License as follows:

       DEPARTMENT OF THE INTERIOR
    COMMISSION TO THE FIVE CIVILIZED TRIBES
       F I L E D
        Dec. 22, 1902
         Tams Bixby,
          Acting Chairman.

I, Ella Bailey, a stenographer to the Commissioner to the Five Civilized Tribes, do hereby certify that the above and foregoing is a true and correct copy of the original now on file with the records of this office.

            Ella Bailey

Subscribed and sworn to before me this 26 day of Sept. 1907

               Frances [Illegible]

Applications for Enrollment of Choctaw Newborn
Act of 1905   Volume IV

N. B. 226

COPY.

Muskogee, Indian Territory, April 10, 1905.

Ephriham Duer,
    Durant, Indian Territory.

Dear Sir:

    There is inclosed you herewith for execution application for the enrollment of your infant child, Ada Arlee Duer, born November 18, 1902.

    The affidavits heretofore filed with the Commission show the child was living on December 20, 1902. It is necessary, for the child to be enrolled, that she was living on March 4, 1905. You will please insert the mother's age in the place left blank for that purpose.

    In having these affidavits executed care should be exercised to see that all the names are written in full as they appear in the body of the affidavit, and in the event that either of the persons signing the affidavit are unable to write, signatures by mark must be attested by two witnesses. Each affidavit must be executed before a Notary Public and the notarial seal and signature of the officer must be attached to each separate affidavit.

Respectfully,

SIGNED

T.B. Needles

SEV 3-10.   Commissioner in Charge.

COPY.   7-NB 226.

Muskogee, Indian Territory, April 28, 1905.

Ephriham Duer,
    Durant, Indian Territory.

Dear Sir:

    Receipt is hereby acknowledged of the affidavits of Mary Duer and Jane Pate to the birth of Ada Arlee Duer, daughter of Ephriham and Mary Duer, November 18, 1902, and the same have been filed with our records as an application for the enrollment of said child.

Respectfully,
SIGNED

Tams Bixby
Chairman.

Applications for Enrollment of Choctaw Newborn
Act of 1905   Volume IV

7-3410

Muskogee, Indian Territory, May 1, 1905.

Ephram Duer,
        Durant, Indian Territory.

Dear Sir:

      Receipt is hereby acknowledged of the affidavits of Mary Duer and John J. Stephens to the birth of William Andrew Duer son of Ephram and Mary Duer, February 20, 1904, and the same has been filed with our records as an application of said child.

        Respectfully,

                Chairman.

Choc New Born 227
      Wanona Estelle Stephenson
      (Born July 3, 1904)

NEW-BORN AFFIDAVIT.

      Number................

...Choctaw Enrolling Commission...

      IN THE MATTER OF THE APPLICATION FOR ENROLLMENT, as a citizen of the Choctaw   Nation, of   Wanona E. Stephenson

born on the 3 day of   July   190 4

Name of father Will F. Stephenson   a citizen of   white
Nation final enrollment No. Daws[sic] Com. Seldner
Name of mother Olive C. Stephenson   a citizen of   Choctaw
Nation final enrollment No. 9805

                      Postoffice   Durant I.T.

Applications for Enrollment of Choctaw Newborn
Act of 1905 Volume IV

AFFIDAVIT OF MOTHER.

UNITED STATES OF AMERICA
INDIAN TERRITORY
Central DISTRICT

I Olive C. Stephenson , on oath state that I am 17 years of age and a citizen by blood of the Choctaw Nation, and as such have been placed upon the final roll of the Choctaw Nation, by the Honorable Secretary of the Interior my final enrollment number being 9805 ; that I am the lawful wife of Will F. Stephenson , who is a citizen of the white Nation, and as such has been placed upon the final roll of said Nation by the Honorable Secretary of the Interior, his final enrollment number being ---------- and that a Female child was born to me on the 3 day of July 190 4; that said child has been named Wanona E Stephenson , and is now living.

Olive C. Stephenson

Witnesseth.
Must be two Witnesses who are Citizens.   WA Durant
G.W. Seeley

Subscribed and sworn to before me this 14 day of January 190 5

James Bower
Notary Public.

My commission expires: Sept 23 1907

AFFIDAVIT OF ATTENDING PHYSICIAN OR MIDWIFE

UNITED STATES OF AMERICA
INDIAN TERRITORY
Central DISTRICT

I, Dr a Practicing Physician on oath state that I attended on Mrs. Olive C. Stephenson wife of Will F Stephenson on the 3 day of July , 190 4 , that there was born to her on said date a Female child, that said child is now living, and is said to have been named Wanona E Stephenson

TL Crissman M.D.
Subscribed and sworn to before me this, the 14 day of January 190 5

James Bower
Notary Public.

WITNESSETH:

Must be two witnesses who are citizens and know the child.   WA Durant
G.W. Seeley

Applications for Enrollment of Choctaw Newborn
Act of 1905 Volume IV

We hereby certify that we are well acquainted with..
a..and know........................to be reputable and of good standing in the community.

{ Must be two citizen witnesses } { W.A. Durant
G.W. Seeley }

BIRTH AFFIDAVIT.

DEPARTMENT OF THE INTERIOR.
COMMISSION TO THE FIVE CIVILIZED TRIBES.

IN RE APPLICATION FOR ENROLLMENT, as a citizen of the Choctaw Nation, of Wanona Estelle Stephenson, born on the 3-d day of July, 1904

Name of Father: William F. Stephenson a citizen of the Non-- Nation.
(nee Seldner)
Name of Mother: Olive C. Stephenson a citizen of the Choctaw Nation.

Postoffice Roff, Ind. Ter.

AFFIDAVIT OF MOTHER.

UNITED STATES OF AMERICA, Indian Territory, }
....DISTRICT. }

I, Olive C. Stephenson, on oath state that I am 17 years of age and a citizen by blood, of the Choctaw Nation; that I am the lawful wife of William F. Stephenson, who is a non citizen, by.................................of the........................ Nation; that a female child was born to me on third day of July, 1904; that said child has been named Wanona Estelle Stephenson, and was living March 4, 1905.

Olive C. Stephenson

Witnesses To Mark:
{

Subscribed and sworn to before me this 20 day of March, 1905

J C Little
Notary Public.

Applications for Enrollment of Choctaw Newborn
Act of 1905 Volume IV

AFFIDAVIT OF ATTENDING PHYSICIAN OR MID-WIFE.

UNITED STATES OF AMERICA, Indian Territory, }
....DISTRICT.}

    I, T. L. Crissman, M. D. , a physician , on oath state that I attended on Mrs. Olie[sic] C. Stephenson , wife of William F. Stephenson on the 3-rd day of July , 1904; that there was born to her on said date a female child; that said child was living March 4, 1905, and is said to have been named Wanona Estelle Stephenson

                                      T.L. Crissman M.D.

Witnesses To Mark:
   { A.F. Stephenson
     WN Jones

    Subscribed and sworn to before me this 21 day of March , 1905

                                J. V. Connell
                                    Notary Public.

                                    7-3445

                Muskogee, Indian Territory, March 16, 1905.

Will F. Stephenson,
    Roff, Indian Territory.

Dear Sir:

    Receipt is hereby acknowledged of your letter of March 9, 1905, in which you state that Wanona Estelle Stephenson was enrolled at Durant by the Choctaw and Chickasaw Enrolling Commission but if it is necessary to make further application for this child you request the necessary blanks.

    In compliance with your request there is inclosed herewith blank application for the enrollment of infant children together with circular giving full information relative thereto.

                    Respectfully,

                                    Chairman.

B. C.
Circular.

Applications for Enrollment of Choctaw Newborn
Act of 1905   Volume IV

7-3445

Muskogee, Indian Territory, March 29, 1905.

William F. Stephenson,
    Roff, Indian Territory.

Dear Sir:

    Receipt is hereby acknowledged of the affidavits of Olive C. Stephenson (Seldner) and T. L. Crissman to the birth of Wanona Estelle Stephenson, daughter of William T. and Olive C. Stephenson, July 3, 1904, and the same have been filed with our records as an application for the enrollment of said child.

                  Respectfully,

                  Chairman.

Choc New Born 228
    Burniss Irene Hampton
    (Born Dec. 18, 1903)

BIRTH AFFIDAVIT.

DEPARTMENT OF THE INTERIOR,
COMMISSION TO THE FIVE CIVILIZED TRIBES.

    In Re Application for Enrollment, as a citizen of the   Choctaw   Nation, of Burniss Irene Hampton , born on the   18   day of December , 1903

Name of Father: John L Hampton   a citizen of the Choctaw   Nation.
                                              by Intermarriage
Name of Mother: Willie m Hampton   a citizen of the   Choctaw   Nation.

                Post-office   Bok chito Ind. Ter.

Applications for Enrollment of Choctaw Newborn
Act of 1905   Volume IV

AFFIDAVIT OF MOTHER.

UNITED STATES OF AMERICA, }
INDIAN TERRITORY,
Central   District.

I, Willie M Hampton , on oath state that I am 29 years of age and a citizen by Marriage , of the Choctaw Nation; that I am the lawful wife of Jno L Hampton , who is a citizen, by Blood of the Choctaw Nation; that a Female child was born to me on 18 day of Dec , 1903 , that said child has been named Burniss Irene Hampton , and is now living.

Willie M Hampton

WITNESSES TO MARK:

Subscribed and sworn to before me this 28 day of May , 1904

[Illegible] Moore
NOTARY PUBLIC.

AFFIDAVIT OF ATTENDING PHYSICIAN OR MID-WIFE.

UNITED STATES OF AMERICA, }
INDIAN TERRITORY,
Central   District.

I, Dr. V.T. Stephens , a Physician , on oath state that I attended on Mrs. Willie M. Hampton , wife of John L Hampton on the 18 day of December, 190 3; that there was born to her on said date a Female child; that said child is now living and is said to have been named Burniss Irene Hampton

V. T. Stephens M.D.

WITNESSES TO MARK:

Subscribed and sworn to before me this 27 day of May , 1904

Chas P. Smith
NOTARY PUBLIC.

Applications for Enrollment of Choctaw Newborn
Act of 1905   Volume IV

NEW-BORN AFFIDAVIT.

Number..........

Choctaw Enrolling Commission.

IN THE MATTER OF THE APPLICATION FOR ENROLLMENT, as a citizen of the Choctaw Nation, of   Burniss Irene Hampton

born on the   18   day of   December   1903

Name of father   John L Hampton   a citizen of   Choctaw
Nation final enrollment No   9828
Name of mother   Willie Hampton   a citizen of   Choctaw
Nation final enrollment No   330

Postoffice   ~~Albany~~   Wade   I.T.

AFFIDAVIT OF MOTHER.

UNITED STATES OF AMERICA,
INDIAN TERRITORY,
Central   DISTRICT

I   Willie M. Hampton   on oath state that I am   29   years of age and a citizen by   Marriage   of the   Choctaw   Nation, and as such have been placed upon the final roll of the   Choctaw   Nation, by the Honorable Secretary of the Interior my final enrollment number being   330   ; that I am the lawful wife of   John L Hampton   , who is a citizen of the   Choctaw   Nation, and as such has been placed upon the final roll of said Nation by the Honorable Secretary of the Interior, his final enrollment number being   9828   and that a   female   child was born to me on the   18   day of   December   190 3 ; that said child has been named   Burniss Irene Hampton   , and is now living.

Willie M Hampton

WITNESSETH:
Must be two Witnesses who are Citizens.
D H Gardner
C P Middleton

Subscribed and sworn to before me this   16   day of   January   190 5

James Bower
Notary Public.

My commission expires   Sept 23/07

233

Applications for Enrollment of Choctaw Newborn
Act of 1905 Volume IV

AFFIDAVIT OF ATTENDING PHYSICIAN OR MIDWIFE

UNITED STATES OF AMERICA
INDIAN TERRITORY
Central DISTRICT

I, V.T. Stephens a Practicing Physician on oath state that I attended on Mrs. Willie M Hampton wife of John L Hampton on the 18 day of December, 190 3, that there was born to her on said date a Female child, that said child is now living, and is said to have been named Burniss Irene Hampton

V.T. Stephens M.D.

Subscribed and sworn to before me this, the 21 day of January 190 5
My Com Exo Apr 25-1907

Al Davis
WITNESSETH: Notary Public.

Must be two witnesses who are citizens and know the child.
{ D H Gardner
C P Middleton

We hereby certify that we are well acquainted with V T Stephens a Practicing Physician and know him to be reputable and of good standing in the community.

Must be two citizen witnesses
{ D.H. Gardner
C P Middleton

BIRTH AFFIDAVIT.

DEPARTMENT OF THE INTERIOR.
COMMISSION TO THE FIVE CIVILIZED TRIBES.

IN RE APPLICATION FOR ENROLLMENT, as a citizen of the Choctaw Nation, of Burniss Irene Hampton, born on the 18th day of December, 1903

Name of Father: John L Hampton a citizen of the Choctaw Nation.
Name of Mother: Mrs. Willie M Hampton a citizen of the Choctaw Nation.

Postoffice Wade Ind. Ter

Applications for Enrollment of Choctaw Newborn
Act of 1905   Volume IV

AFFIDAVIT OF MOTHER.

UNITED STATES OF AMERICA, Indian Territory, }
Central   DISTRICT.

I, Mrs Willie M Hampton, on oath state that I am Thirty years of age and a citizen by Intermarriage, of the Choctaw Nation; that I am the lawful wife of John L Hampton, who is a citizen, by Blood of the Choctaw Nation; that a Female child was born to me on 18th day of December, 1903; that said child has been named Burniss Irene Hampton, and was living March 4, 1905.

Willie M Hampton

Witnesses To Mark:

Subscribed and sworn to before me this 8th day of April, 1905

Chas P Smith
Notary Public.

AFFIDAVIT OF ATTENDING PHYSICIAN OR MID-WIFE.

UNITED STATES OF AMERICA, Indian Territory, }
Central   DISTRICT.

I, V.T. Stephens, a Physician, on oath state that I attended on Mrs. Willie M Hampton, wife of John L Hampton on the 18th day of December, 1903; that there was born to her on said date a female child; that said child was living March 4, 1905, and is said to have been named Burniss Irene Hampton

V.T. Stephens M.D.

Witnesses To Mark:
 James [Illegible]
 J E Traylor

Subscribed and sworn to before me this 11th day of April, 1905

Fred Everett
Notary Public.
My Commission expires Dec. 5th 1908   Cent. Dist Ind Ter.

Applications for Enrollment of Choctaw Newborn
Act of 1905   Volume IV

7-3451

Muskogee, Indian Territory, May 21, 1904.

John L. Hampton,
Bokchito, Indian Territory.

Dear Sir:

Receipt is hereby acknowledged of your letter of the 16th inst., requesting to be advised whether or not your infant daughter, born December 18, 1903, can be enrolled as a citizen by blood of the Choctaw Nation, and if so, you request that a blank for the purpose of making application for enrollment be sent you.

You are informed that under the provisions of the Act of Congress approved July 1, 1902, the Commission is now without authority to receive or consider the original application for enrollment of any person whomsoever as a citizen of the Choctaw or Chickasaw Nation.

A blank application for the enrollment of an infant child however, is enclosed herewith.

Respectfully,

BC.   Commissioner in Charge.

[Letter below typed as given]

Congress approved July 1, 19   ssion is now without
authority to receive or consider   original application for enrollment of any person whomsoever as a citizen of the Choctaw or Chickasaw Nation.

Respectfully,   7-3451

Muskogee, Indian Territory, June 8, 1904.
Chairman.

John L. Hampton,
Bokchito, Indian Territory.

Dear Sir:

Receipt is hereby acknowledged of the affidavits of Willie M. Hampton and V. T. Stephens, relative to the birth of your infant daughter, Nurniss Irene Hampton, December 18, 1903, which it is presumed have been forwarded as an application for the enrollment of said child as a citizen by blood of the Choctaw Nation.

Applications for Enrollment of Choctaw Newborn
Act of 1905   Volume IV

You are informed that under the provisions of the Act of Congress approved July 1, 1902, the Commission is now without authority to receive or consider the original application for enrollment of any person whomsoever as a citizen of the Choctaw or Chickasaw Nation.

Respectfully,

Chairman.

COPY. N.B. 228

Muskogee, Indian Territory, April 7, 1905.

John L. Hampton,
Bokchito, Indian Territory.

Dear Sir:

There is inclosed you herewith for execution application for the enrollment of your infant child, Burniss Irene Hampton, born December 18, 1903.

The affidavits heretofore filed with the Commission show the child was living on May 28, 1904. It is necessary, for the child to be enrolled, that she was living on March 4, 1905. You will please insert the mother's age in the place left blank for that purpose.

In having these affidavits executed, care should be exercised to see that all the names are written in full as they appear in the body of the affidavit, and in the event that either of the persons signing the affidavit are unable to write, signatures by mark must be attested by two witnesses. Each affidavit must be executed before a Notary Public and the notarial seal and signature of the officer must be attached to each separate affidavit.

Respectfully,

SIGNED

T.B. Needles
Commissioner in Charge.

SEV 3-7

Applications for Enrollment of Choctaw Newborn
Act of 1905 Volume IV

COPY. Choctaw N.B.288.

Muskogee, Indian Territory, April 22, 1905.

John L. Hampton,
  Wade, Indian Territory.

Dear Sir:

   Receipt is hereby acknowledged of the affidavits of Willie M. Hampton and V. T. Stephens to the birth of Burniss Irene Hampton, daughter of John L. and Willie M. Hampton, December 18, 1903, and the same have been filed with our records in the matter of the application for the enrollment of said child.

Respectfully,
SIGNED.
Tams Bixby
Chairman.

Choctaw NB 228

Muskogee, Indian Territory, June 28, 1905.

J. L. Hampton,
  Wade, Indian Territory.

Dear Sir:

   Receipt is hereby acknowledged of your letter of June 24, asking if the enrollment of your child, Burniss Irene Hampton has been approved.

   In reply you are advised that the name of Burniss Irene Hampton has been placed upon a schedule of citizens by blood of the Choctaw Nation which has been forwarded the Secretary of the Interior for approval, but the Commission has not yet been notified of Departmental action thereon.

   You will be notified when his[sic] enrollment is approved by the Department.

Respectfully,

Chairman.

Applications for Enrollment of Choctaw Newborn
Act of 1905   Volume IV

Choc New Born 229
    Charles Le Roy Sorrells
    (Born May 7, 1904)

NEW-BORN AFFIDAVIT.

Number..........

...Choctaw Enrolling Commission...

IN THE MATTER OF THE APPLICATION FOR ENROLLMENT, as a citizen of the Choctaw   Nation, of   Charles Leroy Sorrells

born on the 7 day of __May__ 190 4

Name of father George W Sorrells   a citizen of   Choctaw
Nation final enrollment No. 313
Name of mother Catherine Sorrells   a citizen of   Choctaw
Nation final enrollment No. 9555

                              Postoffice   Coalgate I.T.

AFFIDAVIT OF MOTHER.

UNITED STATES OF AMERICA
INDIAN TERRITORY
   Central   DISTRICT

I Catherine Sorrells   , on oath state that I am 37 years of age and a citizen by Blood of the Choctaw Nation, and as such have been placed upon the final roll of the Choctaw Nation, by the Honorable Secretary of the Interior my final enrollment number being 9555 ; that I am the lawful wife of George W Sorrells , who is a citizen of the Choctaw Nation, and as such has been placed upon the final roll of said Nation by the Honorable Secretary of the Interior, his final enrollment number being 313 and that a Male child was born to me on the 7 day of May 190 4; that said child has been named Charles Leroy , and is now living.

                                                                  her
                                       Catherine Sorrells x
Witnesseth.   mark

Must be two ⎤ O.S. Lawrence
Witnesses who ⎬
are Citizens. ⎦ D.A. Lawrence

Applications for Enrollment of Choctaw Newborn
Act of 1905   Volume IV

Subscribed and sworn to before me this 28 day of Jan 190 5

[Name Illegible]
Notary Public.

My commission expires: Dec 19-1905

AFFIDAVIT OF ATTENDING PHYSICIAN OR MIDWIFE

UNITED STATES OF AMERICA
INDIAN TERRITORY
Central   DISTRICT

I, JS Hume a Physician on oath state that I attended on Mrs. Catherine Sorrells wife of Geo W Sorrells on the 7th day of May , 190 4 , that there was born to her on said date a (boy) male child, that said child is now living, and is said to have been named Charles Leroy Sorrells

JS Hume   M.D.

Subscribed and sworn to before me this, the 28 day of Jan 190 5

[Name Illegible]   Notary Public.

WITNESSETH:
Must be two witnesses who are citizens
{ O.S. Lawrence
  D.A. Lawrence

We hereby certify that we are well acquainted with JS Hume a Physician and know him to be reputable and of good standing in the community.

O.S. Lawrence   _____

D A Lawrence   _____

BIRTH AFFIDAVIT.

DEPARTMENT OF THE INTERIOR,
COMMISSION TO THE FIVE CIVILIZED TRIBES.

IN RE Application for Enrollment, as a citizen of the Choctaw Nation, of Charles LeRoy Sorrells , born on the 7th day of May , 1904

Name of Father: George W Sorrells   a citizen of the Choctaw Nation.
Name of Mother: Catherine Sorrells   a citizen of the Choctaw Nation.

Applications for Enrollment of Choctaw Newborn
Act of 1905   Volume IV

Post-Office: Coalgate Ind Ter

AFFIDAVIT OF MOTHER.

UNITED STATES OF AMERICA, }
INDIAN TERRITORY.
Central   District.

I, Catherine Sorrells, on oath state that I am 39 years of age and a citizen by Blood, of the Choctaw Nation; that I am the lawful wife of George Sorrells, who is a citizen, by Marriage of the Choctaw Nation; that a male child was born to me on 7th day of May, 1904, that said child has been named Charles LeRoy, and is now living.

                                    her
                    Catherine Sorrells x
                                    mark

WITNESSES TO MARK:
{ J.H. Carsen
{ Mike Mayes

Subscribed and sworn to before me this 20 *day of* March, 1905.

[Name Illegible]
NOTARY PUBLIC.

AFFIDAVIT OF ATTENDING PHYSICIAN OR MID-WIFE.

UNITED STATES OF AMERICA, }
INDIAN TERRITORY.
Central   District.

I, J.S. Hume, a Physician, on oath state that I attended on Mrs. Catherine Sorrells, wife of George W Sorrells on the 7th day of May, 1904; that there was born to her on said date a male child; that said child is now living and is said to have been named Charles LeRoy Sorrells

JS Hume M.D.

WITNESSES TO MARK:
{ J.H. Carsen
{ Mike Mayes

Subscribed and sworn to before me this 20 *day of* March, 1905.

[Name Illegible]
NOTARY PUBLIC.

Applications for Enrollment of Choctaw Newborn
Act of 1905   Volume IV

7-3331

Muskogee, Indian Territory, March 23, 1905.

George W. Sorrells,
    Coalgate, Indian Territory.

Dear Sir:

    Receipt is hereby acknowledged of the affidavits of Catherine Sorrells and J. S. Hume to the birth of Charles Le Roy Sorrells, son of George W. and Catherine Sorrells, May 7, 1904, and the same have been filed with our records as an application for the enrollment of said child.

                  Respectfully,

                        Chairman.

Choc New Born 230
    Thurman Moore Rabon
    (Born June 2, 1903)

NEW-BORN AFFIDAVIT.

            Number

...Choctaw Enrolling Commission...

    IN THE MATTER OF THE APPLICATION FOR ENROLLMENT, as a citizen of the Choctaw Nation, of Thurman M Rabon

born on the day of 2nd June 190 3

Name of father William T Rabon	a citizen of intermarried Choctaw
Nation final enrollment No. 649	
Name of mother Ora A. Rabon	a citizen of Choctaw
Nation final enrollment No. 649	

                            Postoffice   Bokoshe I.T.

Applications for Enrollment of Choctaw Newborn
Act of 1905   Volume IV

AFFIDAVIT OF MOTHER.

UNITED STATES OF AMERICA
INDIAN TERRITORY
................................DISTRICT

I   Ora A. Rabon   , on oath state that I am   21   years of age and a citizen by   blood   of the   Choctaw   Nation, and as such have been placed upon the final roll of the   Choctaw   Nation, by the Honorable Secretary of the Interior my final enrollment number being   8081   ; that I am the lawful wife of   William T. Rabon   , who is a citizen of the   Choctaw   by marriage Nation, and as such has been placed upon the final roll of said Nation by the Honorable Secretary of the Interior, his final enrollment number being 649   and that a   Male   child was born to me on the day of   2nd of June   190 3; that said child has been named   Thurman M Rabon   , and is now living.

Ora A. Rabon

Witnesseth.

Must be two Witnesses who are Citizens.   } James Taylor
Eugene A Hickman

Subscribed and sworn to before me this   20   day of   Jan   190 5

John R Smoot
Notary Public.

My commission expires:
July 21st 1906

AFFIDAVIT OF ATTENDING PHYSICIAN OR MIDWIFE

UNITED STATES OF AMERICA
INDIAN TERRITORY
Central   DISTRICT

I,   F C Parrott   a   Physician   on oath state that I attended on Mrs. Ora Rabon   wife of   W^m T Rabon   on the 2 day of June , 190 3, that there was born to her on said date a   male   child, that said child is now living, and is said to have been named   Thurman M Rabon

F C Parrott   M.D.

WITNESSETH:

Must be two witnesses who are citizens and know the child.   { James Taylor
Eugene Hickman

Subscribed and sworn to before me this, the   6th   day of   Feb   190 5

John R Smoot   Notary Public.

243

Applications for Enrollment of Choctaw Newborn
Act of 1905   Volume IV

We hereby certify that we are well acquainted with Dr F C Parrott a Physician and know him to be reputable and of good standing in the community.

        { James Taylor
        { Eugene Hickman

BIRTH AFFIDAVIT.

DEPARTMENT OF THE INTERIOR.
COMMISSION TO THE FIVE CIVILIZED TRIBES.

IN RE APPLICATION FOR ENROLLMENT, as a citizen of the Choctaw Nation, of Thurman Moore Rabon , born on the 2nd. day of June 1903 , 1

Name of Father: William Thomas Rabon   a citizen of the Choctaw Nation.
Name of Mother: Ora Almeda Rabon   a citizen of the Choctaw Nation.

      Postoffice   Bokoshe Ind. Ter.

AFFIDAVIT OF MOTHER.

UNITED STATES OF AMERICA, Indian Territory, }
Central   DISTRICT. }

I, Ora Almeda Rabon , on oath state that I am 21 years of age and a citizen by blood , of the Choctaw Nation; that I am the lawful wife of William Thomas Rabon , who is a citizen, by intermarriage of the Choctaw Nation; that a male child was born to me on 2nd. day of June 1903 , 1 ; that said child has been named Thurman Moore Rabon , and was living March 4, 1905.

        Ora Almeda Rabon

Witnesses To Mark:
  { James Taylor
  { Cyrus B Ward

Subscribed and sworn to before me this 24th. day of March 1905 , 190

        C M Bagwell
        Notary Public.

My Commission
Expires March 29-1908

Applications for Enrollment of Choctaw Newborn
Act of 1905 Volume IV

AFFIDAVIT OF ATTENDING PHYSICIAN OR MID-WIFE.

UNITED STATES OF AMERICA, Indian Territory,
Central DISTRICT.

I, F. C. Parrott , a Physician , on oath state that I attended on Mrs. Ora Almeda Rabon , wife of William Thomas Rabon on the 2nd. day of June 1903 , 1........; that there was born to her on said date a male child; that said child was living March 4, 1905, and is said to have been named Thurman Moore Rabon

F.C. Parrott M.D.

Witnesses To Mark:
 { James Taylor
 { Cyrus B. Ward

Subscribed and sworn to before me this 24th. day of March 1905 , 190...

C M Bagwell
Notary Public.

My Commission
Expires March 29-1908

Choc New Born 231
 Tokie Gouger
 (Born Dec. 6, 1903)

BIRTH AFFIDAVIT.

DEPARTMENT OF THE INTERIOR,
COMMISSION TO THE FIVE CIVILIZED TRIBES.

In Re Application for Enrollment, as a citizen of the Choctaw Nation, of Tokie Gouger , born on the 6" day of Dec , 1903

Name of Father: J. J. Gouger   a citizen of the Choctaw Nation.
Name of Mother: Estell Gouger   a citizen of the Choctaw Nation.

Post-office   Stigler, I.T.

Applications for Enrollment of Choctaw Newborn
Act of 1905 Volume IV

AFFIDAVIT OF MOTHER.

UNITED STATES OF AMERICA,
INDIAN TERRITORY,
Central District.

I, Estell Gouger, on oath state that I am 26 years of age and a citizen by blood, of the Choctaw Nation; that I am the lawful wife of J. J. Gouger, who is a citizen, by marriage of the Choctaw Nation; that a Female child was born to me on 6 day of Dec, 190 3, that said child has been named Tokie Gouger, and is now living.

Estell Gouger

WITNESSES TO MARK:

Subscribed and sworn to before me this 21 day of June, 1904

My Commission expires
May 7, 1907

Chas T Walker
NOTARY PUBLIC.

AFFIDAVIT OF ATTENDING PHYSICIAN OR MID-WIFE.

UNITED STATES OF AMERICA,
INDIAN TERRITORY,
Central District.

I, J.D. Murphey, a Physician, on oath state that I attended on Mrs. Estell Gouger, wife of J J Gouger on the 6 day of Dec, 1903; that there was born to her on said date a Female child; that said child is now living and is said to have been named Tokie Gouger

J D Murphey M.D.

WITNESSES TO MARK:

Subscribed and sworn to before me this 21 day of June, 1904

My Commission expires
May 7, 1907

Chas T Walker
NOTARY PUBLIC.

Applications for Enrollment of Choctaw Newborn
Act of 1905   Volume IV

NEW-BORN AFFIDAVIT.

Number................

...Choctaw Enrolling Commission...

IN THE MATTER OF THE APPLICATION FOR ENROLLMENT, as a citizen of the Choctaw Nation, of Tokie Gouger

born on the 6th day of December 190 3

Name of father J.J. Gouger   a citizen of   white
Nation final enrollment No............
Name of mother Estelle Gouger   a citizen of   Choctaw
Nation final enrollment No. 8060

Postoffice   Sans Bois

AFFIDAVIT OF MOTHER.

UNITED STATES OF AMERICA
INDIAN TERRITORY
Central   DISTRICT

I   Estelle Gouger   , on oath state that I am 26 years of age and a citizen by blood of the Choctaw Nation, and as such have been placed upon the final roll of the Choctaw Nation, by the Honorable Secretary of the Interior my final enrollment number being 8060 ; that I am the lawful wife of J. J. Gouger   , who is a citizen of the white Nation, and as such has been placed upon the final roll of said Nation by the Honorable Secretary of the Interior, his final enrollment number being............ and that a female child was born to me on the 6th day of December 190 3; that said child has been named Tokie Gouger , and is now living.

Estelle Gouger

Witnesseth.
 Must be two ⎫ Frank Folsom
 Witnesses who ⎬
 are Citizens. ⎭ Abel Cooper

Subscribed and sworn to before me this 2   day of Jan   190 5

James Bower
Notary Public.

My commission expires:
   Sept 23 1907

247

Applications for Enrollment of Choctaw Newborn
Act of 1905   Volume IV

AFFIDAVIT OF ATTENDING PHYSICIAN OR MIDWIFE

UNITED STATES OF AMERICA
INDIAN TERRITORY
Central   DISTRICT

I, J. D. Murphy a Practicing Physician on oath state that I attended on Mrs. Estelle Gouger wife of J. J. Gouger on the 6 day of December, 190 3, that there was born to her on said date a Female child, that said child is now living, and is said to have been named Tokie Gouger

J.D. Murphy

Subscribed and sworn to before me this, the 2 day of January 190 5

WITNESSETH: James Bower   Notary Public.
Must be two witnesses who are citizens { Joe Carrell
Ben Noel

We hereby certify that we are well acquainted with J.D. Murphy a Practicing Physician and know .... to be reputable and of good standing in the community.

Abel Cooper   W.E. Wallace

BIRTH AFFIDAVIT.
DEPARTMENT OF THE INTERIOR.
COMMISSION TO THE FIVE CIVILIZED TRIBES.

IN RE APPLICATION FOR ENROLLMENT, as a citizen of the Choctaw Nation, of Tokie Gouger, born on the 6th day of December, 190 3

Name of Father: J J Gouger   a citizen of the U.S.   ~~Nation~~.
Name of Mother: Estelle Gouger a citizen of the Choctaw Nation.

Postoffice   Sans Bois, I.T.

Applications for Enrollment of Choctaw Newborn
Act of 1905   Volume IV

AFFIDAVIT OF MOTHER.

UNITED STATES OF AMERICA, Indian Territory, }
Central   DISTRICT.

I, Estelle Gouger, on oath state that I am 26 years of age and a citizen by blood, of the Choctaw Nation; that I am the lawful wife of J J Gouger, who is a citizen, by Intermarried of the Choctaw Nation; that a Female child was born to me on 6 day of December, 1903, that said child has been named Tokie Gouger, and is now living.

                                                  Estelle Gouger

Witnesses To Mark:
{ Boyd Williams
{ Henry Cooper

Subscribed and sworn to before me this 13th day of April, 1905.

My Commission   Henry F Cooper
Expires Oct 29th 1908   Notary Public.

AFFIDAVIT OF ATTENDING PHYSICIAN OR MID-WIFE.

UNITED STATES OF AMERICA, Indian Territory, }
Central   DISTRICT.

I, J D Murphey, a Physician, on oath state that I attended on Mrs. Estelle Gouger, wife of J J Gouger on the 6 day of Dec, 1903; that there was born to her on said date a Female child; that said child is now living and is said to have been named Tokie Gouger

                                                  J.D. Murphey M.D.

Witnesses To Mark:
{ J B Frix
{ Henry F Cooper

Subscribed and sworn to before me this 13th day of April, 1905.

My Commission   Henry F Cooper
Expires Oct 29th 1908   Notary Public.

Applications for Enrollment of Choctaw Newborn
Act of 1905 Volume IV

COPY. N. B. 231

Muskogee, Indian Territory, April 6, 1905.

J. J. Gouger,
    Sansbois, Indian Territory.

Dear Sir:

    There is inclosed you herewith for execution application for the enrollment of your infant child, Tokie Gouger, born December 6, 1903.

    The affidavits heretofore filed with the Commission show the child was living on June 21, 1904. It is necessary, for the child to be enrolled, that she was living on March 4, 1905. You will please insert the mother's age in the place left blank for that purpose.

    In having these affidavits executed, care should be exercised to see that all the names are written in full as they appear in the body of the affidavit, and in the event that either of the persons signing the affidavit are unable to write, signatures by mark must be attested by two witnesses. Each affidavit must be executed before a Notary Public and the notarial seal and signature of the officer must be attached to each separate affidavit.

                  Respectfully,
                  SIGNED.
                  T.B. Needles
SEV 806.   Commissioner in Charge.

---

7 N.B. 231.
Muskogee, Indian Territory, May 25, 1905.

Estelle Gouger,
    Stigler, Indian Territory.

Dear Madam:

    Receipt is hereby acknowledged of your letter of May 21, asking if your infant child, Tokie Gouger, has been approved so that you can file on her allotment.

    In reply to your letter you are advised that the name of your child, Tokie Gouger has been placed upon a schedule of citizens by blood of the Choctaw Nation prepared for forwarding to the Secretary of the Interior. When her enrollment has been approved by the Secretary of the Interior, you will be notified.

    You are advised, however, that pending the approval of her enrollment no selection of allotment can be made for said child.

                  Respectfully,

                        Chairman.

Applications for Enrollment of Choctaw Newborn
Act of 1905   Volume IV

Choc New Born 232
    Elmer Luther Barnett
    (Born April 1, 1904)

BIRTH AFFIDAVIT.

DEPARTMENT OF THE INTERIOR.
COMMISSION TO THE FIVE CIVILIZED TRIBES.

IN RE APPLICATION FOR ENROLLMENT, as a citizen of the Choctaw Nation, of Elmer Luther Barnett, born on the 1st day of April, 1904

Name of Father: Jackson D. Barnett   a citizen of the Choctaw Nation.
Name of Mother: Laura Annie Barnett   a citizen of the Choctaw Nation.

    Postoffice Dibble Ind Ter

AFFIDAVIT OF MOTHER.

UNITED STATES OF AMERICA, Indian Territory,
    Southern   DISTRICT.

    I, Laura Annie Barnett, on oath state that I am 24 years of age and a citizen by marriage, of the Choctaw Nation; that I am the lawful wife of Jackson D. Barnett, who is a citizen, by Blood of the Choctaw Nation; that a male child was born to me on 1st day of April, 1904, that said child has been named Elmer Luther Barnett, and is now living.

                        Laura Annie Barnett

Witnesses To Mark:

    Subscribed and sworn to before me this 8 day of Dec, 1904

                        James M Gordon
                        Notary Public.

Applications for Enrollment of Choctaw Newborn
Act of 1905   Volume IV

AFFIDAVIT OF ATTENDING PHYSICIAN OR MID-WIFE.

UNITED STATES OF AMERICA, Indian Territory,
Southern   DISTRICT.

I, Elizabeth Barnett, a midwife, on oath state that I attended on Mrs. Laura Annie Barnett, wife of Jackson D Barnett on the 1st day of April, 1904; that there was born to her on said date a male child; that said child is now living and is said to have been named Elmer Luther Barnett

                                                        her
                                       Elizabeth x Barnett
Witnesses To Mark: mark
  John Southward
  Ben Daniel

Subscribed and sworn to before me this 8th day of Dec, 1904
                                     James M Gordon
                                            Notary Public.

BIRTH AFFIDAVIT.

DEPARTMENT OF THE INTERIOR.
COMMISSION TO THE FIVE CIVILIZED TRIBES.

IN RE APPLICATION FOR ENROLLMENT, as a citizen of the Choctaw Nation, of Elmer Luther Barnett, born on the 1st day of April, 1904
Name of Father: Jackson D Barnett   a citizen of the Choctaw Nation.
                                                  Choctaw
Name of Mother: Laura Annie Barnett   a citizen of the Intermarried Nation.
                              Postoffice

AFFIDAVIT OF MOTHER.

UNITED STATES OF AMERICA, Indian Territory,
Southern   DISTRICT.

I, Laura Annie Barnett, on oath state that I am 26 years years of age and a citizen by Intermarried, of the Choctaw Nation; that I am the lawful wife of Jack. D. Barnett, who is a citizen, by Blood of the Choctaw Nation; that a male child was born to me on 1st day of April, 1904; that said child has been named Elmer Luther Barnett, and was living March 4, 1905.

                                         Laura Annie Barnett
Witnesses To Mark:

Subscribed and sworn to before me this 12th day of April, 1905
                                     James M Gordon
                                          Notary Public.

Applications for Enrollment of Choctaw Newborn
Act of 1905 Volume IV

AFFIDAVIT OF ATTENDING PHYSICIAN OR MID-WIFE.

UNITED STATES OF AMERICA, Indian Territory,
Southern DISTRICT.

I, John H Howard, a M. D., on oath state that I attended on Mrs. Laura Annie Barnett, wife of Jackson D Barnett on the 1st day of April, 1904; that there was born to her on said date a male child; that said child was living March 4, 1905, and is said to have been named Elmer Luther Barnett

John H. Howard M.D.

Witnesses To Mark:

Subscribed and sworn to before me this 12th day of April, 1905

James M Gordon
Notary Public.
My Commission expires March 1907

COPY. N. B. 232

Muskogee, Indian Territory, April 7, 1905.

Jackson D. Barnett,
Dibble, Indian Territory.

Dear Sir:

There is inclosed you herewith for execution application for the enrollment of your infant child, Elmer Luther Barnett, born April 1, 1904.

The affidavits heretofore filed with the Commission show the child was living on December 8, 1904. It is necessary, for the child to be enrolled, that he was living on March 4, 1905. You will please insert the mother's age in the place left blank for that purpose.

In having these affidavits executed, care should be exercised to see that all the names are written in full as they appear in the body of the affidavit, and in the event that either of the persons signing the affidavit are unable to write, signatures by mark must be attested by two witnesses. Each affidavit must be executed before a Notary Public and the notarial seal and signature of the officer must be attached to each separate affidavit.

Applications for Enrollment of Choctaw Newborn
Act of 1905   Volume IV

SEVS-7.

Respectfully,
SIGNED.

T.B. Needles
Commissioner in Charge.

COPY.　　　　　　　　　　7 NB 232

Muskogee, Indian Territory, April 19, 1905.

Jackson D. Barnett,
    Dibble, Indian Territory.

Dear Sir:

    Receipt is hereby acknowledged of the affidavits of Laura Annie Barnett, and John H. Howard to the birth of Elmer Luther Barnett, son of Jackson D. Barnett and Laura Annie Barnett, April 1, 1904, and the same have been filed with our records as an application for the enrollment of said child.

Respectfully,
SIGNED.

Tams Bixby
Chairman.

7-N. B. 232.

Muskogee, Indian Territory, May 11, 1905.

Jackson D. Barnett,
    Dibble, Indian Territory.

Dear Sir:

    There are enclosed herewith affidavits of Laura Annie Barnett and John H. Howard, M.D., which were heretofore filed with the Commission in connection with the application for the enrollment of your infant child, Elmer Luther Barnett, born April 1, 1904.

    It will be noted that the notary public, before whom the affidavit of the physician was made, omitted his signature and seal. Please have these attached and return the affidavits to this office.

Respectfully,

V. 11/3.　　　　　　　　　　Chairman.

Applications for Enrollment of Choctaw Newborn
Act of 1905   Volume IV

Choctaw N B 232

Muskogee, Indian Territory, May 19, 1905.

Jackson D. Barnett,
    Dibble, Indian Territory.

Dear Sir:

    Receipt is hereby acknowledged of the affidavits of Laura Annie Barnett and John H. Howard to the birth of Elmer Luther Barnett, child of Jackson D. and Laura Annie Barnett, April 1, 1904, corrected by having the signature and seal of the Notary Public before whom the affidavit of John H. Howard was executed affixed thereto and the affidavits have now been filed in the matter of the enrollment of Elmer Luther Barnett.

    Respectfully,

Chairman.

Choc New Born 233
    Cepha Intolabbee
    (Born Apr. 8, 1903)

NEW-BORN AFFIDAVIT.

Number............

...Choctaw Enrolling Commission...

    IN THE MATTER OF THE APPLICATION FOR ENROLLMENT, as a citizen of the Choctaw Nation, of Cepha Intolabbee

born on the 8 day of April 190 3

Name of father   Colbert P. Intolabbee   a citizen of   Choctaw
Nation final enrollment No. 9842
Name of mother   Ada Intolabbee   a citizen of   Choctaw
Nation final enrollment No. 829

    Postoffice   Pirtle I.T.

Applications for Enrollment of Choctaw Newborn
Act of 1905   Volume IV

AFFIDAVIT OF MOTHER.

UNITED STATES OF AMERICA
INDIAN TERRITORY
  Central   DISTRICT

       I   Ada Intolabee[sic]   , on oath state that I am   29   years of age and a citizen by   Marriage   of the   Choctaw   Nation, and as such have been placed upon the final roll of the   Choctaw   Nation, by the Honorable Secretary of the Interior my final enrollment number being   829 ; that I am the lawful wife of   Colbert P Intolabbee   , who is a citizen of the   Choctaw   Nation, and as such has been placed upon the final roll of said Nation by the Honorable Secretary of the Interior, his final enrollment number being   9842   and that a   Female   child was born to me on the   8   day of   April   190 3; that said child has been named   Cepha Intolabbee   , and is now living.

                                            Ada Intolabbe[sic]

Witnesseth.
  Must be two
  Witnesses who } E.E. Dyer
  are Citizens.   John W. McKinney

     Subscribed and sworn to before me this   16   day of   January   190 5

                                 James Bower
                                      Notary Public.
My commission expires: Sept 23, 1907

AFFIDAVIT OF ATTENDING PHYSICIAN OR MIDWIFE

UNITED STATES OF AMERICA
INDIAN TERRITORY
  Central   DISTRICT

    B.W.
  I, ~~W.B.~~ Slover   a   Practicing Physician
on oath state that I attended on Mrs.   Ada Intolabbee   wife of   Colbert P. Intolabbee   on the   8   day of   April   , 190 4, that there was born to her on said date a   Female   child, that said child is now living, and is said to have been named   Cepha Intolabbee

                              B. W. Slover   M.D.
     Subscribed and sworn to before me this, the   16   day of   January   190 5

                                 James Bower
                                    Notary Public.

WITNESSETH:
  Must be two witnesses
  who are citizens and { E.E. Dyer
  know the child.

Applications for Enrollment of Choctaw Newborn
Act of 1905   Volume IV

We hereby certify that we are well acquainted with... a..and know............to be reputable and of good standing in the community.

$\left\{\begin{array}{l}\text{E.E. Dyer}\\ \text{John W. M}^{\text{c}}\text{Kinney}\end{array}\right.$

BIRTH AFFIDAVIT.

DEPARTMENT OF THE INTERIOR.
COMMISSION TO THE FIVE CIVILIZED TRIBES.

IN RE APPLICATION FOR ENROLLMENT, as a citizen of the Choctaw Nation, of Cepha Intolabbee , born on the 8 day of April , 1903

Name of Father: Colbert Intolabbee   a citizen of the Choctaw Nation.
Name of Mother: Ada Intolabbee   a citizen of the Choctaw Nation.

Postoffice   Pirtle I.T.

AFFIDAVIT OF MOTHER.

UNITED STATES OF AMERICA, Indian Territory, ⎱
Central   DISTRICT. ⎰

I, Ada Intolabbee , on oath state that I am 27 years of age and a citizen by Intermarriage , of the Choctaw Nation; that I am the lawful wife of Colbert Intolabbee , who is a citizen, by blood of the Choctaw Nation; that a Female child was born to me on 8 day of April , 1903; that said child has been named Cepha Intolabbee , and was living March 4, 1905.

Ada Intolabbee

Witnesses To Mark:
$\left\{\begin{array}{l}\\ \end{array}\right.$

Subscribed and sworn to before me this 20th day of March , 1905

A. H. Ferguson
Notary Public.

Applications for Enrollment of Choctaw Newborn
Act of 1905   Volume IV

AFFIDAVIT OF ATTENDING PHYSICIAN OR MID-WIFE.

UNITED STATES OF AMERICA, Indian Territory,
Central   DISTRICT.

I, Mrs. Belle Cox, a Midwife, on oath state that I attended on Mrs. Ada Intolabbee, wife of Colbert Intolabbee on the 8 day of April, 1903; that there was born to her on said date a Female child; that said child was living March 4, 1905, and is said to have been named Cepha Intolabbee

Belle Cox

Witnesses To Mark:

Subscribed and sworn to before me this 21 day of March, 1905

J.M. Routh
Notary Public.

7-3454

Muskogee, Indian Territory, March 28, 1905.

C. P. Intolabbee,
  Pirtle, Indian Territory.

Dear Sir:

Receipt is hereby acknowledged of your letter of March 21, 1905, enclosing affidavits of Ada Intolabbee and Belle Cox to the birth of Cepha Intolabbee, daughter of Colbert and Ada Intolabbee, April 8, 1903, and the same have been filed with our records as an application for the enrollment of said child.

Replying to that portion of your letter in which you ask if you and her mother will be allowed to file on land for this child after enrollment is approved without being appointed her guardian, you are advised that under the rules and regulations governing the selection of allotment and designation of homesteads in the Choctaw and Chickasaw Nations citizen fathers are allowed to select allotments for their minor children whose enrollment has been approved by the Secretary of the Interior without being appointed guardian for said children and no reason is seen at this time for making any change in the manner of selecting allotments for children now being enrolled under the provisions of the act of Congress approved March 3, 1905.

You will be notified in the event further evidence is required to enable the Commission to determine the right to enrollment of your child Cepha Intolabbee.

Applications for Enrollment of Choctaw Newborn
Act of 1905   Volume IV

Respectfully,

Chairman.

7-NB-233

Muskogee, Indian Territory, July 12, 1905.

C. P. Intolabbee,
    Pirtle, Indian Territory.

Dear Sir:

    Receipt is hereby acknowledged of your letter of July 8, 1905, asking if the enrollment of your child Cepha Intolabbee has been approved.

    In reply to your letter you are advised that on June 30, 1905, the Secretary of the Interior approved the enrollment of Cepha Intolabbee as a citizen by blood of the Choctaw Nation and selection of allotment may now be made in her behalf in accordance with the rules and regulations governing the selection of allotments and the designation of homesteads in the Choctaw and Chickasaw Nations.

Respectfully,

Commissioner.

Choc New Born 234
    DeWitt D. Battiest
    (Born Feb. 13, 1905)

NEW-BORN AFFIDAVIT.

Number..............

...Choctaw Enrolling Commission...

    IN THE MATTER OF THE APPLICATION FOR ENROLLMENT, as a citizen of the Choctaw Nation, of DeWitt Dyer Battiest born on the 13th day of February 190 5

259

Applications for Enrollment of Choctaw Newborn
Act of 1905 Volume IV

Name of father   Lewis G. Battiest   a citizen of   Choctaw
Nation final enrollment No.   5291
Name of mother   Emma Battiest   a citizen of   Choctaw
Nation final enrollment No.   9923

Postoffice

AFFIDAVIT OF MOTHER.

UNITED STATES OF AMERICA
INDIAN TERRITORY
Central   DISTRICT

I   Emma Dyer, now Battiest   , on oath state that I am   23   years of age and a citizen by   blood   of the   Choctaw   Nation, and as such have been placed upon the final roll of the   Choctaw   Nation, by the Honorable Secretary of the Interior my final enrollment number being   9923 ; that I am the lawful wife of   Lewis G. Battiest   , who is a citizen of the   Choctaw   Nation, and as such has been placed upon the final roll of said Nation by the Honorable Secretary of the Interior, his final enrollment number being   5291   and that a   Male   child was born to me on the 13th day of   February   190 5 ; that said child has been named   DeWitt Dyer Battiest   , and is now living.

Emma Dyer, now Battiest

Witnesseth.
Must be two ⎫
Witnesses who ⎬   Czarina A Homer
are Citizens.   ⎭   Sophia A William

Subscribed and sworn to before me this 23^{d} day of   February   190 5

A. E. Folsom
Notary Public.

My commission expires:

AFFIDAVIT OF ATTENDING PHYSICIAN OR MIDWIFE

UNITED STATES OF AMERICA
INDIAN TERRITORY
Central   DISTRICT

I,   J.S. Fulton   a   Practicing Physician on oath state that I attended on Mrs.   Emma Dyer, now Battiest   wife of   Lewis G. Battiest on the 13th day of   February   , 190 5, that there was born to her on said date a   male child, that said child is now living, and is said to have been named   DeWitt Dyer Battiest

J.S. Fulton   M.D.

Applications for Enrollment of Choctaw Newborn
Act of 1905 Volume IV

WITNESSETH:

Must be two witnesses who are citizens and know the child. { Czarina Homer
Sophia A. William

Subscribed and sworn to before me this, the 24th day of February 190 5

A.E. Folsom   Notary Public.

We hereby certify that we are well acquainted with Dr. J. S. Fulton a Practicing Physician and know him to be reputable and of good standing in the community.

{ Czarina Homer
Sophie A. William

BIRTH AFFIDAVIT.

DEPARTMENT OF THE INTERIOR.
COMMISSION TO THE FIVE CIVILIZED TRIBES.

IN RE APPLICATION FOR ENROLLMENT, as a citizen of the Choctaw Nation, of De Witt D. Battiest, born on the 13th day of February, 1905

Name of Father: Lewis G. Battiest   a citizen of the Choctaw Nation.
Name of Mother: Emma Battiest   a citizen of the Choctaw Nation.

Postoffice   Atoka, Ind. Ter.

AFFIDAVIT OF MOTHER.

UNITED STATES OF AMERICA, Indian Territory,
Central DISTRICT.

I, Emma Battiest, on oath state that I am 23 years of age and a citizen by blood, of the Choctaw Nation; that I am the lawful wife of Lewis G. Battiest, who is a citizen, by blood of the Choctaw Nation; that a male child was born to me on 13th day of February, 1905; that said child has been named De Witt D. Battiest, and was living March 4, 1905.

Emma Battiest

Witnesses To Mark:

Applications for Enrollment of Choctaw Newborn
Act of 1905   Volume IV

Subscribed and sworn to before me this   13th   day of   March   , 1905

[Name Illegible]
Notary Public.

AFFIDAVIT OF ATTENDING PHYSICIAN OR MID-WIFE.

UNITED STATES OF AMERICA, Indian Territory,
Central   DISTRICT.

I,   J. S. Fulton   , a   Physician   , on oath state that I attended on Mrs.   Emma Battiest   , wife of   Lewis G. Battiest   on the   13th   day of   February   , 1905; that there was born to her on said date a   male   child; that said child was living March 4, 1905, and is said to have been named   De Witt D. Battiest

J. S. Fulton

Witnesses To Mark:

Subscribed and sworn to before me this 13 day of   March   , 1905

EA Newman
Notary Public.

7-3482

Muskogee, Indian Territory, March 18, 1905.

Lewis G. Battiest,
Atoka, Indian Territory.

Dear Sir:

Receipt is hereby acknowledged of the affidavits of Emma Battiest nee Dyer and J. S. Fulton to the birth of De Witt D. Battiest, infant son of Lewis G. and Emma Battiest, February 13, 1905, and the same have been filed with our records as an application for the enrollment of said child.

Respectfully,

Chairman.

Applications for Enrollment of Choctaw Newborn
Act of 1905   Volume IV

COPY.   N. B. 234

Muskogee, Indian Territory, April 7, 1905.

Lewis G. Battiest,
    Atoka, Indian Territory.

Dear Sir:

    Referring to the affidavits heretofore forwarded to the birth of DeWitt D. Battiest, it is stated in the affidavit of the mother, Emma Battiest, that she is a citizen by blood of the Choctaw Nation.

    If this is correct, you are requested to state when, where and under what name she was listed for enrollment, the names of her parents and other members of her family for whom application was made at the same time.

                                Respectfully,
                                SIGNED

                                T.B. Needles
SEV4-7   Commissioner in Charge.

Goodwater, I. T. April 14, 1905.

Commission to the Five Civilized Tribes,
    Muskogee, I. T.

                                Gentlemen:

I am in receipt os[sic] your letter under date of April 7th, 1905 in which you requested me to state when, where and under what name my wife was listed for enrollment, the names of her parents etc. In reply you are informed that my wife Emma Battiest was enrolled by the Dawes Commission several years ago, at Durant I. T. under the name of Emma Dyer. The name of my wife's father was Willie Dyer & her mother's name was Phoebe Dyer, both dead. My wife's roll number is 9934 Choctaw by blood.

                              Yours respectfully,

                              (Signed) L.G. Battiest.

Applications for Enrollment of Choctaw Newborn
Act of 1905   Volume IV

Choctaw 3482.

Muskogee, Indian Territory, April 21, 1905.

L. G. Battiest,
    Goodwater, Indian Territory.

Dear Sir:

    Receipt is hereby acknowledged of your letter of April 14, giving the maiden name of your wife, Emma Battiest, and her roll number and this information has enabled the Commission to identify her upon its records as an enrolled citizen by blood of the Choctaw Nation.

    Respectfully,

    Chairman.

Choc New Born 235
    Henry McKinley Roberts
    (Born Dec. 5, 1902)

BIRTH AFFIDAVIT.
DEPARTMENT OF THE INTERIOR.
COMMISSION TO THE FIVE CIVILIZED TRIBES.

IN RE APPLICATION FOR ENROLLMENT, as a citizen of the   Choctaw   Nation of   Henry McKinley Roberts   , born on the   5th day of   December   , 1902

Name of Father: Ben. J. Roberts   a citizen of the   Choctaw   Nation.
Name of Mother: Hattie Roberts   a citizen of the   Choctaw   Nation.

    Postoffice   Bennington I.T.

Applications for Enrollment of Choctaw Newborn
Act of 1905 Volume IV

AFFIDAVIT OF MOTHER.

UNITED STATES OF AMERICA,
INDIAN TERRITORY,
Central   DISTRICT.

I, Hattie Roberts, on oath state that I am 19 years of age and a citizen by birth, of the Choctaw Nation; that I am the lawful wife of Ben. J. Roberts, who is a citizen, by Birth of the Choctaw Nation; that a male child was born to me on 5th day of December, 1902, that said child has been named Henry McKinley Roberts, and is now living.

                                                      her
    WITNESSES TO MARK: Hattie x Roberts
  Isaac Hampton   mark
  W.J. Billy

Subscribed and sworn to before me this 23rd day of December, 1902.

                                        C. C. McClard
                                        Notary Public.

AFFIDAVIT OF ATTENDING PHYSICIAN OR MID-WIFE.

UNITED STATES OF AMERICA,
INDIAN TERRITORY,
Central   DISTRICT.

I, Kacey Homer, a Midwife, on oath state that I attended on Mrs. Hattie Roberts, wife of Ben. J. Roberts on the 5th day of December, 1902 ; that there was born to her on said date a male child; that said child is now living and is said to have been named Henry McKinley Roberts

                                                her
    WITNESSES TO MARK: Kacey x Homer
  Isaac Hampton   mark
  W.J. Billy

Subscribed and sworn to before me this 23rd day of December, 1902.

                                        C. C. McClard
                                        Notary Public.

Applications for Enrollment of Choctaw Newborn
Act of 1905   Volume IV

DEPARTMENT OF THE INTERIOR.
COMMISSIONER TO THE FIVE CIVILIZED TRIBES.

Bennington, Indian Territory, February 2, 1907.

In the matter of the application for the enrollment of Henry McKinley Roberts as a citizen of the Choctaw Nation, under Act of Congress, approved March 4, 1905.

Ben J. Roberts, being first duly sworn and examined, testifies as follows:

ON BEHALF OF THE COMMISSIONER:

Q What is your name?   A Ben J. Roberts.
Q How old are you?   A Forty-seven.
Q What is your postoffice address?   A Bennington.
Q What is the name of your father?   A Jesse.
Q What is the name of your mother?   A Beckie.
Q Are you married?   A Yes, sir, but my wife is dead.
Q What was your wife's name?   A Hattie.
Q What was your wife's father's name?   A Watson Anderson.
Q What is the name of her mother?   A Lucinda Anderson.
Q Was you wife a duly enrolled Choctaw citizen?   A Yes, sir.
Q Under what name was your wife enrolled?   A Hattie Anderson.
Q Has there ever been any filing made for Hattie Anderson?   A Yes, sir.
Q Who filed for her?   A The Commissioners.
Q Was this an arbitrary allotment?   A Yes, sir.
Q Have you ever received an allotment certificate for that filing?   A Yes, sir.
Q Did you have any children by your wife, Hattie Roberts?   A Benjamin.
Q Any more?   A Henry McKinley.
Q Which of these children are the oldest?   A Henry.
Q When was Henry McKinley born?   A December 5, 1902.
Q When was Benjamin born?   A May 22, 1905.
Q Have you ever made application for the enrollment of Benjamin Roberts, your son? A No, sir.
Q Is this boy, Henry McKinley Roberts still living?   A Yes, sir.
Q When did your wife Hattie Roberts die?   A February 22, 1906.
Q Have you remarried since that time?   A No, sir.

(Witness excused)

I, Fay E. Blachert, stenographer to the Commissioner to the Five Civilized Tribes, upon oath, state that I reported the proceedings in the above and foregoing cause and that the same is a true and correct transcript of my stenographic notes taken therein.

Fay E. Blachert

Applications for Enrollment of Choctaw Newborn
Act of 1905   Volume IV

Subscribed and sworn to before me this 3rd day of February, 1907.

            Richard Shanafelt
            Notary Public.

DEPARTMENT OF THE INTERIOR,
COMMISSIONER TO THE FIVE CIVILIZED TRIBES.

Durant, Indian Territory, January 18, 1907.

ooOoo

  In the matter of the application for the enrollment, as a New Born citizen of the Choctaw Nation, under the Act of Congress approved March 3, 1905, of Henry McKinley Roberts, on Card No. 235.

  Testimony taken at Bennington, Indian Territory, December 20, 1906.

  WALTON BILLEY, being duly sworn, by Lacey P. Bobo, Notary Public in and for the Central District of Indian Territory, testified as follows:

BY THE COMMISSIONER:

Q What is your name?   A Walton Billey.
Q What is your age?   A 32.
Q Are you duly enrolled as a citizen by blood of the Choctaw Nation?
A Yes.
Q Were you acquainted with a Choctaw citizen near Bennington, Indian Territory, named Benjamin J. Roberts?
A Yes.
Q What was his wife's name?
A Hattie Roberts, she is dead now, she died in 1905, I have lost the month but I know it was last year.
Q Did this woman leave any new born Choctaw children?
A Yes, Henry McKinley, that's the oldest, and Benjamin Roberts.
Q Is Benjamin J. Roberts the father of Henry McKinley and Benjamin Roberts?
A Yes.
Q Are either of these children dead at the present time?
A No, both living.
Q Which is the older?   A Henry McKinley.
Q How old is Henry McKinley Roberts?
A Next January he will be four years old, I do not know what day but I know it is in January.
Q From the records of the Commission to the Five Civilized Tribes it appears that an application for the enrollment of this Henry McKinley Roberts has been made and is

Applications for Enrollment of Choctaw Newborn
Act of 1905   Volume IV

now pending: Do you know whether application has been made for the enrollment of this child's full brother, Benjamin?
A   No, not for Benjamin, he made application for Henry McKinley.
Q   How long have you known Benjamin J. Roberts, the father of these children, and his wife Hattie?
A   Benjamin the father of the children is my half brother, I have always known him, we have the same mother but a different father.
Q   How near do you live to Benjamin Roberts and his minor children now?   A   About a mile.
Q   Do you state as a positive fact that Henry McKinley Roberts was born before March 4, 1905, and is at the present time living?   A   Yes.
Q   When was this Benjamin Roberts, son of Benjamin J. Roberts and Hattie Roberts, born?
A   Last November he was two years old, I do not know the exact date of his birth, he is going on three years old now.
Q   Do you state as a matter of fact and under oath that Benjamin Roberts, minor son of Benjamin J. Roberts and Hattie Roberts, was born prior to March 4, 1906, and is at the present time living?   A   Yes.
Q   Does the father of these children affiliate with that band of recalcitrant Indians generally known as Snakes?
A   Yes.
                              Witness Excused.

Testimony taken at same place and on same date as above.

J. J. PARKERSON, being duly sworn, by Lacey P. Bobo, Notary Public in and for the Central District of Indian Territory, testified as follows:

BY THE COMMISSIONER:

Q   What is your name?   A   J. J. Parkerson.
Q   How old are you?   A   I am going on 37.
Q   What is your post office?   A   Bennington, I. T.
Q   How long have you lived at or near Bennington, I. T.?
A   I have lived here close to Bennington nine years.
Q   Are you acquainted with one Benjamin J. Roberts, a citizen by blood of the Choctaw Nation?
A   I have known him and his half brother Walton Billey ever since I have been in this ` country.
Q   What is Benjamin J. Robert's wife's name?
A   I do not know, I never knew her only as Mrs. Roberts.
Q   Was she a citizen by blood of the Choctaw Nation?
A   Yes, she was a Choctaw.
Q   Was she regarded as Benjamin J. Roberts' lawful wife?

Applications for Enrollment of Choctaw Newborn
Act of 1905   Volume IV

A Yes sir.
Q Did this woman you knew as Mrs. Roberts have any minor children by Benjamin J. Roberts?   A Yes, sir.
Q What is the name of the younger one?
A Benjamin, Jr.
Q When was Benjamin, Jr., born?
A I could not tell you about that.
A[sic] Do you know him to have been born before March 4, 1906?
A Yes, sir.
Q Is he living at the present time?   A Yes, sir.
Q Do you see this child frequently?
A Why, yes, I see him nearly every day at Walton Billey's house.
Q How old would you judge the child to be?
A I would judge him to be a little over two years old.
Q Had Benjamin J. Roberts any other minor children living?
A Yes, sir, another boy older than that one.
Q What is his name?   A Henry McKinley Roberts.
Q Is Henry McKinley Roberts living at the present time?
A Yes, he is living at the present time, he was yesterday.
Q How old is this child, judging by his size?
A Well, I would judge him to be three or four years old, the biggest boy.
Q Do you state under oath that Henry McKinley Roberts was born before March 4, 1905?   A Yes, sir.
Q With whom do these children at present make their home?
A At Ben Roberts.
Q Is Benjamin Roberts[sic] wife, known to you as Mrs. Roberts, living at the present time?
A No, sir, she is dead.
Q When did she die?
A She died a little over a year ago.
Q Are you related to either Henry McKinley Roberts or Benjamin Roberts, Jr.?
A No, sir.
Q Are you interested directly or indirectly in any estate this child may have by virtue of his enrollment as a citizen by blood of the Choctaw Nation--that is, Henry McKinley Roberts?
A No, sir.

W. P. Covington, being duly sworn, states that the above and foregoing is a full, true and correct transcript of his stenographic notes taken in said case on said date.

Sworn and subscribed to before me, this _____ day of _____ 190 7.

Notary Public.

Applications for Enrollment of Choctaw Newborn
Act of 1905   Volume IV

In the matter of the application for the enrollment, as a citizen by blood of the Choctaw Nation, of Henry McKinley Roberts.

Testimony taken at the home of Benjamin J. Roberts, five miles southwest of Bennington, Indian Territory, December 21, 1906.

BENJAMIN J. ROBERTS, being duly sworn, by Lacey P. Bobo, Notary Public in and for the Central District of Indian Territory, testified as follows:

Jacob Homer, Official Interpreter.

<u>BY THE Commissioner</u>:

Q What is your name?   A Benjamin J. Roberts.
Q How old are you?   A I was born in 1858, old men have told me I was born about that time.
Q What is your wife's name?   A Hattie Roberts.
Q Have you had a child or children born since September 25, 1902 by Hattie Roberts?
A Yes, sir.
Q How many?   A Two.
Q What is the name of the oldest?   A Henry McKinley Roberts, a boy.
Q And the second is Benjamin Roberts, Jr.?   A Yes.
Q When was Henry McKinley Roberts born?
A December 5, 1902.
Q Benjamin Roberts is also a boy?   A Yes, sir, both boys.
Q When was Benjamin Roberts born?   A May 22, 1905.
Q Are both of these children living at the present time?
A Yes, sir, both living.

> Witness directs attention to the presence of two small children, stating they are Henry McKinley and Benjamin Roberts.

Q Have you ever taken any steps looking to the placing of these children on the roll of citizens of the Choctaw Nation?
A I have made application for Henry McKinley, but I have never made application for Benjamin; I made application before a Notary Public but we could not do anything and I just quit and never done anything about Benjamin; there is lots of land but I never could do anything.
Q When did your wife Hattie die?
A February 22, 1906.

> Witness advised that subsequent to July 26, 1906, the Commissioner to the Five Civilized Tribes had no authority to receive applications for the enrollment of New Born Choctaws.

Applications for Enrollment of Choctaw Newborn
Act of 1905   Volume IV

W. P. Covington, being duly sworn states that the above and foregoing is a full, true and correct transcript of his stenographic notes taken in said case on said date.

W. P. Covington

Subscribed and sworn to before me, this 18th day of Jan. 1907.

Lacey P Bobo
Notary Public.

BIRTH AFFIDAVIT.

DEPARTMENT OF THE INTERIOR,
COMMISSIONER TO THE FIVE CIVILIZED TRIBES.

ENROLLMENT OF MINORS.   ACT OF CONGRESS, APPROVED APRIL 26, 1906.

IN RE APPLICATION FOR ENROLLMENT, as a citizen of the   Choctaw   Nation, of   Henry McKinley Roberts   , born on the   5th day of   December , 1902

Name of Father: Ben J. Roberts   a citizen of the   Choctaw   Nation.
                                    Anderson
Name of Mother: Hattie Roberts   formerly   a citizen of the   Choctaw   Nation.

Tribal enrollment of father .... Tribal enrollment of mother ....

Postoffice   Bennington I.T.

AFFIDAVIT OF MOTHER.

UNITED STATES OF AMERICA, Indian Territory, }
   Central   District.

I,   Ross Frazier   , on oath state that I am   30 years of age and a citizen by blood, of the ~~Choctaw Nation; that I am~~ personally acquainted with Hattie Roberts, now deceased ~~the lawful wife of~~   Ben J. Roberts   , who is a citizen, by blood of the   Choctaw   Nation; that a   male   child was born ~~to me~~ her on or about   5th day of December   , 1902, that said child has been named   Henry McKinley Roberts   , and ~~was living March 1, 1906~~ is still living.

Ross Frazier

WITNESSES TO MARK:

Subscribed and sworn to before me this   2nd day of   February , 1907.

Richard Shanafelt
Notary Public.

Applications for Enrollment of Choctaw Newborn
Act of 1905 Volume IV

AFFIDAVIT OF ATTENDING PHYSICIAN OR MID-WIFE.

UNITED STATES OF AMERICA, Indian Territory,
Central District.

I, Sampson Dyer, on oath state that I was personally acquainted with Hattie Roberts now deceased', wife of Ben J. Roberts on the 5 day of December, 1902 ; that there was born to her on said date a male child; that said child is still living March 4, 1906, and is said to have been named Henry McKinley Roberts

Sampson Dyer

WITNESSES TO MARK:

Subscribed and sworn to before me this 2nd day of February , 1907

Richard Shanafelt
Notary Public.

BIRTH AFFIDAVIT.

DEPARTMENT OF THE INTERIOR,
COMMISSIONER TO THE FIVE CIVILIZED TRIBES.

ENROLLMENT OF MINORS. ACT OF CONGRESS, APPROVED APRIL 26, 1906.

IN RE APPLICATION FOR ENROLLMENT, as a citizen of the Choctaw Nation, of Henry McKinley Roberts , born on the 5th day of December , 1902

Name of Father: Ben J. Roberts   a citizen of the Choctaw Nation.
Anderson
Name of Mother: Hattie Roberts formerly a citizen of the Choctaw Nation.

Tribal enrollment of father .... Tribal enrollment of mother ....

Postoffice Bennington I.T.

AFFIDAVIT OF MOTHER.

UNITED STATES OF AMERICA, Indian Territory,
Central District.

I, Asa J Homer , on oath state that I am 50 years of age and a citizen by blood , of the Choctaw Nation; that I was personally acquainted with Hattie Roberts, now deceased the lawful wife of Ben J. Roberts , who is a citizen, by blood of the Choctaw Nation; that a male child was born to her on or about 5

Applications for Enrollment of Choctaw Newborn
Act of 1905   Volume IV

day of December , 1902 , that said child has been named Henry McKinley Roberts , and ~~was living~~ is still living ~~March 4, 1906~~.

As J Homer

WITNESSES TO MARK:

{

Subscribed and sworn to before me this 2nd day of February , 1907

Richard Shanafelt
Notary Public.

AFFIDAVIT OF ATTENDING PHYSICIAN OR MID-WIFE.

UNITED STATES OF AMERICA, Indian Territory,
Central   District.

I, Lane Wilson, , on oath state that I was personally acquainted with   now deceased a ~~attended on~~ ^ Hattie Roberts ^ , wife of Ben J. Roberts on the 5 day of December, 1902 ; that there was born to her on said date a male child; that said child ~~was~~ is still living March 4, 1906, and is said to have been named Henry McKinley Roberts

Lane Wilson

WITNESSES TO MARK:

{

Subscribed and sworn to before me this 2nd day of February , 1907

Richard Shanafelt
Notary Public.

7-3492

Muskogee, Indian Territory, March 3, 1903.

Ben J. Roberts,
  Bennington, Indian Territory.

Dear Sir:

  Referring to the application for enrollment as a citizen of the Choctaw Nation of Henry McKinley Roberts, infant son of Ben J. and Hattie Roberts, born December 5, 1902, which was recently forwarded to this office, your attention is invited to the following provision of the thirty-fourth section of the act of Congress approved July 1, 1902, which was ratified by the citizens of the Choctaw and Chickasaw Nations September 25, 1902:

Applications for Enrollment of Choctaw Newborn
Act of 1905   Volume IV

"During the ninety days first following the date of the final ratification of this agreement, the Commission to the Five Civilized Tribes may receive applications for enrollment only of persons whose names are on the tribal rolls, but who have not heretofore been enrolled by said Commission, commonly known as "delinquents," and such intermarried white persons as may have married recognized citizens of the Choctaw and Chickasaw Nations in accordance with the tribal laws, customs and usages on or before the date of the passage of this Act by Congress, and such infant children as may have been born to recognized and enrolled citizens on or before the date of the final ratification of this agreement; but the application of no person whomsoever for enrollment shall be received after the expiration of the said ninety days."

Under the above legislation, the Commission is without authority to enroll this child.

Respectfully,

Chairman.

COPY.   N.B. 235.

Muskogee, Indian Territory, April 7, 1905.

Benjamin J. Roberts,
    Bennington, Indian Territory.

Dear Sir:

There is enclosed you herewith for execution application for the enrollment of your infant child, Henry McKinley Roberts born December 5, 1902.

The affidavits heretofore filed with the Commission show the child was living December 23, 1902. It is necessary for the child to be enrolled, that he was living on March 4, 1905. It also appears from these affidavits that the mother is a Choctaw by blood, if this is correct you are requested to state when, where and under what name she was listed for enrollment, the names of her parents and other members of her family for whom application was made at the same time. You will please insert the age of the mother in space provided for that purpose.

In having these affidavits executed care should be exercised to see that all the names are written in full as they appear in the body of the affidavit, and in the event that either of the persons signing the affidavit are unable to write, signatures by mark must be attested by two witnesses. Each affidavit must be executed before a Notary Public and the notarial seal and signature of the officer must be attached to each separate affidavit.

Applications for Enrollment of Choctaw Newborn
Act of 1905   Volume IV

LER 7-12

Respectfully,
SIGNED   *T.B. Needles*
Commissioner in Charge.

7-N.B. 235.

Muskogee, Indian Territory, May 11, 1905.

Benjamin J. Roberts,
    Bennington, Indian Territory.

Dear Sir:

    There is enclosed you herewith for execution application for the enrollment of your infant child, Henry McKinley Roberts, born December 5, 1902.

    Your attention is called to the Commission's letter of the 7th ultimo, which contained affidavits similar to those above mentioned, and to which you were requested to furnish information by which the mother of the applicant might be identified. Please have the enclosed affidavits executed and return to this office, at the same time stating when, where and under what name your wife was listed for enrollment, the names of her parents and other members of her family for whom application was made at the same time, and if she has selected an allotment, give her roll number as the same appears on her allotment certificate.

    In having these affidavits executed care should be exercised to see that all the names are written in full as they appear in the body of the affidavit, and in the event that either of the persons signing the affidavit are unable to write, signatures by mark must be attested by two witnesses. Each affidavit must be executed before a Notary Public and the notarial seal and signature of the officer must be attached to each separate affidavit.

Respectfully,

C. 11/4.

Chairman.

Applications for Enrollment of Choctaw Newborn
Act of 1905 Volume IV

7-NB-235

Muskogee, Indian Territory, July 29, 1905.

Benjamin J. Roberts,
Bennington, Indian Territory.

Dear Sir:

Your attention is called to a communication addressed to you by the Commission to the Five Civilized Tribes, under date of May 12, 1905, with which there was inclosed for execution application for the enrollment of your infant child, Henry McKinley Roberts, born December 5, 1902.

In said letter you were advised that the affidavits heretofore filed in this office show that the applicant was living December 23, 1902, and that it was necessary for it to be enrolled that he was living March 4, 1905; you were requested to have the affidavits properly executed and return to this office immediately; you were also requested to furnish information by which your wife Hattie Roberts, may be identified as a citizen by blood of the Choctaw Nation. No reply to this letter has been received.

In the event the child died prior to March 4, 1905, you will please have the inclosed proof of death executed, seeing that all the names are written in full, and if any of the persons signing the affidavits are unable to write, signatures by mark must be attested by two witnesses. Each affidavit must be executed before a Notary Public and the notarial seal and signature of the officer must be attached to each separate affidavit.

If the child was living on March 4, 1905, you are requested to have the application heretofore mailed you, executed, forwarding same to this office immediately, as no further action can be taken relative to the enrollment of your said child until the evidence requested is supplied.

Respectfully,

LM 7/29

Commissioner.

7-NB-235

Muskogee, Indian Territory, February 4, 1907.

Benjamin J. Roberts,
Bennington, Indian Territory.

Dear Sir:

Please advise this office at once the maiden name of your former wife Hattie Roberts, the names of her parents, and if allotment has been selected for her please state her roll number as it appears upon her allotment certificate.

Applications for Enrollment of Choctaw Newborn
Act of 1905   Volume IV

This matter should receive <u>immediate</u> attention.

Respectfully,

Commissioner.

Choc New Born 236
    Brewster Lewis
    (Born Oct. 15, 1903)

BIRTH AFFIDAVIT.

DEPARTMENT OF THE INTERIOR.
COMMISSION TO THE FIVE CIVILIZED TRIBES.

IN RE APPLICATION FOR ENROLLMENT, as a citizen of the Choctaw Nation, of Brewster Lewis, born on the 15th day of Oct, 1903

Name of Father: Charles S Lewis   a citizen of the Choc Nation.
Name of Mother: Cynthia Eudora Lewis   a citizen of the Choc Nation.

Postoffice   Peck I.T.

AFFIDAVIT OF MOTHER.

UNITED STATES OF AMERICA, Indian Territory,
  Central   DISTRICT.

    I, Cynthia Eudora Lewis, on oath state that I am 23 years of age and a citizen by Intermarriage, of the Choctaw Nation; that I am the lawful wife of Charles S Lewis, who is a citizen, by blood of the Choctaw Nation; that a male child was born to me on 15th day of October, 1903; that said child has been named Brewster Lewis, and was living March 4, 1905.

                               Cynthia Eudora Lewis

Witnesses To Mark:

    Subscribed and sworn to before me this 13th day of March, 1905

                             W.H. Angell
                                Notary Public.

Applications for Enrollment of Choctaw Newborn
Act of 1905 Volume IV

AFFIDAVIT OF ATTENDING PHYSICIAN OR MID-WIFE.

UNITED STATES OF AMERICA, Indian Territory,
Central DISTRICT.

I, T J Long, a physician, on oath state that I attended on Mrs. Cynthia Eudora Lewis, wife of Charles S Lewis on the 15th day of October, 1903; that there was born to her on said date a male child; that said child was living March 4, 1905, and is said to have been named Brewster Lewis

T. J. Long M.D.

Witnesses To Mark:

Subscribed and sworn to before me this 13th day of March, 1905

W.H. Angell
Notary Public.

7-3494

Muskogee, Indian Territory, March 6, 1905.

Charles S. Lewis,
Peck, Indian Territory.

Dear Sir:

Receipt is hereby acknowledged of the affidavits of Cynthia Eudora Lewis and T. J. Long to the birth of Worcester[sic] Lewis infant son of Charles S. and Cynthia E. Lewis, October 15, 1903, and the same have been filed with our records as an application for the enrollment of said child.

Respectfully,

Chairman.

Applications for Enrollment of Choctaw Newborn
Act of 1905   Volume IV

7-3494

Muskogee, Indian Territory, March 27, 1905.

Charles S. Lewis,
    Peck, Indian Territory.

Dear Sir:

    Receipt is hereby acknowledged of your letter without date in which you state that the correct name of your child is Brewster not Worcester Lewis.

    In reply to your letter you are advised that the records of the Commission show that the name of your child for whom application was recently made is Brewster Lewis, son of Charles S. and Cynthia Eudora Lewis.

        Respectfully,

        Chairman.

Choc New Born 237
    Morris Stanley McClendon
    (Born June 8, 1904)

DEPARTMENT OF THE INTERIOR.
Commission to the Five Civilized Tribes.

---o-o---

    IN RE Application for Enrollment, as a citizen of the   Choctaw   Nation, of Morris Stanley McClendon   born   June 8 , 190 4.

Name of father: T. L. McClendon   , a citizen of the   United States
Name of mother: Annie McClendon   , a citizen of the   Choctaw Nation
Postoffice: Washington, I.T.

AFFIDAVIT OF MOTHER

---o-o---

UNITED STATES OF AMERICA, :
    INDIAN TERRITORY,   : SS.
        SOUTHERN DISTRICT. :

Applications for Enrollment of Choctaw Newborn
Act of 1905   Volume IV

I   Annie McClendon   , on oath state that I am   30   years of age and a citizen of   Choctaw Nation   , that I am the lawful wife of   T.L. McClendon   , who is a citizen of   United States   ; that a   male   child was born to me on the   8th day of   June 1904   ; that said child has been named   Morris Stanley McClendon   , and is now living.

Witnesses to signature: Annie McClendon
E. E. Gillam
O H Loomis

Subscribed and sworn to before me this, the   3   day of   March   , 1905.
My Commission
Expires Nov. 17, 1908   O. H. Loomis
                                                              Notary Public.

AFFIDAVIT OF ATTENDING PHYSICIAN OR MIDWIFE.

---o-o---

UNITED STATES OF AMERICA, :
        INDIAN TERRITORY,   : SS.
        SOUTHERN DISTRICT. :

I,   Nancy E. Kerr   , a midwife, on oath, states that I attended on Mrs.   Annie McClendon   , wife of   T.L. McClendon   , on the   8th day of   June   , 190 4 , that there was born to her on said date, a   Male   child; that said child is now living, and is said to have been named   Morris Stanley McClendon

                                        Nancy E Kerr
                                        Midwife.
Witnesses to Signature:
E. E. Gillam
O.H. Loomis

Subscribed and sworn to before me this, the   3rd day of   March   , 1905.
My Commission
Expires Nov. 17, 1908   O. H. Loomis
                                                 Notary Public.

Applications for Enrollment of Choctaw Newborn
Act of 1905   Volume IV

BIRTH AFFIDAVIT.

DEPARTMENT OF THE INTERIOR,
COMMISSION TO THE FIVE CIVILIZED TRIBES.

IN RE Application for Enrollment, as a citizen of the   Choctaw   Nation, of   Morris Stanley McClendon , born on the   8th day of   June   , 1904

Name of Father: T.L. McClendon   a citizen of the   Choctaw   Nation.
Name of Mother: Annie McClendon   a citizen of the   Choctaw   Nation.

Post-Office: Washington I.T.

AFFIDAVIT OF MOTHER.

UNITED STATES OF AMERICA,
   INDIAN TERRITORY.
Southern   District.

I,   Annie McClendon   , on oath state that I am   30   years of age and a citizen by   blood   , of the   Choctaw   Nation; that I am the lawful wife of   T.L. McClendon   , who is a citizen, ~~by~~............of the   United States   Nation; that a   male   child was born to me on   8th day of   June   , 1904 , that said child has been named   Morris Stanley McClendon   , and is now living.

Annie McClendon

WITNESSES TO MARK:

Subscribed and sworn to before me this   10th *day of*   April   , 1905.

Geo W Miller
NOTARY PUBLIC.

AFFIDAVIT OF ATTENDING PHYSICIAN OR MID-WIFE.

UNITED STATES OF AMERICA,
   INDIAN TERRITORY.
Southern District   District.

I,   Nancy E Kerr   , a   midwife   , on oath state that I attended on Mrs.   Annie McClendon   , wife of   T.L. McClendon   on the   8th day of June , 1904 ; that there was born to her on said date a   male   child; that said child is now living and is said to have been named   Morris Stanley McClendon

Applications for Enrollment of Choctaw Newborn
Act of 1905 Volume IV

WITNESSES TO MARK:

{

Subscribed and sworn to before me this 10th day of April , 1905.

Geo W Miller
NOTARY PUBLIC.

7-3540

Muskogee, Indian Territory, March 7, 1905.

Annie McClendon,
    Washington, Indian Territory.

Dear Madam:

    Receipt is hereby acknowledged of your affidavit and the affidavit of Nancy E. Kerr to the birth of Morris Stanley McClendon son of Annie and T. L. McClendon June 8, 1904, and the same have been filed with our records as an application for the enrollment of said child.

    Respectfully,

    Commissioner in Charge.

COPY.   N.B. 237.

Muskogee, Indian Territory, April 7, 1905.

T. L. McClendon,
    Washington, Indian Territory.

Dear Sir:

    There is enclosed you herewith for execution application for the enrollment of your infant child Morris Stanley McClendon, born June 8, 1904.

    The affidavits heretofore filed with the Commission show the child was living March 3, 1905. It is necessary for the child to be enrolled, that he was living on March 4, 1905. You will please insert the age of the mother in space provided for that purpose.

    In having these affidavits executed care should be exercised to see that all the names are written in full as they appear in the body of the affidavit, and in the event that

Applications for Enrollment of Choctaw Newborn
Act of 1905 Volume IV

either of the persons signing the affidavit are unable to write, signatures by mark must be attested by two witnesses. Each affidavit must be executed before a Notary Public and the notarial seal and signature of the officer must be attached to each separate affidavit.

LER 7-10

Respectfully,
SIGNED
T.B. Needles
Commissioner in Charge.

Choctaw 3540.

Muskogee, Indian Territory, April 15, 1905.

T. L. McClendon,
    Purcell, Indian Territory.

Dear Sir:

    Receipt is hereby acknowledged of your letter of April 10, enclosing the affidavits of Annie McClendon and Nancy E. Kerr to the birth of Morris Stanley McClendon, son of F[sic] L. and Annie McClendon, June 8, 1904, and the same have been filed with our records as an application for the enrollment of said child.

Respectfully,

Chairman.

Applications for Enrollment of Choctaw Newborn
Act of 1905   Volume IV

Choc New Born 238
>Chas. Franklin Beal
>(Born Oct. 23, 1902)

The Sate[sic] of Texas,
County of Fannin.

>To any Judge of the District or County Court, Justice of the Peace, or regularly licenses or ordained Minister of the Gospel, GREETING:-

>You are hereby authorized to solemnize the rites of matrimony between W. C. Beal and D. E. Wingate, and made due return of this license to my office within sixty days, certified according to law.

>Given under my hand and seal of office at Bonham this the 1st day of September, 1883.

>>J. H. Oliphint Clerk County
>>Court, Fannin County.

>I, W. L. Fuqua, a minister of the Cumberland Presbyterian Church hereby certify that I solemnized the rites of matrimony between W. C. Beal and Miss D. E. Wingate on the 2nd day of September, 1883.

>>W. L. Fuqua.

Issued Sept., 1st, 1883.
Recorded Sept. 11th, 1883

>>(STAMP)

The State of Texas,   )
>>>)
County of Famin[sic].   )

>I, T. F. Gray, County Clerk of Fannin County, Texas, do hereby certify that the foregoign[sic] is a true copy of the marriage license and the return thereon issued to W. C. Beal and D. E. Wingate as is of record in Book "E" page 5 of the marriage records of Fannin County, Texas.

>(Seal)   T. F. Gray, Co. Clerk.
Per C. R. Inglish[sic], Deputy.   Fannin County, Texas.

Applications for Enrollment of Choctaw Newborn
Act of 1905   Volume IV

BIRTH AFFIDAVIT.

Department of the Interior,
COMMISSION TO THE FIVE CIVILIZED TRIBES.

IN RE APPLICATION FOR ENROLLMENT, as a citizen of the   Choctaw   Nation, of   Chas. Franklin Beal   , born on the   23   day of   Oct   , 190 5

Name of Father: Wm C. Beal   a citizen of the   Choctaw   Nation.
Name of Mother: D. E. Beal   a citizen of the .... Nation.

Post-Office: Silo Ind. Ter.

AFFIDAVIT OF MOTHER.

UNITED STATES OF AMERICA, }
  INDIAN TERRITORY,
   Cent.   District.

I,   D. E. Beal   , on oath state that I am   36   years of age and a citizen by intermarriage , of the   Choctaw   Nation; that I am the lawful wife of   Wm C. Beal   , who is a citizen, by Blood   of the   Choctaw   Nation; that a   male   child was born to me on   23   day of   Oct   , 190 2, that said child has been named   Chas Franklin Beal`   , and is now living.

D E Beal

WITNESSES TO MARK:
{

Subscribed and sworn to before me this   20   day of   Nov   , 190 2

G. F. Dick
Notary Public.

AFFIDAVIT OF ATTENDING PHYSICIAN OR MID-WIFE.

UNITED STATES OF AMERICA, }
  INDIAN TERRITORY,
   Central   District.

I,   E. G. Pate   , a   M. D.   , on oath state that I attended on Mrs ...., wife of Wife of W^m C Beal   on the 23 day of Oct, 190 2; that there was born to her on said date a   male   child; that said child is now living and is said to have been named   Chas Franklin Beal

E.G. Pate M.D.

WITNESSES TO MARK:
{

285

Applications for Enrollment of Choctaw Newborn
Act of 1905 Volume IV

Subscribed and sworn to before me this 20 *day of* Nov , 190 2

G. F. Dick
Notary Public.

BIRTH AFFIDAVIT.

DEPARTMENT OF THE INTERIOR.
COMMISSION TO THE FIVE CIVILIZED TRIBES.

IN RE APPLICATION FOR ENROLLMENT, as a citizen of the Choctaw Nation, of Charley Beal , born on the 23 day of Oct , 1902

Name of Father: William C Beal   a citizen of the Choctaw Nation.
Name of Mother: Donna Beal   a citizen of the U.S. Nation.

Postoffice Silo Ind Territory

AFFIDAVIT OF MOTHER.

UNITED STATES OF AMERICA, Indian Territory,
Central Judical[sic]   DISTRICT.

I, Donna Beal , on oath state that I am 38 years of age and a citizen by ...., of the United States Nation; that I am the lawful wife of William C Beal , who is a citizen, by Blood of the Choctaw Nation; that a male child was born to me on 23 day of Oct , 1902; that said child has been named Charley Beal , and was living March 4, 1905.

Donna Beal

Witnesses To Mark:

Subscribed and sworn to before me this 29 day of March , 1905

F. M. Kizer
Notary Public.

Applications for Enrollment of Choctaw Newborn
Act of 1905 Volume IV

AFFIDAVIT OF ATTENDING PHYSICIAN OR MID-WIFE.

UNITED STATES OF AMERICA, Indian Territory, }
Central Judicial   DISTRICT.

I, E.G. Pate, a Physician, on oath state that I attended on Mrs. Donna Beal, wife of William C Beal on the 23 day of Oct, 1902; that there was born to her on said date a male child; that said child was living March 4, 1905, and is said to have been named Charley Beal

E.G. Pate M.D.

Witnesses To Mark:
{

Subscribed and sworn to before me this 29 day of March, 1905

F. M. Kizer
Notary Public.

BIRTH AFFIDAVIT.

DEPARTMENT OF THE INTERIOR.
COMMISSION TO THE FIVE CIVILIZED TRIBES.

IN RE APPLICATION FOR ENROLLMENT, as a citizen of the Choctaw Nation, of Chas Franklin Beal, born on the 23rd day of October, 1902

Name of Father: William C Beal   a citizen of the Choctaw Nation.
Name of Mother: Donnie[sic] Beal   a citizen of the U.S. Nation.

Postoffice   Silo Ind. Ter.

AFFIDAVIT OF MOTHER.

UNITED STATES OF AMERICA, Indian Territory, }
Central   DISTRICT.

I, Donnie Beal, on oath state that I am 38 years of age and a citizen by ...., of the United States Nation; that I am the lawful wife of William C Beal, who is a citizen, by blood of the Choctaw Nation; that a male child was born to me on 23rd day of October, 1902; that said child has been named Chas Franklin Beal, and was living March 4, 1905.

Witnesses To Mark:
{

Applications for Enrollment of Choctaw Newborn
Act of 1905 Volume IV

Subscribed and sworn to before me this 12 day of April, 1905

Donnie Beal
Notary Public.

AFFIDAVIT OF ATTENDING PHYSICIAN OR MID-WIFE.

UNITED STATES OF AMERICA, Indian Territory, }
Central DISTRICT. }

I, EG Pate, a Physician, on oath state that I attended on Mrs. Donna Beal, wife of William C Beal on the 23rd day of October, 1902; that there was born to her on said date a male child; that said child was living March 4, 1905, and is said to have been named Chas Franklin Beal

E.G. Pate MD

Witnesses To Mark:
{

Subscribed and sworn to before me this 12 day of April, 1905

F M Kizer
Notary Public.

BIRTH AFFIDAVIT.

DEPARTMENT OF THE INTERIOR.
COMMISSION TO THE FIVE CIVILIZED TRIBES.

IN RE APPLICATION FOR ENROLLMENT, as a citizen of the Choctaw Nation, of Chas Franklin Beal, born on the 23rd day of October, 1902

Name of Father: William C Beal a citizen of the Choctaw Nation.
Name of Mother: Donnie[sic] Beal a citizen of the United States Nation.

Postoffice Silo I.T.

AFFIDAVIT OF MOTHER.

UNITED STATES OF AMERICA, Indian Territory, }
Central Judicial DISTRICT. }

I, Donnie Beal, on oath state that I am 38 years of age and a citizen by ...., of the United States Nation; that I am the lawful wife of William C

Applications for Enrollment of Choctaw Newborn
Act of 1905 Volume IV

Beal   , who is a citizen, by blood   of the   Choctaw   Nation; that a male   child was born to me on   23rd   day of   October   , 1902; that said child has been named   Chas Franklin Beal   , and was living March 4, 1905.

                                        Donnie Beal

Witnesses To Mark:
{
    Subscribed and sworn to before me this 20 day of   April   , 1905

                                        FM Kizer
                                            Notary Public.

AFFIDAVIT OF ATTENDING PHYSICIAN OR MID-WIFE.

UNITED STATES OF AMERICA, Indian Territory, }
   Central Judicial   DISTRICT.}

I,   E G Pate   , a   Physician   , on oath state that I attended on Mrs. Donnie Beal   , wife of   William C Beal   on the 23rd   day of October , 1902; that there was born to her on said date a   male   child; that said child was living March 4, 1905, and is said to have been named Chas Franklin Beal

                                        E.G. Pate MD

Witnesses To Mark:
{
    Subscribed and sworn to before me this 20 day of   April   , 1905

                                        F M Kizer
                                            Notary Public.

                                                    7-3498.

                        Muskogee, Indian Territory, November 24, 1902.

William C. Beal,
    Silo, Indian Territory.

Dear Sir:

        Receipt is hereby acknowledged of the application for enrollment of Charles Franklin Beal, infant son of William C. and D.E. Beal, born October 23, 1902.

        You are informed that the Commission is without authority to enroll this child as a citizen of the Choctaw Nation, it appearing that said child was born October 23,

Applications for Enrollment of Choctaw Newborn
Act of 1905   Volume IV

1902, subsequent to the ratification by the citizens of the Choctaw and Chickasaw Nations on September 25, 1902, of an act of Congress approved July 1, 1902 (32 Stats., 841).

Section twenty-eight thereof provides as follows:

"The names of all persons living on the date of the final ratification of this agreement entitled to be enrolled as provided in section 27 hereof shall be placed upon the rolls made by said Commission; and no child born thereafter to a citizen or freedman and no person intermarried thereafter to a citizen shall be entitled to enrollment or to participate in the distribution of the tribal property of the Choctaws and Chickasaws."

Respectfully,

Acting Chairman.

COPY.   N.B. 238

Muskogee, Indian Territory, April 7, 1905.

William C. Beal,
Silo, Indian Territory.

Dear Sir:

There is inclosed you herewith for execution application for the enrollment of your infant child, Chas. Franklin Beal, born October 23, 1902.

The affidavits heretofore filed with the Commission show the child was living on November 20, 1902. It is necessary, for the child to be enrolled, that he was living on March 4, 1905. You will please insert the age of the mother in space provided for that purpose.

It is also noted from the above mentioned affidavit that the mother's name is "D. E. Beal" while on the records of this office it appears that your wife is "Donnie Beal". If D. E. Beal and Donnie Beal are one and the same person, you will please insert the name Donnie Beal, as it appears on the records of this office, in the place, in the inclosed application, left for that purpose.

In case that D. E. Beal and Donnie Beal are different persons, it will be necessary that you file in this office the original or a certified copy of the license and certificate of marriage of yourself and D. E. Beal.

In having these affidavits executed care should be exercised to see that all the names are written in full as they appear in the body of the affidavit, and in the event that

Applications for Enrollment of Choctaw Newborn
Act of 1905 Volume IV

either of the persons signing the affidavit are unable to write, signatures by mark must be attested by two witnesses. Each affidavit must be executed before a Notary Public and the notarial seal and signature of the officer must be attached to each separate affidavit.

Respectfully,
SIGNED

T.B. Needles

LM 7-5. Commissioner in Charge.

Choctaw 3498.

Muskogee, Indian Territory, April 12, 1905.

William C. Beal,
    Silo, Indian Territory.

Dear Sir:

    Receipt is hereby acknowledged of the affidavits of Donna Beal and E. G. Pate to the birth of Charley Beal, son of William C. and Donna Beal, October 23, 1902, and the same have been filed with our records as an application for the enrollment of said child.

Respectfully,

Commissioner in Charge.

COPY. 7 N B 238

Muskogee, Indian Territory, April 17, 1905.

William C. Beal,
    Silo, Indian Territory.

Dear Sir:

    Receipt is hereby acknowledged of the affidavits of Donie[sic] Beal and E. G. Pate to the birth of Charles Franklin Beal son of William C. and Donnie Beal.

    You are advised, however, that the mother signed her affidavit upon the line which should have been used by the Notary Public for his signature and there is inclosed herewith for execution another blank partially made out which please have acknowledged and returned to this office as early as practicable.

Applications for Enrollment of Choctaw Newborn
Act of 1905 Volume IV

EB 4-17

Respectfully,
SIGNED

Tams Bixby
Chairman.

7-3498

Muskogee, Indian Territory, April 19, 1905.

William C. Beal,
 Silo, Indian Territory.

Dear Sir:

Receipt is hereby acknowledged of the affidavits of Donnie Beal and E. G. Pate to the birth of Charles Franklin Beal son of William C. and Donnie Beal, October 23, 1902, and the same have been filed with our records as an application for the enrollment of said child.

Respectfully,

Chairman.

COPY.

7 NB 238

Muskogee, Indian Territory, April 26, 1905.

William C. Beal,
 Silo, Indian Territory.

Dear Sir:

Receipt is hereby acknowledged of the affidavits of Donnie Beal and E. G. Pate to the birth of Chas. Franklin Beal, son of William C. and Donnie Beal, October 23, 1902, and the same have been filed with our records as an application for the enrollment of said child.

Respectfully,
SIGNED

Tams Bixby
Chairman.

Applications for Enrollment of Choctaw Newborn
Act of 1905 Volume IV

Choc New Born 239
    Junetta Nail
    (Born June 1, 1903)

BIRTH AFFIDAVIT.

DEPARTMENT OF THE INTERIOR.
COMMISSION TO THE FIVE CIVILIZED TRIBES.

IN RE APPLICATION FOR ENROLLMENT, as a citizen of the Choctaw Nation, of June Etta Nail , born on the 1 day of June , 190 3

Name of Father: Jessie Nail   a citizen of the Choctaw Nation.
Name of Mother: Mary Ann Nail   a citizen of the Choctaw Nation.

Postoffice   Coopeland[sic] I.T.

AFFIDAVIT OF MOTHER.

UNITED STATES OF AMERICA, Indian Territory, }
    Cent   DISTRICT.

I, Mary Ann Nail , on oath state that I am 23 years of age and a citizen by Marriage , of the Choctaw Nation; that I am the lawful wife of Jessie Nail , who is a citizen, by blood of the Choctaw Nation; that a female child was born to me on 1 day of June , 1903, that said child has been named June Etta Nail , and is now living.

    Mary Ann Nail

Witnesses To Mark:
JW Jones H.M. Clark

Subscribed and sworn to before me this 10 day of January , 1905.

    JW Jones
    Notary Public.

AFFIDAVIT OF ATTENDING PHYSICIAN OR MID-WIFE.

UNITED STATES OF AMERICA, Indian Territory, }
    Cent   DISTRICT.

I, Effie Swaffer , a midwife , on oath state that I attended on Mrs. Mary Ann Nail , wife of Jessie Nail on the 1 day of June , 1903;

Applications for Enrollment of Choctaw Newborn
Act of 1905   Volume IV

that there was born to her on said date a   female   child; that said child is now living and is said to have been named   June Etta Nail

                                      Effie Swaffar

Witnesses To Mark:
JW Jones   H.M. Clark

        Subscribed and sworn to before me this 10 day of January , 1905.

                                JW Jones
                                    Notary Public.

NEW BORN AFFIDAVIT

No _____

CHOCTAW ENROLLING COMMISSION

IN THE MATTER OF THE APPLICATION FOR ENROLLMENT as a citizen of the Choctaw Nation, of   Junetta Nail   born on the 1st day of   June   190 3

   Name of father Jessie Nail   a citizen of   Choctaw   Nation, final enrollment No. 10059
   Name of mother Mary Ann Nail   a citizen of   Choctaw   Nation, final enrollment No. 665

                            Copeland   Postoffice.

AFFIDAVIT OF MOTHER

UNITED STATES OF AMERICA
   INDIAN TERRITORY
Central DISTRICT

   I Mary Ann Nail   , on oath state that I am 23   years of age and a citizen by   Marriage   of the   Choctaw   Nation, and as such have been placed upon the final roll of the   Choctaw   Nation, by the Honorable Secretary of the Interior my final enrollment number being 665 ; that I am the lawful wife of Jessie Nail , who is a citizen of the   Choctaw   Nation, and as such has been placed upon the final roll of said Nation by the Honorable Secretary of the Interior, his final enrollment number being

Applications for Enrollment of Choctaw Newborn
Act of 1905   Volume IV

10059   and that a Female child was born to me on the 1st day of June   190 3; that said child has been named Junetta Nail , and is now living.

WITNESSETH: her   Mary Ann Nail
  Must be two witnesses { Maria x Cardwell
  who are citizens   mark
                                        Mary Priscilla Hodges
     Subscribed and sworn to before me this, the 10th   day of February , 190 5

                                                                [Illegible] Williams
                                                                          Notary Public.
My Commission Expires:
   Sept 5th 1905

Affidavit of Attending Physician or Midwife

UNITED STATES OF AMERICA, ⎫
       INDIAN TERRITORY,   ⎬
   Central   DISTRICT ⎭

   I, Effie Na. Swaffar   a   Midwife
on oath state that I attended on Mrs. Mary Ann Nail   wife of   Jessie Nail
on the 1st   day of June   , 190 3, that there was born to her on said date a   Female
child, that said child is now living, and is said to have been named Junetta Nail

                                              Effie Swaffar   M. D.

     Subscribed and sworn to before me this the 10th   day of February   1905

                                                   [Illegible] Williams
                                                            Notary Public.

WITNESSETH:
  Must be two witnesses   { Mary Priscilla Hodges
  who are citizens and   her
  know the child.   Maria x Cardwell
                                          mark
     We hereby certify that we are well acquainted with   Mrs Effie N Swaffar
a   Midwife   and know   her   to be reputable and of good standing in the community.

                                   Must be two citizen { Mary Priscilla Hodges
                                   witnesses.   her
                                                                 Maria x Cardwell
                                                                         mark

Applications for Enrollment of Choctaw Newborn
Act of 1905 Volume IV

BIRTH AFFIDAVIT.

DEPARTMENT OF THE INTERIOR.
COMMISSION TO THE FIVE CIVILIZED TRIBES.

IN RE APPLICATION FOR ENROLLMENT, as a citizen of the Choctaw Nation, of Junetta Nail, born on the 1st day of June, 1903

Name of Father: Jesse Nail　　　　a citizen of the Choctaw Nation.
Name of Mother: Mary Ann Nail　　a citizen of the Choctaw Nation.

Postoffice　Copeland, I.T.

AFFIDAVIT OF MOTHER.

UNITED STATES OF AMERICA, Indian Territory,
Central　　　　DISTRICT.

I, Mary Ann Nail, on oath state that I am 23 years of age and a citizen by intermarriage, of the Choctaw Nation; that I am the lawful wife of Jesse Nail, who is a citizen, by blood of the Choctaw Nation; that a female child was born to me on 1st day of June, 1903; that said child has been named Junetta Nail, and was living March 4, 1905.

　　　　　　　　　　　　　　　　　　　　Mary Ann Nail

Witnesses To Mark:

Subscribed and sworn to before me this 21st day of March, 1905

　　　　　　　　　　　W.H. Angell
　　　　　　　　　　　　Notary Public.

AFFIDAVIT OF ATTENDING PHYSICIAN OR MID-WIFE.

UNITED STATES OF AMERICA, Indian Territory,
Central　　　　DISTRICT.

I, Effie N. Swaffar, a midwife, on oath state that I attended on Mrs. Mary Ann Nail, wife of Jesse Nail on the 1st day of June, 1903; that there was born to her on said date a female child; that said child was living March 4, 1905, and is said to have been named Junetta Nail

　　　　　　　　　　　　　　　　　　Effie N Swaffar

Witnesses To Mark:

Applications for Enrollment of Choctaw Newborn
Act of 1905 Volume IV

Subscribed and sworn to before me this 1st day of April , 1905

[Illegible] Williams
Notary Public.

COPY. N.B. 239

Muskogee, Indian Territory, April 7, 1905.

Jesse Nail,
    Copeland, Indian Territory.

Dear Sir:

    There is enclosed you herewith for execution application for the enrollment of your infant child, June Etta Nail, born June 1, 1903.

    The affidavits heretofore filed with the Commission show the child was living January 10, 1905. It is necessary, for the child to be enrolled, that she was living on March 4, 1905. You will please insert the age of the mother in space provided for that purpose.

    In having these affidavits executed care should be exercised to see that all the names are written in full as they appear in the body of the affidavit, and in the event that either of the persons signing the affidavit are unable to write, signatures by mark must be attested by two witnesses. Each affidavit must be executed before a Notary Public and the notarial seal and signature of the officer must be attached to each separate affidavit.

Respectfully,
SIGNED. *T.B. Needles*
LER 7-8   Commissioner in Charge.

Choctaw 3544.

Muskogee, Indian Territory, April 12, 1905.

Jesse Nail,
    Copeland, Indian Territory.

Dear Sir:

    Receipt is hereby acknowledged of the affidavits of Mary Ann Naile[sic] and Effie N. Snaffar[sic] to the birth of Junetta Nail, daughter of Jesse and Mary Ann Nail,

Applications for Enrollment of Choctaw Newborn
Act of 1905   Volume IV

June 1, 1903, and the same have been filed with our records as an application for the enrollment of said child.

Respectfully,

Commissioner in Charge.

COPY.   Choctaw N.B. 239

Muskogee, Indian Territory, April 17, 1905.

Jesse Nail,
  Copeland, Indian Territory.

Dear Sir:

Receipt is hereby acknowledged of your letter of April 12, in which you ask if the affidavits to the birth of your child, Junetta Nail, had been received, or if it would be necessary for you to go before the enrolling Commission.

In reply to your letter you are advised that the affidavits heretofore forwarded to the birth of your child, Junetta Nail, June 1, 1903, have been filed with our records as an application for the enrollment of said child and if further evidence is necessary to enable the Commission to determine the right to enrollment of this child, you will be advised.

It will not be necessary, however, for you to appear before one of the enrolling parties unless you so desire.

Respectfully,
SIGNED

Tams Bixby
Chairman.

COPY.   Choctaw N.B. 239

Muskogee, Indian Territory, April 18, 1905.

Jesse Nail,
  Copeland, Indian Territory.

Dear Sir:

Receipt is hereby acknowledged of your letter of April 12, in which you ask if the affidavits to the birth of your child, Junetta Nail, had been received, or if it would be necessary for you to go before the enrolling Commission.

Applications for Enrollment of Choctaw Newborn
Act of 1905   Volume IV

In reply to your letter you are advised that the affidavits heretofore forwarded to the birth of your child, Junetta Nail, June 1, 1903, have been filed with our records as an application for the enrollment of said child and if further evidence is necessary to enable the Commission to determine the right to enrollment of this child, you will be advised.

It will not be necessary, however, for you to appear before one of the enrolling parties unless you so desire.

Respectfully,
SIGNED

Tams Bixby
Chairman.

Choc New Born 240
    Daisy Ruby Lauchner
    (Born May 15, 1905[sic])

BIRTH AFFIDAVIT.

DEPARTMENT OF THE INTERIOR.
COMMISSION TO THE FIVE CIVILIZED TRIBES.

IN RE APPLICATION FOR ENROLLMENT, as a citizen of the   Choctaw   Nation, of Daisy Ruby , born on the 15th day of May , 1903

Name of Father: Grant Lauchner   a citizen of the   ----   Nation.
Name of Mother: Lella[sic] V Lauchner   a citizen of the   Choctaw   Nation.

Postoffice   Kingston I.T.

AFFIDAVIT OF MOTHER.

UNITED STATES OF AMERICA, Indian Territory,
    Southern   **DISTRICT.**

I, Lella V Lauchner , on oath state that I am   22   years of age and a citizen by   blood   , of the   Choctaw   Nation; that I am the lawful wife of Grant Lauchner , who is a citizen, by ——— of the ——— Nation; that a   female   child was born to me on   15th day of May   , 1903; that said child has been named Daisy Ruby   , and was living March 4, 1905.

299

Applications for Enrollment of Choctaw Newborn
Act of 1905   Volume IV

Lela V Lauchner

Witnesses To Mark:

Subscribed and sworn to before me this 18th day of March   , 1905

DR Johnston
Notary Public.

AFFIDAVIT OF ATTENDING PHYSICIAN OR MID-WIFE.

UNITED STATES OF AMERICA, Indian Territory,
Southern   DISTRICT.

I, Margaret Lauchner   , a ══════   , on oath state that I attended on Mrs. Grant Lauchner   , wife of Grant Lauchner   on the 15th day of May   , 1903; that there was born to her on said date a   female   child; that said child was living March 4, 1905, and is said to have been named Daisy Ruby

Margaret Lauchner

Witnesses To Mark:

Subscribed and sworn to before me this 18th day of March   , 1905

DR Johnston
Notary Public.

Applications for Enrollment of Choctaw Newborn
Act of 1905 Volume IV

Choc New Born 241
    Allen Terrell Human
    (Born June 11, 1903)

NEW-BORN AFFIDAVIT.

Number..................

Choctaw Enrolling Commission.

IN THE MATTER OF THE APPLICATION FOR ENROLLMENT, as a citizen of the Choctaw Nation, of   Allen Terrell Human

born on the   11 day of   June   190 3

Name of father   Jesse M Human   a citizen of   Choctaw
Nation final enrollment No   15301
Name of mother   Mattie E Human   a citizen of   Choctaw
Nation final enrollment No   1004

                  Postoffice   Durant I.T.

AFFIDAVIT OF MOTHER.

UNITED STATES OF AMERICA,
    INDIAN TERRITORY,
  Central   DISTRICT

    I   Mattie E Human   on oath state that I am 38 years of age and a citizen by Intermarriage   of the   Choctaw   Nation, and as such have been placed upon the final roll of the   Choctaw   Nation, by the Honorable Secretary of the Interior my final enrollment number being   1004 ; that I am the lawful wife of   Jesse M. Human , who is a citizen of the   Choctaw   Nation, and as such has been placed upon the final roll of said Nation by the Honorable Secretary of the Interior, his final enrollment number being   15301   and that a   male child was born to me on the   11 day of   June   190 3 ; that said child has been named   Allen Terrell Human , and is now living.

                                  Mattie E Human

WITNESSETH:
  Must be two
  Witnesses who   A. Frank Ross
  are Citizens.   J. B. Human

    Subscribed and sworn to before me this   16th   day of   January   190 5

                                  Charles A Phillips
                                           Notary Public.

My commission expires   Feb 8th 1908

Applications for Enrollment of Choctaw Newborn
Act of 1905   Volume IV

AFFIDAVIT OF ATTENDING PHYSICIAN OR MIDWIFE

UNITED STATES OF AMERICA
INDIAN TERRITORY
Central   DISTRICT

I, Jas. C. Terrell a Physician on oath state that I attended on Mrs. Mattie E Human wife of Jesse M. Human on the 11th day of June , 190 3 , that there was born to her on said date a Male child, that said child is now living, and is said to have been named Allen Terrell Human

                            Jas. C. Terrell   M.D.

Subscribed and sworn to before me this, the 16th day of January 190 5

                          Charles A Phillips
                              Notary Public.

WITNESSETH:
Must be two witnesses who are citizens and know the child.

    A. Frank Ross
    J B Human

We hereby certify that we are well acquainted with Jas C Terrell a Physician and know him to be reputable and of good standing in the community.

                         A Frank Ross
                         J B Human

BIRTH AFFIDAVIT.

DEPARTMENT OF THE INTERIOR.
COMMISSION TO THE FIVE CIVILIZED TRIBES.

IN RE APPLICATION FOR ENROLLMENT, as a citizen of the Choctaw Nation, of Allen Terrell Human , born on the 11th day of June , 1903

Name of Father: Jesse M Human   a citizen of the Choctaw Nation.
Name of Mother: Mattie E Human   a citizen of the Choctaw Nation.

                        Postoffice   Durant, Ind. Ter.

Applications for Enrollment of Choctaw Newborn
Act of 1905   Volume IV

AFFIDAVIT OF MOTHER.

UNITED STATES OF AMERICA, Indian Territory, }
Central Jud.   DISTRICT.

I,   Mattie E Human   , on oath state that I am   38   years of age and a citizen by Intermarriage , of the   Choctaw   Nation; that I am the lawful wife of Jesse M Human   , who is a citizen, by Blood   of the   Choctaw   Nation; that a   male   child was born to me on   11th day of   June   , 1903; that said child has been named   Allen Terrell Human   , and was living March 4, 1905.

                                              Mattie E Human

Witnesses To Mark:
{

    Subscribed and sworn to before me this 20 day of   March   , 1905

                                              W. T. Sprowls
                                                  Notary Public.

AFFIDAVIT OF ATTENDING PHYSICIAN OR MID-WIFE.

UNITED STATES OF AMERICA, Indian Territory, }
Central Jud.   DISTRICT.

I,   James C Terrell   , a   Physician   , on oath state that I attended on Mrs. Mattie E Human   , wife of   Jesse M Human   on the 11 day of June , 1903; that there was born to her on said date a   male   child; that said child was living March 4, 1905, and is said to have been named   Allen Terrell Human

                                              Jas. C. Terrell

Witnesses To Mark:
{

    Subscribed and sworn to before me this 15 day of   March   , 1905

                                              [Name Illegible]
                                                Notary Public.

Applications for Enrollment of Choctaw Newborn
Act of 1905 Volume IV

7-3575

Muskogee, Indian Territory, March 25, 1905.

Jesse M. Human,
    Durant, Indian Territory.

Dear Sir:

    Receipt is hereby acknowledged of the affidavits of Mattie E. Human and James C. Terrell to the birth of Allen Terrell Human, son of Jesse M. and Mattie E. Human, June 11, 1903, and the same have been filed with our records as an application for the enrollment of said child.

    Respectfully,

    Chairman.

Choctaw N B 105
241

Muskogee, Indian Territory, May 19, 1905.

W. T. Sprowls,
    Attorney at Law,
        Durant, Indian Territory.

Dear Sir:

    Receipt is hereby acknowledged of your letter of May 15, stating that early in March you forwarded application for the enrollment of the infant child of John B. Human and in the same envelope application for the enrollment of the infant child of Jesse M. Human; that J. M. Human has received acknowledged[sic] of application for the enrollment of his child but that no such acknowledgment has been received by J. B. Human and you request to be advised if the application for the enrollment of his child has not been received.

    In reply to your letter you are advised that the affidavits heretofore forwarded to the birth of Allen Terrell Human, child of J. M. Human, and Eugenia Basil Human, child of John B. Human, have been filed with our records as applications for the enrollment of said children and their names have been placed upon a schedule of citizens by blood of the Choctaw Nation prepared for forwarding to the Secretary of the Interior.

    Respectfully,

[End of current file]

Applications for Enrollment of Choctaw Newborn
Act of 1905   Volume IV

Choc New Born 242
  Minnie V. Davis
  (Born March 4, 1905)

Cancelled
Record transferred to Choc
  New Born 790 Act of Congress
  approved April 26, 1906.
           July 19, 1906

CHOCTAW 242
NEW BORN
ACT OF CONGRESS APPROVED MARCH 30, 1905.

Minnie V. Davis
(Born March 4, 1905)

NEW BORN

CANCELLED

Record transferred to
Choctaw New born 790.
ACT OF CONGRESS APPROVED MARCH 30, 1905.

JUL 19 1906

Applications for Enrollment of Choctaw Newborn
Act of 1905   Volume IV

Choc New Born 243
    Lora B. Izard
    (Born Jan. 6, 1904)

BIRTH AFFIDAVIT.

DEPARTMENT OF THE INTERIOR.
COMMISSION TO THE FIVE CIVILIZED TRIBES.

    IN RE APPLICATION FOR ENROLLMENT, as a citizen of the Choctaw Nation, of Lora B. Izard, born on the 6 day of Jan, 1904.

Name of Father: Silas P. Izard   a citizen of the Choctaw Nation.
Name of Mother: Mary L. Izard   a citizen of the U.S. Intermarriedtion.

    Postoffice Milburn Ind. Ty.

AFFIDAVIT OF MOTHER.

UNITED STATES OF AMERICA, Indian Territory, }
    Southern   DISTRICT.

    I, Mary L Izard, on oath state that I am 26 years of age and a citizen by Intermarriage, of the Choctaw Nation; that I am the lawful wife of Silas P. Izard, who is a citizen, by Blood of the Choctaw Nation; that a Female child was born to me on 6 day of Jan, 1904, that said child has been named Lora B. Izard, and is now living.

                Mary L Izard

Witnesses To Mark:
{

    Subscribed and sworn to before me this 16 day of March, 1905.

                S.J. Powell
                    Notary Public.

AFFIDAVIT OF ATTENDING PHYSICIAN OR MID-WIFE.

UNITED STATES OF AMERICA, Indian Territory, }
    Southern   DISTRICT.

    I, J.J. Clark M.D., a Physician, on oath state that I attended on Mrs. Mary L Izard, wife of Silas P Izard on the .... day of ....,

Applications for Enrollment of Choctaw Newborn
Act of 1905   Volume IV

190__; that there was born to her on said date a   Female   child; that said child is now living and is said to have been named Lora B. Izard

J.J. Clark M.D.

Witnesses To Mark:
{

Subscribed and sworn to before me this 16 day of March , 1905.

S.J. Powell
Notary Public.

BIRTH AFFIDAVIT.
DEPARTMENT OF THE INTERIOR.
COMMISSION TO THE FIVE CIVILIZED TRIBES.

IN RE APPLICATION FOR ENROLLMENT, as a citizen of the   Choctaw   Nation, of   Lora B. Izard   , born on the 6" day of January , 1904

Name of Father: Silas P Izard   a citizen of the Choctaw   Nation.
Name of Mother: Mary L Izard   a citizen of the Choctaw   Nation.

Postoffice   Milburn Ind. Ter.

AFFIDAVIT OF MOTHER.

UNITED STATES OF AMERICA, Indian Territory, }
Southern   DISTRICT.   }

I, Mary L Izard , on oath state that I am 26 years of age and a citizen by Intermarriage , of the Choctaw   Nation; that I am the lawful wife of Silas P Izard, who is a citizen, by Blood   of the Choctaw   Nation; that a Female child was born to me on 6" day of January , 1904; that said child has been named   Lora B. Izard   , and was living March 4, 1905.

Mary L Izard

Witnesses To Mark:
{

Subscribed and sworn to before me this 10 day of April , 1905

S J Powell
Notary Public.

Applications for Enrollment of Choctaw Newborn
Act of 1905   Volume IV

AFFIDAVIT OF ATTENDING PHYSICIAN OR MID-WIFE.

UNITED STATES OF AMERICA, Indian Territory,
Southern   DISTRICT.

I, J.J. Clark   , a   Physician   , on oath state that I attended on Mrs. Mary L Izard   , wife of Silas P Izard   on the 6" day of January , 1904; that there was born to her on said date a   Female   child; that said child was living March 4, 1905, and is said to have been named   Lora B. Izard

J.J. Clark

Witnesses To Mark:

Subscribed and sworn to before me this 10 day of April   , 1905

S J Powell
Notary Public.

7-3537

Muskogee, Indian Territory, March 20, 1905.

Silas P. Izard,
   Milburn, Indian Territory.

Dear Sir:

Receipt is hereby acknowledged of the affidavits of Mary L. Izard and J. J. Clark to the birth of Lora B. Izard, daughter of Silas P. and Mary L. Izard, January 6, 1904, and the same have been filed with our records as an application for the enrollment of said child.

Respectfully,

Chairman.

Applications for Enrollment of Choctaw Newborn
Act of 1905   Volume IV

COPY.   N.B. 243.

Muskogee, Indian Territory, April 7, 1905.

Silas P. Izard,
    Milburn, Indian Territory.

Dear Sir:

    There is enclosed you herewith for execution application for the enrollment of your infant child, Lora B. Izard, born January 6, 1904.

    In the affidavits heretofore filed the physician ommited[sic] the date of the birth of the applicant. He must state definitely the date on which the child was born.

    In having the affidavits executed care should be exercised to see that all the names are written in full as they appear in the body of the affidavit, and in the event that either of the persons signing the affidavit are unable to write, signatures by mark must be attested by two witnesses. Each affidavit must be executed before a Notary Public and the notarial seal and signature of the officer must be attached to each separate affidavit.

Respectfully,
SIGNED
T.B. Needles
Commissioner in Charge.

LER 7-7

[The following letter does not belong with the current applicant.]

Choctaw 3639.

Muskogee, Indian Territory, April 11, 1905.

Thomas Stark,
    Bennington, Indian Territory.

Dear Sir:

    Receipt is hereby acknowledged of the affidavit of Josephine Stark and B. C. Rutherford to the birth of Bessie Leola Stark, daughter of Thomas and Josephine Stark, October 4, 1902, and the same have been filed with our records as an application for the enrollment of said child.

Respectfully,

Commissioner in Charge.

Applications for Enrollment of Choctaw Newborn
Act of 1905 Volume IV

COPY. Choctaw N.B. 243.

Muskogee, Indian Territory, April 18, 1905.

Silas P. Izard,
    Milburn, Indian Territory.

Dear Sir:

    Receipt is hereby acknowledged of the affidavits of Mary L. Izard and J. J. Clark to the birth of Lora B. Izard, daughter of Silas P. and Mary L. Izard, January 6, 1904, and the same have been filed with our records as an application for the enrollment of said child.

        Respectfully,
        SIGNED.
        Tams Bixby
        Chairman.

Choc New Born 244
    Bessie Leola Starks
    (Born Oct. 4, 1902)

THE   CHOCTAW   NATION

In the Circuit Court the Third Judicial District, Regular August Term 1899 a Petition of Thos Starks being presented by his Attorney in said Court, for a

BILL OF DIVORCE,

setting forth the facts, etc., and after the Court hearing the Testimony in regard to the Petition do order and decree that a Bill of Divorce be issued to the applicant, Thos Starks.

    THEREFORE, I do issue a Bill of Divorce to said applicant Thos Starks forever releasing him from the bonds of Matrimony heretofore existing between Thos Stark[sic] and Hettie Stark.

    Given under my hand and seal of office, this the 15 day of August 1899.

        Will Everidge
        District Clerk.

Applications for Enrollment of Choctaw Newborn
Act of 1905 Volume IV

I, Wilma Smith a stenographer to the Five Civilized Tribes, do hereby certify that the above and foregoing is a true and correct copy of the original now on file with the records of this office.

Wilma Smith

Subscribed and sworn to before me this the 31st day of May 1907.

HE Hains
Notary Public.

Bennington, I. T. Sept. 20, 1901.

This certificate that I W. J. B. Lloyd a minister of the gospel did on the sixth (6) day of December 1900 perform the ceremony and publish the bans of Matrimony uniting in marriage Thomas Starks and Miss Josephine Stover.

certificate given this the 20 day of Sept. 1901 by W. J. B. Lloyd a minister of gospel. Credentials Recorded in Book A page 101.

Endorsed on back.

DEPARTMENT OF THE INTERIOR,
COMMISSION TO THE FIVE CIVILIZED TRIBES.
F I L E D
SEP 23 1901

Tams Bixby Acting Chairman.

I, Wilma Smith a stenographer to the Five Civilized Tribes, do hereby certify that the above and foregoing is a true and correct copy of the original now on file with the records of this office.

Wilma Smith

Subscribed and sworn to before me this the 31st day of May 1907.

HE Hains
Notary Public.

Applications for Enrollment of Choctaw Newborn
Act of 1905 Volume IV

BIRTH AFFIDAVIT.

DEPARTMENT OF THE INTERIOR,
COMMISSION TO THE FIVE CIVILIZED TRIBES.

IN RE APPLICATION FOR ENROLLMENT, as a citizen of the Choctaw Nation, of Leola Bessie Stark, born on the 4th day of October, 1902

Name of Father: Thomas Stark   a citizen of the Choctaw Nation.
Name of Mother: Josephine Stark   a citizen of the Choctaw Nation.

Post-Office: Bennington I.T.

AFFIDAVIT OF MOTHER.

UNITED STATES OF AMERICA,
INDIAN TERRITORY,
Central District.

I, Josephine Stark, on oath state that I am 25 years of age and a citizen by Marriage, of the Choctaw Nation; that I am the lawful wife of Thomas Stark, who is a citizen, by Birth of the Choctaw Nation; that a female child was born to me on the 4th day of October, 190 2, that said child has been named Leola Bessie Stark, and is now living.

                           Josephine Stark

WITNESSES TO MARK:

Subscribed and sworn to before me this 27th day of November, 1902

                           C. C. McClard
                                NOTARY PUBLIC.

AFFIDAVIT OF ATTENDING PHYSICIAN OR MID-WIFE.

UNITED STATES OF AMERICA,
INDIAN TERRITORY,
Central District.

I, Josephine Taylor, as Midwife, on oath state that I attended on Mrs. Josephine Stark, wife of Thomas Stark on the 4th day of October, 190 2; that there was born to her on said date a female child; that said child is now living and is said to have been named Leola Bessie Stark

                           Josephine Taylor

WITNESSES TO MARK:

Applications for Enrollment of Choctaw Newborn
Act of 1905   Volume IV

Subscribed and sworn to before me this 27th day of November, 1902

C. C. McClard
NOTARY PUBLIC.

BIRTH AFFIDAVIT.

DEPARTMENT OF THE INTERIOR,
COMMISSION TO THE FIVE CIVILIZED TRIBES.

IN RE Application for Enrollment, as a citizen of the Choctaw Nation, of Bessie L. Starks, born on the 4 day of October, 1902

Name of Father: Thomas Starks   a citizen of the Choctaw Nation.
Name of Mother: Josephine Starks   a citizen of the Choctaw Nation.

Post-Office:..

AFFIDAVIT OF MOTHER.

UNITED STATES OF AMERICA, }
    INDIAN TERRITORY.
  Central   District.

I, Josephine Starks, on oath state that I am 25 years of age and a citizen by Marriage, of the Choctaw Nation; that I am the lawful wife of Thomas Starks, who is a citizen, by blood of the Choctaw Nation; that a female child was born to me on 4th day of October, 190 3[sic], that said child has been named Bessie L Starks, and is now living.
                                              her
                                  Josephine x Starks
WITNESSES TO MARK: mark
  { W^m C [Illegible]
    Fred V Kincade

Subscribed and sworn to before me this 22nd *day of* December, 1902

T. C. Humphrey
NOTARY PUBLIC.

Applications for Enrollment of Choctaw Newborn
Act of 1905 Volume IV

BIRTH AFFIDAVIT.

DEPARTMENT OF THE INTERIOR,
COMMISSION TO THE FIVE CIVILIZED TRIBES.

IN RE Application for Enrollment, as a citizen of the Choctaw Nation, of Bessie Leola Stark, born on the 4th day of October, 1902

Name of Father: Thomas Stark   a citizen of the Choctaw Nation.
Name of Mother: Josephine Stark   a citizen of the Choctaw Nation.

Post-Office: Bennington I.T.

AFFIDAVIT OF MOTHER.

UNITED STATES OF AMERICA,
   INDIAN TERRITORY.
Central District.

I, Josephine Stark, on oath state that I am 25 years of age and a citizen by Marriage, of the Choctaw Nation; that I am the lawful wife of Thomas Stark, who is a citizen, by Blood of the Choctaw Nation; that a Female child was born to me on 4th day of October, 1902, that said child has been named Bessie Leola Stark, and is now living.

                                                     her
                                        Josephine x Starks
WITNESSES TO MARK: mark
   J.W. Lloyd
   J.E. Sides

Subscribed and sworn to before me this 24th day of December, 1902

                                      C. C. McClard
                                          NOTARY PUBLIC.

AFFIDAVIT OF ATTENDING PHYSICIAN OR MID-WIFE.

UNITED STATES OF AMERICA,
   INDIAN TERRITORY.
Central District.

I, Josephine Taylor, a s Midwife, on oath state that I attended on Mrs. Josephine Stark, wife of Thomas Stark on the 4th day of

Applications for Enrollment of Choctaw Newborn
Act of 1905   Volume IV

October   , 1902 ; that there was born to her on said date a   Female   child; that said child is now living and is said to have been named   Bessie Leola Stark

Josephine Taylor

WITNESSES TO MARK:
{

   Subscribed and sworn to before me this   24th day of   December   , 1902

C. C. McClard
NOTARY PUBLIC.

BIRTH AFFIDAVIT.

DEPARTMENT OF THE INTERIOR.
COMMISSION TO THE FIVE CIVILIZED TRIBES.

IN RE APPLICATION FOR ENROLLMENT, as a citizen of the   Choctaw   Nation, of   Bessie Leola Stark   , born on the   4th day of   October   , 1902

Name of Father: Thomas Stark   a citizen of the   Choctaw   Nation.
Intermarried
Name of Mother: Josephine Stark   an   a citizen of the   Choctaw   Nation.

Postoffice   Bennington I.T.

AFFIDAVIT OF MOTHER.

UNITED STATES OF AMERICA, Indian Territory, }
   Central   DISTRICT. }

I,   Josephine Stark   , on oath state that I am   26   years of age and a citizen by   marriage   , of the   Choctaw   Nation; that I am the lawful wife of   Thomas Stark   , who is a citizen, by Blood   of the   Choctaw   Nation; that a   Female   child was born to me on the 4th day of   October   , 1902; that said child has been named   Bessie Leola Stark   , and was living March 4, 1905.

Josephine Stark

Witnesses To Mark:
{

   Subscribed and sworn to before me this   6th day of   April   , 1905

C.C. McClard
Notary Public.

Applications for Enrollment of Choctaw Newborn
Act of 1905   Volume IV

AFFIDAVIT OF ATTENDING PHYSICIAN OR MID-WIFE.

UNITED STATES OF AMERICA, Indian Territory,
Central   DISTRICT.

I, B. C. Rutherford, a Physician, on oath state that I attended on Mrs. Josephine Stark, wife of Thomas Stark on the 4th day of October, 1902; that there was born to her on said date a Female child; that said child was living March 4, 1905, and is said to have been named Bessie Leola Stark

B C Rutherford M.D.

Witnesses To Mark:

Subscribed and sworn to before me this 6th day of April, 1905

C.C. McClard
Notary Public.

N.B. 244.

COPY.

Thomas Starks,
　　　Bennington Indian Territory.

Dear Sir:

　　　There is enclosed you herewith for execution application for the enrollment of your infant child, Bessie Leola Starks, born October 4, 1902.

　　　The affidavits heretofore filed with the Commission show the child was living December 24, 1902. It is necessary, for the child to be enrolled, that she was living on March 4, 1905. You will please insert the age of the mother in space provided for that purpose.

　　　In having these affidavits executed care should be exercised to see that all the names are written in full as they appear in the body of the affidavit, and in the event that either of the persons signing the affidavit are unable to write, signatures by mark must be attested by two witnesses. Each affidavit must be executed before a Notary Public and the notarial seal and signature of the officer must be attached to each separate affidavit.

Respectfully,
SIGNED.
T.B. Needles
Commissioner in Charge.

LER 7-9-

Applications for Enrollment of Choctaw Newborn
Act of 1905 Volume IV

COPY. 7 NB 244

Muskogee, Indian Territory, April 27, 1905.

Thomas Stark,
    Bennington, Indian Territory.

Dear Sir:

    Receipt is hereby acknowledged of your letter of April 20, 1905, in which you state that a short time ago you forwarded application for the enrollment of your child B. Leola Stark and ask if it will be necessary for you to execute the blank recently sent you in the matter of her enrollment.

    In reply to your letter you are advised that affidavits executed in the matter of the enrollment of your child Bessie L. Stark on April 6, 1905, are in proper form and have been filed with our records in the matter of the enrollment of said child; it will not therefore be necessary for you to execute the affidavits recently forwarded you.

    Respectfully,
    SIGNED

Tams Bixby
Chairman.

Choc New Born 245
    Glenn M. Terry
    (Born July 11, 1903)

BIRTH AFFIDAVIT.

DEPARTMENT OF THE INTERIOR.
COMMISSION TO THE FIVE CIVILIZED TRIBES.

IN RE APPLICATION FOR ENROLLMENT, as a citizen of the Choctaw Nation, of Glenn M Terry, born on the 11th day of July, 1903

non
Name of Father: Elisha S Terry   a citizen of the .... Nation.
Name of Mother: Malinda Walker   a citizen of the Choctaw Nation.

Postoffice Bradley, I.T.

Applications for Enrollment of Choctaw Newborn
Act of 1905 Volume IV

AFFIDAVIT OF MOTHER.

UNITED STATES OF AMERICA, Indian Territory, }
Southern DISTRICT. }

I, Malinda Walker "Terry", on oath state that I am 30 years of age and a citizen by Blood, of the Choctaw Nation; that I am the lawful wife of Elisha S Terry, who is not a citizen, by of the Nation; that a male child was born to me on 11th day of July, 1903; that said child has been named Glenn M Terry, and was living March 4, 1905.

                                                  Malinda Walker Terry

Witnesses To Mark:

Subscribed and sworn to before me this 22 day of Mch, 1905

                                                  R M Cochran
                                                    Notary Public.

AFFIDAVIT OF ATTENDING PHYSICIAN OR MID-WIFE.

UNITED STATES OF AMERICA, Indian Territory, }
Southern DISTRICT. }

I, Nannie Shelby, a mid wife, on oath state that I attended on Mrs. Malinda Walker Terry, wife of Elisha S Terry on the 11th day of July, 1903; that there was born to her on said date a male child; that said child was living March 4, 1905, and is said to have been named Glenn M Terry

                                                  Nannie Shelby

Witnesses To Mark:

Subscribed and sworn to before me this 22 day of Mch, 1905

                                                  R M Cochran
                                                  Notary Public.

Applications for Enrollment of Choctaw Newborn
Act of 1905   Volume IV

7-3646

Muskogee, Indian Territory, March 31, 1905.

Elisha S. Terry,
    Bradley, Indian Territory.

Dear Sir:

    Receipt is hereby acknowledged of the affidavits of Malinda Walker Terry and Nannie Shelby to the birth of Glenn M. Terry, son of Elisha S. and Malinda Walker Terry, July 11, 1903, and the same have been filed with our records as an application for the enrollment of said child.

Respectfully,

Chairman.

Choc New Born 246
    Edith Irene McKinnon
    (Born Aug. 11, 1904)
    Mary Virgil McKinnon
    (Born Oct. 25, 1902)

BIRTH AFFIDAVIT.
DEPARTMENT OF THE INTERIOR.
COMMISSION TO THE FIVE CIVILIZED TRIBES.

IN RE APPLICATION FOR ENROLLMENT, as a citizen of the   Choctaw   Nation, of   Mary Virgil McKinnon   , born on the   25   day of Oct   , 190 2

Name of Father: Geo. Gipson McKinnon   a citizen of the .... Nation.
Name of Mother: Lula McKinnon   a citizen of the   Choctaw   Nation.

Postoffice   Erin Springs I.T.

Applications for Enrollment of Choctaw Newborn
Act of 1905   Volume IV

AFFIDAVIT OF MOTHER.

UNITED STATES OF AMERICA, Indian Territory, }
Southern   DISTRICT.

I, Lula McKinnon, on oath state that I am 32 years of age and a citizen by Blood, of the Choctaw Nation; that I am the lawful wife of Geo. Gipson McKinnon, who is a citizen, by .... of the .... Nation; that a Female child was born to me on 25 day of Oct., 1902, that said child has been named Mary Virgil McKinnon, and is now living.

Lula McKinnon

Witnesses To Mark:
{

Subscribed and sworn to before me this 16 day of Nov, 1904

I.W. Eagan
Notary Public.

AFFIDAVIT OF ATTENDING PHYSICIAN OR MID-WIFE.

UNITED STATES OF AMERICA, Indian Territory, }
.... DISTRICT.

I, S. P. Patterson, a Physician, on oath state that I attended on Mrs. Lula M McKinnon, wife of George Gipson McKinnon on the 25 day of October, 1902; that there was born to her on said date a Female child; that said child is now living and is said to have been named Mary Virgil McKinnon

S P Patterson

Witnesses To Mark:
{

Subscribed and sworn to before me this 23 day of December, 1904

PE High
Notary Public.

Applications for Enrollment of Choctaw Newborn
Act of 1905 Volume IV

BIRTH AFFIDAVIT.

DEPARTMENT OF THE INTERIOR.
COMMISSION TO THE FIVE CIVILIZED TRIBES.

IN RE APPLICATION FOR ENROLLMENT, as a citizen of the   Choctaw   Nation, of   Edith Irene McKinnon , born on the 11th day of August , 190 4

Name of Father: G. G. McKinnon   a citizen of the .... Nation.
Name of Mother: Lula McKinnon   a citizen of the   Choctaw   Nation.

Postoffice   Lindsay In'd Territory

AFFIDAVIT OF MOTHER.

UNITED STATES OF AMERICA, Indian Territory, }
Southern   DISTRICT. }

I, Lula McKinnon , on oath state that I am 33 years of age and a citizen by Blood , of the   Choctaw Nation; that I am the lawful wife of   G. G. McKinnon who is a citizen, by .... of the .... Nation; that a   Female   child was born to me on Eleventh day of August , 1904, that said child has been named Edith Irene McKinnon , and is now living.

Lula McKinnon

Witnesses To Mark:
{

Subscribed and sworn to before me this 24th day of   March , 1905

F.E. Rice
Notary Public.

AFFIDAVIT OF ATTENDING PHYSICIAN OR MID-WIFE.

UNITED STATES OF AMERICA, Indian Territory, }
Southern   DISTRICT. }

I,   Thomas M. Gipson   , a   Physician   , on oath state that I attended on Mrs. Lula McKinnon   , wife of G. G. McKinnon   on the 11th day of August , 1904; that there was born to her on said date a   female   child; that said child is now living and is said to have been named Edith Irene McKinnon

Thomas M Gipson M.D.

Witnesses To Mark:
{

Applications for Enrollment of Choctaw Newborn
Act of 1905   Volume IV

Subscribed and sworn to before me this 24th day of   March   , 1905

                            F.E. Rice
                            Notary Public.

BIRTH AFFIDAVIT.

DEPARTMENT OF THE INTERIOR.
COMMISSION TO THE FIVE CIVILIZED TRIBES.

IN RE APPLICATION FOR ENROLLMENT, as a citizen of the   Choctaw   Nation, of   Mary Virgil McKinnon   , born on the   25"   day of October   , 190 2

Name of Father: George Gipson McKinnon   a citizen of the United States Nation.
Name of Mother: Lula McKinnon   a citizen of the   Choctaw   Nation.

                Postoffice   Erin Springs I.T.

AFFIDAVIT OF MOTHER.

UNITED STATES OF AMERICA, Indian Territory,
....DISTRICT.

I, Lula McKinnon   , on oath state that I am   33   years of age and a citizen by blood   , of the   Choctaw   Nation; that I am the lawful wife of   George Gipson McKinnon   , who is a citizen, by ——— of the United States Nation; that a   female   child was born to me on   25"   day of   October   , 1902, that said child has been named   Mary Virgil McKinnon   , and was living March 4, 1905.

                          Lula McKinnon
Witnesses To Mark:

Subscribed and sworn to before me this   26   day of   April   , 1905

                          F.E. Rice

Applications for Enrollment of Choctaw Newborn
Act of 1905   Volume IV

United States of America,
Indian Territory,   AFFIDAVIT;-
Southern District.

Personally appeared before me F. E. Rice, a Notary Public within and for the Southern District of the Indian Territory, G. L. Holland and Villey Holland, who being by me duly sworn according to law each for themselves on oath state, that they are of lawful age and reside near the town of Lindsay, in the afore-said district and Territory,; That there was born to Lula McKinnon, wife of George Gipson McKinnon, on the 25th day of October 1902, a female child, that said child was named Mary Virgil McKinnon, and was living on March 4th, 21905, further; affiants each for themselves state that they have not any interest in the foregoing matter.

G. L. Holland
Villey Holland

Subscribed and sworn to before me this 26 day of April, 1905.

F. E. Rice
Notary Public.

7-3342

Muskogee, Indian Territory, March 29, 1905.

Lula McKinnon,
     Erin Springs, Indian Territory.

Dear Madam:

Receipt is hereby acknowledged of your letter of March 21, 1905, stating that you have two children born since September 25, 1902, that the attending physician for the oldest one has gone away and it will be almost impossible to get his affidavit; that you have his affidavit made in December 1904, and you wish to be advised if this will be all that is necessary in the matter of the enrollment of said child.

In reply to your letter you are advised that you should forward the affidavits referred to in your letter to the Commission as early as practicable and the same will be received and considered as applications for the enrollment of the children therein names. You can then have executed and returned to the Commission affidavits to the birth of said children on the inclosed blanks, and if you cannot secure the affidavit of the attending physician and there was no nurse in attendance at the birth of said child, you should forward the affidavit of two disinterested persons who know of the birth of said child.

Respectfully,

2 B.C.   Chairman.

Applications for Enrollment of Choctaw Newborn
Act of 1905   Volume IV

9-497
7-3342

Muskogee, Indian Territory, March 31, 1905.

F. E. Rice,
    Lindsay, Indian Territory.

Dear Sir:

    Receipt is hereby acknowledged of the affidavits of Maude Turnbull and S. H. Wilson to the birth of John B. Turnbull, son of Dick and Maud[sic] Turnbull, March 7, 1904; also the affidavits of Lula McKinnon and Thomas M. Gipson to the birth of Edith Irene McKinnon daughter of G. G. and Lula McKinnon, August 11, 1904, and the same have been filed with our records as an application for the enrollment of said children.

Respectfully,

Chairman.

Choctaw 3342.

Muskogee, Indian Territory, April 10, 1905.

George Gipson McKinnon,
    Erin Springs, Indian Territory.

Dear Sir:

    Receipt is hereby acknowledged of the affidavits of Eula[sic] McKinnon and S. P. Patterson to the birth of Mary Virgil McKinnon, daughter of George Gipson and Lula M. McKinnon, October 25, 1902, and the same have been filed with our records as an application for the enrollment of said child.

Respectfully,

Commissioner in Charge.

Applications for Enrollment of Choctaw Newborn
Act of 1905   Volume IV

COPY.   7 N B 717

Muskogee, Indian Territory, April 15, 1905.

George Gipson McKinnon,
    Erin Springs, Indian Territory.

Dear Sir:

There is inclosed you herewith for execution application for the enrollment of your infant child, Mary Virgil McKinnon, born October 25, 1902.

The affidavits heretofore filed with the Commission show the child was living on December 23, 1904. It is necessary, for the child to be enrolled, that she was living on March 4, 1905. Please insert the mother's age in the space provided for that purpose.

In having these affidavits executed care should be exercised to see that all the names are written in full as they appear in the body of the affidavit, and in the event that either of the persons signing the affidavit are unable to write, signatures by mark must be attested by two witnesses. Each affidavit must be executed before a Notary Public and the notarial seal and signature of the officer must be attached to each separate affidavit.

Respectfully,
SIGNED

Tams Bixby
Chairman.

LM 15-110.

COPY.

Choctaw N.B. 246.
Muskogee, Indian Territory, May 1, 1905.

F. E. Rice,
    Lindsey, Indian Territory.

Dear Sir:

Receipt is hereby acknowledged of your letter of April 26, enclosing the affidavits of Lula McKinnon, G. L. Holland and Villey Holland to the birth of Mary Virgil McKinnon, daughter of George Gipson and Lula McKinnon, October 25, 1902, and the same have been filed with our records in the matter of the enrollment of said child.

Respectfully,
SIGNED

Tams Bixby
Chairman.

Index

ABERNATHY
  Mrs N D 12
ADAMES
  James 188
ADAMS
  G W 9,12
  Geo 82
  Thomas 189,190
AINSWORTH
  N B 41,42
ALLEN
  J F 205
ANATUBBY
  Jane 193
  Lankford 193
ANDERSO
  Noel 159
ANDERSON
  Hattie 272
  Josie 134,135,136
  Lucinda 266
  Noel 160,161
  Oscar 133,134,135,136
  Rufus 133,134,135,136
  Sellen Coley 135
  Silen 133,134
  Sillan Coley 136
  Watson 266
  William P 206,207
ANGELL
  W H 52,148,277,278,296
ANSLEY
  W H 42
ARMSTRONG
  J H 128,130,132,133
  J H, MD 128,130,131
ARNOTE & LESTER 165
ARPELA
  Letice 193

BAGWELL
  C M 244,245
BAILEY
  Ella 225
BAIN
  Mrs M H 198
BAKER

  Oscar J 119
BARBOUR
  D P 48
  David P 44,45,46,47,49,50,51,52
  Hester 50
  Hester A 44,45,46,47,48,49,52
  John Lawson 44,45,46,47,48,49, 50,51,52
BARNETT
  Elizabeth 251,252
  Elmer Luther 251,252,253,254,255
  Jackson D 251,252,253,254,255
  Laura Annie 251,252,253,254,255
  Robert R 174
BATTIEST
  De Witt D 261,262
  DeWitt D 259,263
  DeWitt Dyer 259,260
  Emma 260,261,262,263,264
  L G 263,264
  Lewis G 260,261,262,263
BEAL
  Bonnie 290
  Charles Franklin 289,291,292
  Charley 286,287,291
  Chas Franklin 284,285,287,288, 289,290,292
  D E 285,289,290
  Donna 286,287,288,289,291
  Donnie 287,288,289,290,291,292
  W C 284
  William C 286,287,288,289, 290,291,292
  Wm C 285
BELL
  Lizzie F 212,213
BENCH
  Alton B 31
  Alton Brooks 24,25,27,28,31
  Altonbrooks 23
  Bettie 23,24,25,26,27,28,29,31
  John D 23,24,25,26,27,28,29,30,31
  Lee O 23,24,26,27,29,30,31
BENNETT
  Robt R 203
BENTON
  James 129

Index

BILLEY
  Walton 267,268,269
BILLINGSLEY
  A 66
BILLY
  W J 265
BIXBY
  Tams 7,31,54,58,59,64,70,71,73,
  74,105,113,133,140,145,146,150,165,
  210,211,218,220,225,226,238,254,292,
  298,299,310,311,317,325
BLACHERT
  Fay E 266
BLUE
  Willie 189
  Willy 190
BOBO
  Lacey P 267,268,270,271
BOLGER
  P C 93
BOLING
  John F 87,88
BOLLING
  Frank Alfred 76,77,78,79,80,81,
  87,88
  John F 76,77,78,79,80,81,82,83,84,
  85,86,87
  Lewis Layfayette 87
  Louis Lafayett 76,83,84,88
  Louis Layfayett 81,82,87
  Louis Layfayette 84,85,86
  Nancy I 76,77,78,79,80,81,82,83,
  84,85,86,87,88
  W C 77
BOND
  Clarence 37,38,39,40
  Henry J 37,38,39,40
  Lizzie 37,38,39,40
BONESTUT
  F J 138
BOWER
  James 25,26,27,42,57,169,170,
  171,189,190,228,233,247,248,256
BOWMAN
  J H 56
BRASHEARS
  Minnie 152

BRASHERS
  Minnie 152
BROWN
  Agnes 100,102,103,105
  William H 79
BUNCH
  William H 85
  William J 79,85
BURNEY
  George 208
BURNS
  J P 11,12
BURRIS
  Rebecca 166,167
BYINGTON
  Silas 37,38
BYNUM
  J N 82
CAMP
  Vinson 209,210
CAMPELUBE
  Columbus 168,170,171
CAMPULUBE
  Columbus 169
CARDWELL
  Maria 295
  Marie 295
CARNEY
  Nellie 169,170
  Rosa 169
CARRELL
  Joe 248
CARSON
  J H 241
CARTER
  Frances 175,177
  Nellie 172
  Rosa 168,170,171,174
  Rose 170
CASE
  Addie F 212,213
  Lee 212,213
  Lucy 212,213
CASS
  Osborne N 16,17
CASTLEBERRY

Index

Mary E 153
CATHEY
   Azalee 135,136
CHARLES
   A J 199
   R J 198,199,200
CLABORN
   H E 5
CLARK
   Edwin O 94,95,97,99
   H M 293,294
   J J 308,310
   J J, MD 306,307
COCHRAN
   R M 318
COFFMAN
   J 129
   J A 130
   John A 127,128,130,131,132,133
   Joseph Osbon ... 127,128,129,130,131, 132,133
   Sarah E 127,128,129,130,131, 132,133
COLBERT
   Edward 124,125,126
   Harriet 124,125,126,127
   Lena 124,125,126
   Lenner 124
COLEY
   Sellen 135
   Silen 133,134
COLLINS
   Daisy 73
   Daisy Lee 68,69,75
   John F 68,69,70,71,72,73,74,75
   John Foley 68
   Viola 68,69,70,71,72,73,74,75
CONNELL
   J V 230
COOK
   T H 142
COOPER
   Abel 247,248
   Henry 27,249
   Henry F 249
   James 25,26,27
CORN

Jackson 206,207
CORNELISON
   D S 82
COS
   Dr W A 155
COTTON
   R P 143,144
COVINGTON
   W P 269,271
COX
   Belle 258
   W A 156
   William A 136,137,139,140
   William A, MD 137
COYLE
   Andrew H 155
   Mrs E E 155
   Mrs M E 155
CRABTREE
   Anna 34
CRISSMAN
   T L 231
   T L, MD 228,230
CULBERSON
   James 148,188
CUNNINGHAM
   J N 153
   William H 148

DABNEY
   Dr J A 38
   J A 38,39
   J A, MD 38,39
DALBY
   H L 108,110,111,112
   H L, MD 109
DALTON
   E M 94,96
DANIEL
   Ben 252
DAUGHERTY
   D D 9
DAVDSON
   Wm B 47
DAVIDSON
   Wm B 45,46,49,50
DAVIS

Al 234
D E 89,90
Dave E 89
Dr Wm 205
Maggie E 89,90
Minnie V 305
Mrs M E 90
Susie 89,90
Wiliam 211
William 207,208,209,210
William, MD 207
DENTON
  Nancy I 80,81,86
DICK
  G F 285,286
DICKERSON
  J H 225
DIFENDAFER
  Chas T 48,175
DILBECK 220
  Emeline 214,217,218,219
  Emiline 215,216
  Emma 218
  J M 218
  Martha Iler 214,215,217,218, 219,220
  Martha Iler Irine 215,216
  S M 214,215,217,219,220
  Stephen M 215,216
DUER
  Ada Arlee 221,222,223,226
  Ephram 223,224,227
  Ephriam 221,222,225
  Ephriham 222,223,226
  Mary 221,222,223,224,226,227
  William Andrew 221,223,224,227
DUNLAP
  J D 141
  James D 136,137,138,139,140
  Susan L 136,137,138,139,140
  Wallace Green McCurtain ... 136,137, 138,139,140,141
DURANT
  W A 228,229
DYER
  E E 256,257
  Emma 260,261,262,263

Phoebe 263
Sam 263
Sampson 263272
Sarah 263
Willie 263
EAGAN
  J W 320
ELKINS
  O C 38
ELLIOT
  Leonard 144
  Maude E 144
  Richard H 144
ELLIOTT
  Amanda 143,145
  J H 213
  Leonard 141,142,143,144,145,146
  Manda 141,142
  R H 146
  Richard 145
  Richard H .. 141,142,143,144,145,146
  William 213
EMOS
  John 194,195
EPLER
  E G 69
  E G, MD 69
ESTES
  Alfred Henry 182,183
  Joe S 182
  Lorena 182
EVERETT
  Fred 235
EVERIDGE
  Will 310
FARRET
  Minnie 25,26
FERGUSON
  A H 257
FETTER
  Abbie 197,198
  Abigail 199,200,201,202,203
  Amanda May 197,200,201,202,204
  Manda May 197
  Mandy May 198

Nina Belle............... 197,199,201,202, 203,204
O B 197,198,204
Oliver B 200,201,202,203
Olliver B 199
Wm 203
FETTERS
Harry... 199
FIELD
C E.. 69
FOLSOM
Alex.. 137
Alice 60,61,62,63,64
Allice 62,64
A E 206,260,261
F E 225
Frank... 247
Maud......................... 60,61,62,63,64
Robert....................... 60,61,62,63,64
FOLSON
Maud.. 64
FRANKLIN
Wirt..............43,44,67,97,98,126,138, 153,156,157,166,167,172,173,174,176, 177,182,183,200,201,202,203
FRAZIER
Ross 271
FRETWELL
Dell 147,149
FULTON
Dr J S 261
J S.. 260,262
J S, MD...................................... 260
FUQUA
W L.. 284

GADNEY
J A 40
GAFFORD
T F 134
GARDNER
D H 233,234
GARLAND
C C 16,17
Marcy L 22
Mary L.........15,16,17,18,19,20,21,22
Virginia................. 15,16,17,19,20,21

Virginnia 17,18,22
W G... 15,17
William G....15,16,17,18,19,20,21,22
William J 22
Wm G..................................... 16,18
GILLAMAN
E W 280
GILLUM
Emeline 217,220
GIPSON
Thomas M 321,324
Thomas M, MD 321
GIVENS
J I...................................179,180,181
GOIN
Jeff.. 188
GOLD
S M 78,80,81,84,85,87
GOODENOUGH
A D 135,136
GOODWIN
Geo M 139
GORDON
James M 251,252,253
GORE
Maggie 159,160,161,162,163,165
GOUGER
Estell................................... 245,246
Estelle.....................247,248,249,250
J J 245,246,247,248,249,250
Tokie 245,246,247,248,249,250
GRACE
B F... 28,29
GRAY
T F 284
GREEN
R B 191
GREENSTREET
T J.. 69
GULLEY
Cora A 179,180

HAINS
H E 311
HALL
Daisy C...91,92,93,94,95,96,97,98,99
Ella 47,49,50,52

331

Index

R R 129,130,131
Theodore B 95,96
Theodore Byron 91,92,98,99
W S 91,92,97,98
William S 92,96,97,98,99
William S, Jr 91,93,94,96,97,99
William S, Sr 93,94,95,96
HAMPTON 233
  Ben B 34
  Burniss Irene 231,232,233,234,
235,237,238
  Elizabeth 158,159,160,161,
162,163,165
  Henry 158,159
  Henry G 157,158,161,162,164,165
  Isaac 265
  J L 238
  Jno L 232
  John L 231,232,233,234,235,
236,237,238
  Noel 157,160,161,163,165
  Sweeney 158,159,160,161,162,
163,164,165
  Willie 233
  Willie M 231,232,234,235,236,238
HANCOCK
  Willis 103
HARKIN
  (Illegible) 103
HARLEY
  Earl 65
HARLIN
  Logan 5
HARRIS
  W L 119
HARTSHORNE
  David C 41,43
  G E 41,42,43,44
  G E, MD 42
  G W 43
  George Ewing 41,43,44
  Mrs David C 42,43,44
HEDGECOCK
  T L 10,11,12,13,14,90
  T L, MD 10,11,13
HEMBREE
  Amy 204,205,206,207,208,
209,210,211
  Rebecca Jencey 207,208,210
  Rebecca Jency 204,205
  Rebecca Jincey 207
  Rebecca Jincy 206,209,210,211
  William 204,205,206,207,208,
209,210,211
HENDERSON
  Jos B 79,81,85,86
  Marion 212
HERMAN
  J B 302
HICKER
  Daisy 106,107
  Edward 106,107
HICKMAN
  Eugene 243,244
  Eugene A 243
HIGH
  P E 320
HINTON
  John H 72,75
HODGES
  Mary Priscilla 295
HOLDER
  Cathrine 25
HOLLAND
  G L 323,325
  Villey 323,325
HOMER
  Asa J 272
  Czarina 260,261
  Jacob 270
  Kacey 265
HORNER
  E A 216
HOWARD
  Alice 114
  John H 253,254,255
  John H, MD 253,254
HUDSON
  Charles H 110
HULSEY
  Earnest T ... 108,109,110,111,112,113
  Marion T 108,109,110,111,112
  Mary A 108,109,110,111,112,113
  Mary E 110

Index

Mr 113
HUMAN
   Allen Terreell 304
   Allen Terrell 301,302,303,304
   Eugenia Basil............................. 304
   J B.. 301,304
   J M.. 304
   Jesse M 301,302,303,304
   John B....................................... 304
   Mattie C.................................... 303
   Mattie E 301,302,303,304
HUME
   J S....................................... 240,241,242
   J S, MD............................... 240,241
HUMPHREY
   T C.................................... 60,158,313
HUNTER
   Cecelia......................... 201,202,203

INGLISH
   C R 284
INTOLABBE
   Ada 256
INTOLABBEE
   Ada 256,257,258
   C P 258,259
   Cepha.............. 255,256,257,258,259
   Colbert................................. 257,258
   Colbert P 256
INTOLABEE
   Ada 255,256
   Colbert P 255
ISAACS
   C R 6
IZARD
   Lora B............... 306,307,308,309,310
   Mary L 306,307,308,310
   Silas [.. 307
   Silas P 306,308,309,310

JAMES
   C W 225
   Florence 225
JASPER
   Jno W 65
JEFFERSON
   Sikey 105

Siky 101,105
Smallwood........................... 101,105
JOHNSON
   B J 1,2,3,6
   B S.. 221,222
   Daniel E.................................... 176
   E 184,185,186
   E, MD................................. 184,186
   Eliza A....................................... 176
   O L 48,49,175
   P S 88
JOHNSTON
   D P 300
   Dr James C 199
   James C 199
   P S 78,79,80,81,82,84,85,86,87
   P S, MD............78,80,81,82,84,85,86
JONES
   Ben 5
   C C 16,17,18,19,22,61,62,63,64
   J N 17,18,20,62,63
   Jno 293,294
   Tilson 209,210
   W N 230

KEENER
   A F 205
   A F M 32,33
KEMP
   Frances 175,176,177
   Joseph..................... 175,176,177,178
   Mr... 175
   Warren.......................... 176,177,178
KENNEDY
   D S 38,39
KENUP
   Willis.. 208
KERR
   Nancy E 280,281,282,283
KINCADE
   Alice 118
   Joe 118
   Mary 118
   Sissie 118
KING
   Charley 93,94,95,96
   H C 66,67

Index

H C, MD 66,67
KINKADE
  Fred V 158,313
KIZER
  F M 286,287,288,289

LANTZ
  John M 28,29,30
LATIMER
  Allie B 151,152,153,154
  Ames S 154
  A B 152
  J S 152
  James S 151,152,153,154
  Marie Kathleen 151,152,153,154
LAUCHNER
  Daisy Ruby 299,300
  Grant 299,300
  Lela V 300
  Lella 299
  Margarett 300
  Mrs Grant 300
LAWRENCE
  D A 239,240
  O S 239,240
LE FLORE
  Houston 193
  Joseph 193
  Selina 193
LEE
  Robert E 5,191
LEFLORE
  Felix 54,55,57
  Houston 187,188
LEFLORE
  Houston 189
LEFLORE
  Houston 189
LEFLORE
  Houston 190
LEFLORE
  Houston 190
LEFLORE
  Houston 191
LEFLORE
  Houston 191
LEFLORE
  Houston 192
LEFLORE
  Houston 192
  Jno W 10,11,12,13
  Jno Wesley 9,11
  John W 13,14
  John Wesley 9
LEFLORE
  John Wesley 9
LEFLORE
  John Wesley 10,12,13,14
  John Wesley, Jr 12,13
  Joseph 187,188,189,190
LEFLORE
  Joseph 190
LEFLORE
  Joseph 191
LEFLORE
  Joseph 191,192
LEFLORE
  Joseph 192
  Laura 10,11
  Laura E 9,10,12,13,14
  Selina 187,188,189
LEFLORE
  Selina 190
LEFLORE
  Selina 190,191
LEFLORE
  Selina 191
LEFLORE
  Selina 192
  T L 11,12
LESTER
  E F 159,161,162,163,164,165
LEWIS
  Alice 114,120
  Alice E 117
  Alice J 115,116,117,118,119,
120,121,122
  Brewster 277,278,279
  Charles S 277,278,279
  Cynthia E 278
  Cynthia Eudora 277,278,279
  Ethel 114,120,122
  Ethel E 114,115,118,120,121,
122,123

Ethel Eugenia .. 115,116,119,122,123
H E 121,122
Howard 114,118,119,120,122
Howard E 115,116,117,118,
120,123
J L 9,10,11,12,13,89,90
Joseph 121
Lena 126,127
Salina 125,126
Silas 130
William 121
William J 115,116,117,118
William Joseph 114,116,117,
120,121
Woodson 126
Worcester 278,279
LITTLE
J C 229
LLOYD
J W 314
W J B 311
LOCKE
Victor M, Jr 201,202
LONG
T J 278
T J, MD 278
LOOMIS
O H 280
LORING
Lulie 6

MCCAIN
C E 214,215,216,217,218
MCCARTHY
Elchy 142
Elciy 142
MCCARTY
Elsie 144
A F 143
J V 144
Maude E 144
Mrs Elcie 143,145
MCCLARD
C C 265,312,313,314,315,316
MCCLENDON
Annie 279,280,281,282,283
F L 283

Morris Stanley ..279,280,281,282,283
T L 279,280,281,282,283
MCCURTAIN
Thomas 3,4
MCDONALD
J B 205
MCFERRIN
Margaret 122
Margret 119
MCKENNON
Mary Virgil 319
MCKINNEY
John W 256,257
MCKINNON
Edith Irene 319,321,324
G G 321,324
Geo Gipson 319,320
George Gipson..320,322,323,324,325
Lula 319,320,321,322,323,324,325
Lula M 324
Mary Virgil 319,320,322,323,
324,325
MANNING
T T 109
MANSFIELD, MCMURRAY &
CORNISH 59,74
MARRYMAN
Walter 4
MARTIN
C C 179,181
C C, MD 179,181
Dr C C 180
MATHEWS
John W 34,35
Lorena 34
MATTHEWS
John W 32,33,34,35,36
Losera 32,33,34,35,36
Rosa 32,33,34,35
MAXEY
J F 124,125,126
MAYES
Mike 241
MAYTUBBY
Peter, Jr 201,202
MEEK
Calvin W 207

335

Index

MENTZER
  J L 143,144
MERRYMAN
  Benjamin C 1,2,5,6,7,8
  Benjamin Colbert 2,3,4,5,7
  Benjiman Colbert 4
  F A 55
  Florance A 56
  Florence A 58
  Martha 53
  Martha B 53,54,55,56,57,58,59
  Mary 1,2,3,4,5,6,7
  Walter 1,2,4,5,7
  Walter G 2,3,5,6,7
  Walter J 8
  William B 53,54,55,56,57,58,59
  Wm B 55
MIDDLETON
  C P 233,234
MILLENS
  Rutha 7
MILLER
  Geo W 281
MILLUS
  John B 5
  Ruth 2,5,7
  Rutha 3,4,6
MITCHELL
  Eli E 42
MOORE
  (Illegible) 232
  Corine 186
  Corinne 183,184,185,186,187
  H M 187
  Herbert M 183,184,185,186
  Lena 183,184,185,186
  Selina 147,149,150
MURPHEY
  J D 246,249
  J D, MD 246,249
MURPHY
  J D 248

NACHTEL
  Geo W 174
NAIL
  Jesse 296,297,298
  Jessie 293,294,295
  June Etta 293,294,297
  Junetta 293,294,295,296,297,
  298,299
  Junr Etta 293
  Lillie 168,170,171,173,174
  Mary Ann 293,294,295,296
  Robert 168,169,171,172,173,174
  Rosa 168,169,170,171,172,173,174
  Silas 171,172,173
  Silas W 168,169,170,171
  Wilas 174
NAILE
  Mary Ann 297
NEEDLES
  T B 8,14,21,30,35,51,53,54,55,
  63,70,87,88,104,112,120,132,140,145,
  164,177,193,219,226,237,250,254,
  263,275,283,291,297,309,316
NESSMITH
  David 65,66,67
  Mary B 65
  Mary V 66,67
  Mrs 66
  Susan Myrtle 65,66,67
NEWMAN
  E A 262
NOEL
  Ben 248
NORVELL
  E E 117,118
  Elijah E, MD 117
OGLESBY
  Minnie 195,196
  W J 194,195,196
OLDS
  E O 146
OLIPHINT
  J H 284
PARKER
  Gabe E 52
  P M 215
PARKERSON
  J J 268
PARROTT

Dr F C 244
F C 243,245
F C, MD 245
PATE
  E G 285,287,288,289,291,292
  E G, MD 285,287,288,289
  Jane 222,223,226
  Mary 225
PATTERSON
  J N 155
  S P 320
PATTRSON
  S P 324
PAXSON
  Janetta 183
  Jennetta 182
PERKINS
  L H 78,79,84
PHILLIPS
  Charles A 223,224,301,302
  A Denton 128
  G W 149
POE
  J 147,149,152
POPE
  Frank 168,169,170,171
  Gilbert 194,195,196,197
  Lucy 194,195,196,197
  Mutien 194,195,196,197
POWELL
  S J 306,307,308
PRATHER
  C B 34,208,209,210
PRIDDY
  M W 78,83
PRINCE
  John 218
  Phema 214,215,216,218
  Phemy 217,220
PUSLEY
  John 178,179,180,181
  Lizzie 179,180
  Mrs 179
  Nancy B 181
  Nannie B 178,179,180,181
  Silas 159,160,161
  Willie 179
  Willie Lee 178,179,180,181
QUIGLEY
  J P 118
RABON
  J W 184,185
  Ora 243
  Ora A 242,243
  Ora Almeda 244,245
  Rufus 184,185
  Thurman M 242,243
  Thurman Moore 242,244,245
  William T 242,243
  William Thomas 244,245
  Wm T 243
REAGAN
  R L 124,125
  Robert L 126
REICHERT
  William 115,116,117,118
REYNOLDS
  Bell 198
RICE
  F C 321,322,324,325
  F E 323
  T J 82
RIDDLE
  Florence 154,155,156,157
  G W 151,152
  Lee Ray 154,155,156,157
  Mrs Richard 155
  Richard 154,155,157
  Richard R 152,156,200,202
  Thomas 200,202,203
RIPLEY
  Sallie 197
RIPLY
  Sallie 196
RISTEEN
  H C 15,114
ROBERTS
  Beckie 266
  Ben 269
  Ben J 264,265,266,271,272,273
  Benjamin 266,267,268
  Benjamin J 267,268,269,270,

Index

274,275,276
Benjamin, Jr.................. 268,269,270
Hattie 264,265,266,267,268,270,
271,272,273,276
Henry McKinley.... 264,265,266,267,
268,269,270,271,272,273,274,275
Jesse.. 266
Mrs 268,269
ROCKETT
   Louis.. 137
RODEN
   A J 23,24
ROSS
   A Frank................................ 301,302
ROUTH
   J M... 258
RUTHERFORD
   B C 309,316
   B C, MD 316

SAM
   Fannie 194,196
SCANTLER
   J M.. 46,47
SEELEY
   G W 228,229
SELDNER 227
   Olive C 229,231
SELF
   Jno H 38
   John H 37
SHANAFELT
   Richard 267,271,272,273
SHELBY
   Nannie 318,319
SHULER
   Ira M.. 66
SIDES
   J E... 314
SILMON
   Lee 41,42,194,195
SLOVER
   B W 256
   B W, MD 256
SMITH
   Chas P................................. 232,235
   Dr... 47,48

Eliza Ann...................................... 77
J Wesley 72
S M... 45,50
S M, MD 45
Wilma.. 311
SMOOT
   Jno R 243
   John R 243
SNAFFAR
   Effie N 297
SNAKES 268
SORRELLS
   Catherine 239,240,241,242
   Charles Le Roy............................ 239
   Charles Leroy 239
   Charles LeRoy............................ 240
   Charles Leroy 240
   Charles LeRoy............................ 241
   Geo W 240
   George.. 241
   George W 239,240,241,242
SORRELS
   Charles Le Roy........................... 242
SOUTHWARD
   John 252
SPARKS
   Capitola............................... 166,167
   Cornelia Maye 166,167
   John F 166
SPEARS
   Mary 43
SPROWLS
   W T 303,304
STAFFORD
   Anna 33,34,35
   R B 32,33
   W R 32,33
STALLABY
   Silaney................................ 106,107
STARK.. 309
   Bessie L 317
   Bessie Leola 314,315,316
   Hettie... 310
   Josephine 309,312,314,315,316
   Leola Bessie 312
   Thomas 309,312,314,315,316,317
   Thos... 310

STARKS
- Bessie L 313
- Bessie Leola 316
- Bessue Keika 310
- Josephine 313
- Thomas 311,313,316
- Thos 310

STEPHENS
- Burniss Irene 236
- Dr V T 232
- John J 224,227
- John J, MD 224
- V T 234,235,236,238
- V T, MD 232,234,235

STEPHENSON
- A F 230
- Olie C 230
- Olive C 227,228,229,231
- Wannona E 227,228
- Wanona Estelle 227,229,230,231
- Will F 227,228,230
- William F 229,230,231
- William T 231

STIGLER
- J S 25,27

STONE
- C L 101,103

STOVER
- Josephine 311

SWAFFAR
- Effie 293,294,295
- Effie N 296

SWAFFER
- Effie N 295

TALLEY
- Isham C 107

TAYLOR
- James 243,244,245
- John 93,94,95,96
- Josephine 312,314,315

TERRELL
- James C 303,304
- Jas C 302,303
- Jas C, MD 302

TERRY
- Edna 221,222

- Elisha S 317,318,319
- Glenn M 317,318,319
- Malinda 318
- Malinda Walker 318,319

THOMAS
- A S 92,94,96,97,98,99
- A S, MD 94,96

THOMPSON
- Beula 99,100,101,102,103,104,105
- Beulah 105
- Malinda 99,100,101,102,103,104,105
- Monroe 91,92
- Nelson .. 99,100,101,102,103,104,105

TIFFER
- S G 191

TIGNOR
- J D 78,83

TINEY
- L C 184

TOLBERT
- N J 130

TOOLE
- J Y 78,83

TRAYLOR
- J T 235

TURNBULL
- Dick 324
- John B 324
- Maud 324
- Maude 324
- Simeon 129

TURNER
- T B 24,25,27,28,29,31
- T B, MD 24,25,27,28,29

VAIL
- Minnie 146
- Willie 146

VAUGHN
- E J 38

WACHTEL
- George W 203

WADE
- Eastman 146
- Eastman 147,148,149,150,152
- Eli 151,152

Index

Ellen 146,147,148,149,150
Ethel 146,147,148,149,150
Ethel W 150
WADLEY
   George L 46,47
WALKER
   Chas T 246
   Malinda 317
WALLACE
   W E 248
WARD
   Charlee 172
   Cyrus B 244,245
WEAVER
   Claude 112
   S W 216
WELCH
   R A 124,125
WESTHOFF
   E W 142
   Mrs E W 142
WILLIAM
   Sophia A 260,261
WILLIAMS
   (Illegible) 295,297
   Boyd 249
   J E 108
   Joe B 100,102,106
WILLKITT
   N J 56
WILSON
   A C 82
   Lane 273
   R M 158
   S H 324
   Sam 273
WINGATE
   D E 284
   Miss D E 284
WINLOCK
   Risal 118
WOOLEY
   W Y 213
WRIGHT
   Watson 3,4
YOTA

Cellis 191
Cillis 191,193
YOTAH
   Sillis 188

www.ingramcontent.com/pod-product-compliance
Lightning Source LLC
Chambersburg PA
CBHW020241030426
42336CB00010B/571